Musical Healing in Cultural Contexts

Musical Healing in Cultural Contexts

Edited by

PENELOPE GOUK

Routledge
Taylor & Francis Group
LONDON AND NEW YORK

First published 2000 by Ashgate Publishing

Published 2016 by Routledge
2 Park Square, Milton Park, Abingdon, Oxfordshire OX14 4RN
711 Third Avenue, New York, NY 10017, USA

First issued in paperback 2016

Routledge is an imprint of the Taylor & Francis Group, an informa business

British Library Cataloguing in Publication Data

Musical Healing in Cultural Contexts
1. Music therapy—Cross-cultural studies.
I. Gouk, Penelope.
615.8'5154

Library of Congress Cataloging-in-Publication Data

Musical healing in cultural contexts/edited by Penelope Gouk.
Includes bibliographical references (pp. 197–216) and index.
ISBN 1–84014–279–0 (hb)
1. Music therapy. 2. Traditional medicine. 3. Music and society.
I. Gouk, Penelope.
ML3920.M89997 2000
615.8'5154—dc21 99–40654
CIP

ISBN 13: 978-1-138-27672-7 (pbk)
ISBN 13: 978-1-84014-279-2 (hbk)

Contents

List of figures and tables

Figures

Tables

Notes on contributors

Linda Phyllis Austern is Associate Professor of Musicology at Northwestern University. She has published extensively on music, literature and cultural issues in sixteenth- and seventeenth-century England, with occasional forays into other periods and locations. She received her PhD from the University of Chicago and has been the recipient of numerous fellowships and grants from such agencies as the American Council of Learned Societies, the British Academy, and the National Endowment for the Humanities. She is currently completing a book entitled *Music in English Intellectual Culture 1550–1650* and editing a collection of essays on *Music, Sensation and Sensuality.*

Charles Burnett is Professor of the History of Arabic Influence in the West at the Warburg Institute, and a Fellow of the British Academy. He is author of *The Introduction of Arabic Learning into England* (London, 1997), and *Magic and Divination in the Middle Ages* (a collection of articles, Aldershot, 1996), and co-editor (with Danielle Jacquart) of *Constantine the African and ᶜAlī ibn al-ᶜAbbās al-Maǧūsī: The Pantegni and Related Texts* (Leiden, 1994). His interest in the history of music therapy represents the joining of his academic research with his experience as a practising musician.

Steven M. Friedson is Professor of Music and Adjunct Professor of Anthropology at the University of North Texas, and Research Associate at the International Centre for African Music and Dance, University of Ghana. He is the author of *Dancing Prophets: Musical Healing in Tumbuka Healing* (Chicago, 1996), and producer of the documentary *Prophet Healers of Northern Malawi* (1989). He is currently working on a book on music and healing in West Africa based on his research in the Volta region of Ghana.

Penelope Gouk is a Wellcome Researcher in the History of Medicine at the University of Manchester, and also plays the violin. She took her PhD at the Warburg Institute, and went on to become a Postdoctoral Research Fellow at the University of Oxford and Director of The Achievement Project (1990–95). She has published extensively on early modern European intellectual and material culture, and is currently working on music and healing and the use of musical models in medical and scientific thought. Her most recent book, *Music, Science and Natural Magic in Seventeenth-Century England* (New Haven and London, 1999), explores the use of musical models by English natural philosophers and their relationship to natural magic.

John M. Janzen is Professor of Anthropology at the University of Kansas, Lawrence, and Director of the African Studies Resource Center. He has held positions at McGill University, and guest lectureships at the University of Capetown and the American University of Cairo. He received his PhD from the University of Chicago, and has studied at the University of Paris. His long-time research interest has been on Central African health and healing, including the widespread use of song-dance, widely called 'ngoma'. Most recently he has turned his attention to African approaches to dealing with the aftermath of war and severe trauma.

Cheryce Kramer is currently a Research Fellow at the Wellcome Institute for the History of Medicine. In 1998 she completed her PhD dissertation at the University of Chicago on 'A Fool's Paradise: The Psychiatry of *Gemüth* in a Biedermeier Asylum'. Besides her academic education, she has also had extensive training as a classical guitarist and dancer. Her scholarly interests revolve around questions of culture, identity and perception and how each relates to the other.

George Rousseau took his PhD at Princeton and has taught at the universities of Harvard, University of California at Los Angeles, Cambridge, Oxford, Leiden and Aberdeen, and is currently Research Professor of the Humanities at De Montfort University. He is also a trained keyboard player who has performed in concerts. His primary interest is in the interface of literature and medicine, for which his work has recently been awarded a three-year Leverhulme Trust Fellowship in 1999–2001. The author of many studies dealing with medicine and the humanities, his most recent book, written jointly with Roy Porter, is *Gout: The Patrician Malady* (New Haven and London, 1998).

Lyn Schumaker is a Wellcome Lecturer at the University of Manchester, currently researching the history of Western and African medicine in Zambia. Her 1994 PhD at the University of Pennsylvania dealt with the fieldwork of the Manchester School anthropologists at the Rhodes–Livingstone Institute in Northern Rhodesia (Zambia) from 1937 to 1964. She has taught African history at the University of Stirling, and in 1994 took up a postdoctoral research fellowship at the Wellcome Unit for the History of Medicine at the University of Manchester. Her book *Africanizing Anthropology: Fieldwork, Networks and the Making of Cultural Knowledge in Central Africa* will be published by Duke University Press.

Henry Stobart is a lecturer in Music at the Royal Holloway, University of London, and is an ethnomusicologist specializing in the music of the Bolivian Andes. He originally trained as a performing musician and remains active as a performer with the Early Music ensemble SIRINU, with whom he has toured and broadcast widely, and recorded five CDs. Following his PhD entitled 'Sounding the Seasons: Music Ideologies and the Poetics of Production in an Andean Hamlet' (1995), written at St John's College, Cambridge, he was Adrian Research Fellow at Darwin College, Cambridge. He is co-editor of *SOUND*, a volume of multi-disciplinary approaches to the acoustic world (Cambridge, 1999), and is co-editing a series of essays on knowledge and learning in the Andes.

Acknowledgements

First of all my appreciation goes to fellow contributors of this book, not only for being so willing to collaborate in this venture in the first place, but also for assisting in the lengthy process of turning a set of conference papers into a finished volume. Thanks are also due to the other participants at the August 1997 meeting on 'Music, Healing and Culture: Towards a Comparative Perspective' who are not represented in this book. Their contribution to our thinking on this subject is gratefully acknowledged. I am particularly indebted to Rachel Ecclestone for introducing me to the world of professional music therapy, and for looking critically at my work from this perspective.

I would also like to thank the Wellcome Trust for its generous financial support of this project, which has been undertaken as part of my work as Wellcome Researcher and Lecturer at the University of Manchester. Additional funding for the August 1997 symposium was also provided by the Wellcome Trust and Renaissance Trust.

Figure 7.2 has been reproduced by gracious permission of Her Majesty Queen Elizabeth II; Figure 7.3 by permission of the National Gallery of Art Library, David K. E. Bruce Fund; Figure 8.1 by Hugo Huber, Achern. We have made every effort to secure permission to reproduce all copyright material anywhere in this volume. Any omissions will be gladly rectified in future editions.

Penelope Gouk
Manchester, 1999

CHAPTER ONE

Introduction

Penelope Gouk

This volume is a collaborative work by a group of scholars whose goal is to promote interdisciplinary and cross-cultural discussion of the healing powers of music.[1] How do people use music to heal themselves or others, and how do such practices change through time and space? Are the healing powers of music universal, or culturally specific? There is something about music's effects on people which arouses interest far beyond the confines of any single profession, and clearly has tremendous appeal to a broader public. It is no accident that virtually all contributors to this volume have been trained in music or dance and still practise their skills non-professionally. We feel that the central part that such activities play in people's lives, and the benefits (or otherwise) that they bring, should be more widely recognized.

The origins of this book go back to 1995, when I embarked on a study of the relationship between music and healing in the early modern period (fifteenth–eighteenth centuries). It seemed appropriate to discover how colleagues in history, musicology, anthropology and other social science disciplines were addressing the kind of issues I was interested in, as well as practitioners themselves. What soon became evident is that although there is a wealth of literature by music therapists, other arts-therapy professionals, psychologists, psychiatrists and neuroscientists about music's healing properties, comparatively little on this area has been produced by scholars engaged in social, cultural and historical studies.[2] Organizing a meeting seemed the obvious starting point for generating wider interest in this theme within the scholarly community, and the symposium on 'Music, Healing and Culture: Towards a Comparative Perspective' (London, 20–21 August 1997) was the outcome.[3] This occasion provided a rare, but extremely welcome, opportunity for dialogue between those whose primary concern is to treat patients, and those whose job it is to reflect on such processes and place them in cultural context. One of the most fruitful sessions was the final plenary discussion where we addressed the practicalities involved in producing a book. It became clear that our aim was twofold: first, and foremost, to generate interest among those who do not think of themselves as being experts in this area (e.g. the majority of historians, anthropologists and cultural scholars), and second, to introduce those who are experts to some alternative models of practice, both past as well as present.

Inevitably, there are limits to what can be achieved in any collection of essays. It important to acknowledge that what this book does *not* claim to do is survey current practices within music therapy or related forms of therapy. By the term 'music therapy' I mean the activities of qualified practitioners working with clients/patients who cannot deal with specific psychical or physical conditions without professional assistance. Such activities involve patient assessment procedures, goal-oriented treatment processes and appropriate forms of evaluation.[4] None of the essays here is by a qualified music therapist, although the 1997 symposium included a presentation on the profession's search for an adequate theoretical foundation.[5] To learn more about the enormous variety of music-therapy work which takes place in psychiatric units, hospitals for severely learning-disabled people, schools for children with special needs and other medical and educational institutions worldwide, it is advisable to consult the profession's own literature.[6] Likewise, there is no account here of the widespread use of music *in* medicine, namely the use of music therapy in the treatment and prevention of physical illness and disease. Music is routinely used in hospitals as a support or adjunct to other forms of treatment, if not as the primary form of intervention (e.g. in surgery, pediatry, intensive care, labour and delivery, terminal illness), and new applications are constantly being developed.[7] This is an area about which medical historians know almost nothing, and would provide a fascinating subject for future research, not just by music therapists interested in the origins of their profession.

The type of 'music therapy' that this volume *does* take some account of, however, is the general, non-expert kind – the only form which really existed before a recognized body of music-therapy professionals came into being. In this context, the term 'therapy' is being used to denote the general therapeutic effect which can be gained from being involved in any form of musical/artistic performance, either as a participant or audience. The critical difference between this kind of activity and 'proper' music therapy (as defined in the previous paragraph) is that it does not need the intervention of a trained therapist, and is chiefly a form of *recreation*: that is, an act or experience selected by the individual to meet personal wants in his or her leisure time, or as part of a liberal education. This kind of therapy potentially includes all creative activity, and regardless of the efforts of professionals to stabilize the boundaries of their discipline, it inevitably overlaps with their domain of expertise. Hence the choice of *Musical Healing* as the start of our book's title: this reflects a bias towards thinking of music as a form of healing (i.e. making strong, whole again) rather than just in terms of therapy (i.e. techniques of intervention involving distinct goals and desired outcomes). What might be especially interesting to explore is the changing relationship between these two domains, and how the differences between them have been constituted on both sides of the professional–lay divide.

As I have already indicated, there is no shortage of texts addressing the healing powers and therapeutic applications of music, in whatever sense these terms might be used. It is altogether harder to find material which locates such practices in any kind of historical or cultural setting. This is perhaps not surprising, since most people conducting research into this area are concerned with developing new therapies and have little time for history. Significantly, the most recent contributions to the study of musical healing have come from anthropology and ethnomusicology, most notably Marina Roseman's *Healing Sounds from the Malaysian Rainforest* (1991), John Janzen's *Ngoma: Discourses of Healing in Central and Southern Africa* (1992) and Steven Friedson's *Dancing Prophets: Musical Experience in Tumbuka Healing* (1996). Little further needs to be said about these books in this introduction, not just because Janzen and Friedson are among our contributors, but also because the influence of their work (and that of Roseman's) is manifest throughout the volume. The literature which is worth remarking on here is altogether more Eurocentric in focus, but nevertheless still has a lot to offer new readers.

Published just over fifty years ago, *Music and Medicine* (1948), edited by Dorothy Schullian and Max Schoen, was the first multi-author work in English devoted to the subject. The book comprises sixteen articles by scholars from a range of disciplines (see Table 10.1), together with an extensive bibliography by Schullian that merits further analysis in its own right. *Music and Medicine* is extremely important for what it represents both intellectually and institutionally, and accordingly has been made the focus of the final essay here. As I explain in Chapter 10, the book's appearance not only signalled a new phase of academic interest in music's healing powers, but more significantly marked the emergence of music therapy as a fully accredited profession in the United States. Typical of its time and place, the book celebrated the advanced status of Western medical science in contrast to more 'primitive' forms of health care, but at the same time traced the origins of music therapy to ancient Greece. Half a century later, such ethnocentric and élitist assumptions are no longer tenable, but we should not underestimate the difficulty of framing an alternative set of questions about music's capacity to heal. What such questions might be are considered in more detail below.

The only substantial historical work to appear since Schullian and Schoen's volume is Werner Friedrich Kümmel's *Musik und Medizin: Ihre Wechselbeziehungen in Theorie und Praxis von 800 bis 1800* (1977). Based on research for the author's Habilitationsschrift at the Frankfurt medical school, the book surveys texts covering a thousand-year period and includes an impressive bibliography as well as illustrative material. As the author himself points out, there are few works which address music and medicine in any systematic sense, and Dorothy Schullian's classified bibliography is the only real precedent for his own. In taking a long-term view of the subject, Kümmel privileges continuity rather than discontinuity, and the decision to organize his material thematically further reinforces the impression of an unchanging medico-musical tradition before 1800. Among his key themes are music and the pulse; music and medical education; the foundations of the diatetic-therapeutic functions of music; music as an aid to health, and its role in therapy (music therapy as such being a modern development). Within each subject area he cites sources from across different centuries, and thereby shows just how long-standing certain ideas actually are. For example, the role of music as link between body and soul, its use as both a stimulant and a sedative, and its particular associations with mental diseases, can be traced throughout the period. Readers should be aware that many of the issues touched on in this introduction (see below) were already being discussed in antiquity, and that Kümmel has also addressed them in some depth.[8]

A disadvantage of this thematic approach, however, is that it is hard to see what changes in thinking and practice have occurred over time, or whether in a given period or place there have been significant *disagreements* about music's healing powers. Kümmel has taken an important first step by identifying sources which range from popular medical handbooks to learned treatises on music theory. But precisely because his discussions move easily back and forth across centuries, across countries, and across professional boundaries, the reader can have no sense of why any individual author wrote what he did (they are all male, I think), in what context it arises in his own work, how it fits into larger discourses, and whether it was commonplace or unusual for its time. Thus, for example, we may note that during this entire period books on music theory almost invariably include a passing reference to the healing properties of music – along with its other social and moral benefits – in their introductory material. This literary convention followed the pattern set by Boethius' *Fundamentals of Music* (6th century AD), and in virtually every case the author has nothing substantial to say on the subject. From the medical perspective, it is also noteworthy that while the value of music as a liberal art is a common literary trope (again this derives from Boethius), in fact it is conspicuously absent from the formal medical curriculum.[9]

Where then, might we ask, does music fit into the field of medical knowledge and practice? And has musical healing been more widely practised in some cultures rather than others? Peregrine Horden's response to this challenge has been to edit a volume on *Music as Medicine*, which complements the present collection.[10] His essays are organized chiefly chronologically, but their geographical range moves beyond Europe to embrace Islam, Hinduism, and Korean shamanism. With such material at our disposal we may begin to track major historical changes, and also to compare different belief systems and practices. Another strength of Horden's collection is that it explores some particularly important themes in depth. For example, the phenomenon of tarantism, its effects and methods of cure, has been a recurring topic of interest in the European medical community since the sixteenth century.[11] The influence of Marsilio Ficino (1433–99), whose *Three Books on Life* (1489) seems to be the original source of this interest, is another significant theme in Horden's volume.[12] Not altogether surprisingly, this enigmatic Renaissance philosopher also appears in the present collection (see below, as well as Chapters 5, 6 and 7), as indeed does tarantism (Chapter 10).

Given this overlap of interests, and especially since three authors have contributed to both volumes (Austern, Gouk, Kramer), the question of how our books actually differ from each other naturally arises. Part of the answer is already evident in the choice of titles: while *Music as Medicine* is explicitly described as a 'history of music therapy', *Musical Healing* foregrounds 'cultural contexts' and avoids the term 'music therapy' for reasons already explained. This is not to say that we consider history unimportant (indeed quite the reverse!), or that music therapy should be marginalized. However, 'doing history', or indeed practising any other kind of discipline presupposes a set of categories and assumptions that is worth making explicit if we really want to create a truly interdisciplinary approach, much less a cross-cultural one. The nature and purpose of history, for example, has traditionally been to hold up individuals, groups or nations as examples to propagate moral and religious values. Within the Christian tradition, history has also been understood as a goal-directed process, and since Francis Bacon's time as a cumulative product of mankind through the centuries.[13] We are unable to escape the consequences of this kind of cultural grounding, but at least can acknowledge its effects.

Merely substituting the phrase 'cultural contexts' for 'history' is no solution to the problem, although it perhaps forces us to confront it more directly. Neither is it adequate simply to juxtapose historical and anthropological essays, as if by doing so we might overcome cultural bias. After all, the very categories history and anthropology themselves imply a shared set of assumptions about these subjects and how they are to be treated. Indeed, one theme which emerged strongly from our discussions at the London symposium was the need to combine disciplinary approaches. As we considered case studies from Africa and South America, for example, it became clear that the 'traditional' practices being described by anthropologists were inextricably bound up with histories of European global expansion. At the same time we also recognized that, in chronological terms at least, the most modern (or rather contemporary) beliefs represented in this volume are non-Western, based on ethnographic work carried out in post-colonial societies whose peoples have been exposed to European technologies since the sixteenth century. An unexpected link between Stobart's account of an Andean village and the African papers by Janzen and Schumaker, for example, was the impact mining had made on these communities and their means of self-expression. Having made this connection, we went on to consider more generally the relationship between pain and suffering experienced through oppression and the transformative and healing roles that music seems to play within many different societies. How such transformations are effected, the forms they can take, and whether they can be ascribed to 'music' at all, clearly merits further collaborative enquiry. The findings presented in this volume might usefully complement debates within the music-therapy profession, for whom such questions are of direct and immediate importance.

Any serious investigation of these issues obviously has to include sustained and continuing discussion about what is actually meant by the word 'music', and indeed all the other terms and categories that are so central to this book. The point is not to fix meanings on which everyone can agree; rather, it is to acknowledge the effect that words have in shaping what is known and the consequences that this must have on our enterprise. Something inevitably changes when non-verbal experiences are put into words, and especially when one language is translated into another. For example, as Henry Stobart points out in Chapter 2, there are no Andean equivalents for the English concepts of 'music' or 'sound', which have no use in a culture where the *quality* and *context* of sound are more important than any general form of classification. Since this is also the case for many other societies, ethnomusicologists are accustomed to grappling with the problems that arise from taking 'music' as a starting point for research, but beyond this disciplinary specialism the majority of scholars remain unaware that such problems even exist. Clearly we are unable to dispense altogether with categories like 'music' or 'sound', but it is at least desirable to reflect on how and where such terms are currently used, how their meanings may have changed through time, and what alternatives might exist.

Having acknowledged the limitations of any single discipline in addressing musical healing, we considered the best way to ground our discussion was to formulate a shared set of questions which could usefully be applied across disciplines and also cultures. The following questions were circulated to contributors in advance of the 'Music, Healing and Culture' symposium, and we have presented them here the hope that they might generate further questions and debate:

- What words and images are used by those who want to describe and explain the powers and effects of music? In any given cultural setting, what kind of people do this, and why is it important to them?
- Of the various effects ascribed to music in a given culture, which are considered as medical or therapeutic in nature?
- What kind of identity does someone have who uses music for healing, and in what contexts is this activity judged as specifically medical, rather than musical or religious?
- In what ways do individuals and groups use certain kinds of music to improve the well-being of themselves and others?
- What, if any, relationship is there between the long-established intellectual tradition celebrating the therapeutic powers of music and what people have actually practised?
- Where does music fit into institutionalized medicine (e.g. in hospitals): by whom, for whom, where, and when? Is there anything distinctive about the social contexts where such practices were/are legitimated?
- How does the emergence of 'music therapy' as a recognized profession fit into wider accounts of professionalization and competing claims for authority within and on the margins of the medical community?

Obviously, no individual was expected to touch on every issue, and as it turns out not all the above questions are fully addressed in this volume. Nevertheless, the strategy of asking questions proved useful in that it became possible to identify three over-arching themes which linked all the precirculated papers and now provide a framework for this book. The first theme, 'identities', focuses on roles assumed by, or conferred on, participants in the process of musical healing. The second theme, 'sites and technologies of performance', is concerned with locating these actors within particular settings, and identifying the tools or instruments they use, including musical ones. The third, and arguably the most difficult theme to tackle, is 'conceptualizing the non-verbal'. On the one hand this refers to the way people talk *about* music and its effects (including the power to heal), and on the other it considers the way people *use* music as a means of grasping things which by their very nature cannot be verbalized. Whatever language might be involved (e.g. psychoanalytical, religious, artistic), the embodied act of making music opens up realms within and beyond individuals, providing access to the unconscious, to the soul, to the divine, or to the spirit realm; in short mediating between the material and immaterial worlds. As I shall suggest in the final section of this introduction, exactly how such experiences are understood and articulated depends on broader cultural understandings of the nature of bodies and their relationship to the world as a whole.

Identities

From a late twentieth-century perspective it appears entirely natural to seek for meaningful, and perhaps new, relationships between music and medicine through some kind of rapprochement between individuals who have higher qualifications in these fields. The concept of identity can thus be framed entirely within the structure of the professions. Classic medical roles, like those of the 'physician', 'doctor' or 'nurse', for example, are somehow to be meshed with those of the 'musician', 'composer' or 'instrumentalist'.[14] In reality, such simple occupational designations have always obscured enormous differences (as well as similarities) in experience among practitioners of these arts through time and space. Independently from each other, historians of both medicine and music have begun to consider particular communities of practitioners in sociologically nuanced terms. As yet, however, there has been no concerted attempt to discover how members of such communities might construct their own identities in relation to each other, nor to see how those active in the so-called medical marketplace might draw on the production and consumption of musical wares.

The main reason for this neglect is simple: musicologists, like most professional as well as amateur musicians (including doctors), are chiefly concerned with musical works, products whose qualities are judged in aesthetic terms. Music therapists, on the other hand, think about music chiefly in terms of process, as a means through which they may heal people. The quality of the 'music' created in such a context may be irrelevant to this desired outcome. Judged by conventional aesthetic standards, the 'musical' products of a patient's self-expression are normally thought to be of little worth, and consequently what therapists do to facilitate creativity in their clients does not merit scholarly attention. Mindful of such tensions, contributors to this volume were invited to reflect on the self-identities of the practitioners they were concerned with, and how, if at all, they perceived music as therapeutically relevant.

The dominant authorial voice emerging from Charles Burnett's account of Islamic sources in Chapter 5 is that of the court physician, whose knowledge of cures is directed towards maintaining the health of his aristocratic patron. Within this cultured environment both doctor and patient are assumed to be musically sophisticated, and music is a recognized branch of astrological medicine. On the basis of his training and experience, the doctor is able to prescribe listening to certain kinds of music, both for dietary regimes and curative purposes. Underpinning this particular area of specialist medical knowledge is the asylum, an institution which enabled the physician systematically to observe the effects of specific therapies as well as to classify mental diseases themselves with some rigour. As is well known to students of Islamic culture, organized institutional care for the mentally ill developed in the Islamic world long before the Latin West. The European scholars who were first responsible for transmitting Arabic medical learning had no conception of specialist mental hospitals, nor were they interested in the therapeutic potential of musical technologies that might be used within such an environment. As a result they did not bother to translate the relevant material on this subject, which in contrast to other areas of Arabic learning only began to be taken seriously in the late fifteenth century.

To be sure, there are isolated accounts of wealthy patrons using music as part of their daily regimen, and references to its beneficial effect on melancholic spirits abound. But Marsilio Ficino was the first – and, I would suggest, practically the only – Western medical theorist who actually went beyond literary platitudes in his attempt to recreate an ancient kind of spiritual medicine, a form of theurgy (i.e. the invocation of gods), in which music played a fundamental role. The music–spirit theory expounded in his *Three Books on Life* was taken up enthusiastically by court poets and composers in the later sixteenth century, but seems to have been ignored by most academic physicians of the time.[15] The first specialist medical works devoted to music's effects and its potential role in curing disease appeared in the mid-eighteenth century, and the benefits of music for mental health were increasingly noted. Yet it was only from the mid-nineteenth century that any systematic attempts were made to incorporate music into asylum life. As Cheryce Kramer's discussion of the regime in Illenau suggests (Chapter 8), it was a form of treatment that remained largely confined to the wealthy. The majority of asylums simply could not have afforded what many perceived as a luxury for their inmates, especially since they were charitable institutions for the poor. Both the widespread clinical application of music and the eventual emergence of a distinct profession of music therapists depended on the massive expansion of state funding for medicine in the twentieth century.

This pattern of European experience can be usefully contrasted with African examples. In Chapter 3 John Janzen focuses on the role of the *ganga*, or 'doctor of medicine' who often directs the ngoma healing rituals widely practised in central and southern Africa. Using a case study of a healing session in Greater Capetown (1982), Janzen explains how those who come to take on this role start out as sufferers themselves. By means of a lengthy apprenticeship, novices eventually acquire the ability to discern spirits through 'music' and to achieve the sufferer's release from them. However, 'music', even if understood to embrace singing, dancing and drumming, is an inadequate category for grasping what 'doing ngoma' fully entails. For not only do Western definitions of music tend to imply performers before an audience, but they also take no account of the spirits which can be evoked through the bodily movement, drumming, sound and words emanating from the participants. Such spirits also have no place in modern Western medical practice, and the idea of a healer who takes on the identity of a spirit, who *is* the disease even as (s)he dances, is virtually unimaginable in a Christian society where interaction with demons has always been forbidden.

Yet Steven Friedson's study of the *nchimi*, or 'prophet' in Chapter 4 shows an alternative reality which the Timbuka of the northern region of Malawi believe to be compatible with their Christian faith. Indeed, with their capacity for divination the *nchimi* see themselves as following the tradition of Old Testament prophets. These healers are called to their vocation through a spirit affliction, for which the only cure is to enter the world of dancing prophets (the alternative being madness and death). Again there is a period of apprenticeship, during which the novice learns the techniques of divinatory trance through which spirits become accessible. This indigenous form of healing practice coexists alongside Western medicine because it successfully treats 'African diseases' (i.e. those caused by witchcraft and spirits) for which modern medicine has no remedy.

The roles touched on here – ranging from the ninth-century Arabic court physician to the nineteenth-century German asylum doctor or the late twentieth-century Tumbukan *nchimi* – already indicate there is a correlation between the way healers and their patients identify themselves and interact with each other, and the way they understand the human body and its relationship to the world more generally.[16] As I shall consider more fully in the final section below, Western biomedicine appears to work on a very different set of cultural assumptions than the traditional forms of healing described in Chapters 2 to 4. A further dimension to Western medicine is that (for the most part, anyway) it is practised by experts using highly sophisticated apparatus in specialized institutions. Just thinking in isolation about the various identities conferred on practitioners and patients, healers and sufferers is clearly inadequate for our purposes. It is also essential to consider where and by what means the healing process may – or may not – be enacted. Whether a particular activity is identified as medical or not depends almost entirely on its setting, and it is to these spatial and technical aspects that we now turn.

Sites and technologies of performance

The places where musical healing can occur are clearly not restricted to clinics, hospitals and special educational institutions. Although only qualified professionals may provide therapy in these contexts, it can be argued that any musician is potentially a healer, almost anywhere. This is because even just listening to music – for example in the concert hall, in the privacy of one's own home, or even in a hospital ward – is often experienced as therapeutic. Between these two extremes of clinical expertise and self-treatment it seems that there are many different institutional settings – public and private, secular and sacred, indoor and outdoor – in which musical healing can occur. Although we have begun to touch on these geographical issues in this collection, much more attention is required before proper comparative work can be undertaken.

For example, there is a distinct asymmetry between the kinds of spaces that anthropologists on the one hand, and historians of modern Western medicine on the other, have been prepared to recognize as sites of healing. Such imbalance is demonstrated even in this volume. Although institutions like hospitals and clinics are at least touched on here, no serious attention is given to churches as potential sites of healing, nor to religious communities in which music is recognized as a means of healing as well as an integral part of worship. As my final chapter points out, exactly the same imbalance prevailed in *Music and Medicine* fifty years ago, and is a consequence of the clear boundary that has been drawn between professional medical and religious roles, and the secularization of academic life. Any discussion of music's power to communicate with the divine, or to heal the soul, is firmly outside the realm of medical discourse. Consequently such issues are normally overlooked in historical and sociological studies pertaining to modern Western medicine. That it is still so hard even to notice what is being left out of the picture should remind us of the power that institutionalized disciplines exercise over thought.

A similar power is exercised by technologies of performance, by which I mean the tools and instruments used to facilitate human interactions. What roles do particular technologies serve in the process of healing? Are they regarded as central or peripheral to this process as a whole? Does it matter what kinds of instrument are being used, and are some technologies recognized as more effective than others? Finally, and perhaps most importantly, in what ways have advances in technology affected *understandings* of healing as well as the means by which it may be accomplished? As my discussion of 'conceptualizing the non-verbal' suggests below, the widespread dissemination of new kinds of mechanical or electronic devices has consistently opened up new possibilities for understanding how human bodies work and interact with their environment (Descartes's *l'homme machine* is the classic example of this phenomenon).[17] The technologies used to record, store and transmit sounds have tended to receive less attention as physiological models than those used for visual processes, but in the wake of recent developments in the cognitive sciences this imbalance is being rectified.[18] In short, we see that instrumental technologies shape the cognitive world as much as they shape the material and social world.

In the case of musical healing, the instrumental technologies to be considered not only include material artefacts – most obviously instruments designed to make music – but also the voice, which is itself a powerful instrument for human expression. Rousseau, for example, is among those who would privilege voice over all other musical instruments in its capacity for therapeutic potential. (I will come back later to consider divergent views on the relative merits of voices and instruments.) Despite this potential, however, the voice itself has largely resisted scientific and scholarly analysis, and in Chapter 6 George Rousseau challenges us to consider why this should be the case. Some answers to this question may be found in the long-established and continuing debate about the hierarchy of the senses, as well as in the importance that science and philosophy have accorded to the sight.[19] Within this tradition, the written, rather than spoken (or sung), word has been given privileged emphasis. And even when the sense of hearing is taken seriously, the voice as such is still in danger of being lost within the larger category of things heard. Thus, as Rousseau observes, the *metaphor* of the voice is frequently invoked by literary authors when they write about texts written by other authors. Yet the *actual* voice, including the anatomical apparatus which produces and interprets vocal sounds, has largely been omitted from postmodern discussions about the body and its cultural representations. Having suggested what a cultural history of the voice might begin to look like if it were developed, Rousseau concentrates on the musical qualities of the inflected, or melodious voice, and its perceived effects on listeners. At the same time he also asks whether recent technological advances may be diminishing, rather than enhancing, these qualities: perhaps the widespread use of electronic mail and computerized voices may lead to the loss of the 'natural' inflected voice and its particular power. How a natural voice is to be distinguished from an artificial one, and what makes it melodious rather than otherwise, are important questions to be investigated.

What Rousseau alludes to as the 'Rodalina school of soothing', namely the songs that musicians have created to express pain and suffering, provides a rich crop of literary as well as aural evidence that is ripe for investigation. Linda Austern takes us further into this territory in Chapter 7. She claims that over the last four hundred years, at least, unrequited love and erotic melancholy have provided the chief stimulus for works of this genre.[20] Comparing song settings by three early seventeenth-century composers (John Dowland, Claudio Monteverdi and Barbara Strozzi) with examples of late twentieth-century rock ballads (Robert Palmer, The Smashing Pumpkins, Pat Benatar), Austern shows a remarkable consistency in the way musicians have communicated feelings of anguish, sorrow and despair. Certain kinds of melodic and rhythmic structure are used to express emotional states which are recognized and shared by the audience as well as composers themselves. Although this musical language seems inherently 'natural' in the way it mirrors our innermost feelings, it is nevertheless a highly sophisticated cultural artefact which has been developed and refined over centuries. As Kramer emphasizes at the end of Chapter 8, in order for any kind of song to have an effect there must be a shared phenomenal framework organizing the musical experience for participants. Both the music itself and the emotions it arouses are culturally negotiated as well as being mutually interdependent on each other.[21] It appears that music not only provides a context in which a language of the emotions can come into being, but also gives actual shape and meaning to the emotions themselves, to what it means to be human.

The role of cultural expectations in determining what seems natural is also evident from the way that male and female voices are differentiated. Gender is a crucial factor in determining how and where particular voices can be used, as well as the effects they may have. Austern shows us that in contexts where the production of music is overwhelmingly shaped by (heterosexual) male desires, there is a corresponding emphasis on men's suffering and the ambiguous roles that women play within this male world. For example, until quite recently most of the songs performed on stage by women have been composed by men, just as it has been men who have judged the quality of their singing. In such a context it is not altogether surprising to find that women's voices have been considered naturally more soothing or arousing than men's, or that this difference has been ascribed to their maternal or sexual roles. As women themselves increasingly take control of musical production, it remains to be seen whether the voices they create for themselves will be significantly different, and in what alternative ways they might be used to heal.

Thus far we have considered the voice chiefly as an instrument for articulating individual suffering, or as a therapeutic tool. The classic melancholic song expresses private grief, even though it might be giving comfort to millions of people at the same time (e.g. as a live broadcast or recorded performance on CD, tape or video). This mode of therapy contrasts strikingly with the communal process of 'doing ngoma' described by Janzen. In this form of healing, which is ubiquitous across much of Africa, sufferers pour out their troubles and are responded to by a group in a call-and-response mode that not only collapses Western distinctions between performer and audience but resists classification as song, dance or instrumental music. This problem of classification can also lead us to look more closely at the precise role that particular musical instruments are thought to play in the process of healing, as well as the importance of words and music in relation to each other.

For example, drums are so fundamental to African healing that the word for drum, *ngoma*, is also the name given to a wide complex of healing activities known as 'rites of affliction'. Across the sub-Saharan continent drums clearly take on a variety of roles within this healing complex, and in some cases are absent altogether. In the *vimbuza* rites of Malawi described by Friedson, the ngoma drums are central, being seen as the 'batteries of the spirits', as the Tumbuka themselves put it (using the metaphor of a transistor radio to envisage this process). A unique rhythmic mode is associated with each kind of spirit that enters the prophet, and it is through the drums that this transformative energy is created and harnessed. Yet as Janzen points out, to assume that African healing always involves spirit possession or trance would be quite mistaken, and it would be similarly misguided to focus on the agency of drums alone. In the Capetown ngoma sessions he describes, for example, the drum appears merely supportive of the rhythms initiated by the singing–dancing group, and it is the words of their songs as much as their rhythms which constitute the expression and cure of the patient's ills. Disagreement about the relative importance of words and music appears to be as typical among African healers as among European opera buffs and academics (compare Janzen, Rousseau, Austern).

Lyn Schumaker in Chapter 9 points out that the musical technologies used in healing ngomas are also found in *beni ngoma*, the drum bands and dance associations historically widespread over central and eastern Africa. While Janzen and others have identified this activity merely as a form of entertainment, she sees it instead as a means of healing the collective body comparable to the ngoma rituals for the individual body. Her argument is supported by an analysis of the *kalela* dance, a form of 'smart' dance performed in Zambian mining communities which is particularly associated with Western standards of hygiene and self-presentation. In *kalela* the lyrics of the songs articulate the political woes of the community, and in conjunction with the drums that go 'deep in the heart', bring about a transformation of identity expressed through dancing. The reworking of European technologies, including uniforms, military discipline and a dominating drumbeat, provides a powerful means of reworking relationships within local African communities. Even though *kalela* is not explicitly recognized as medical by its performers, it appears to function as a cure for public afflictions from witchcraft to bad political leadership.

Although drums have a positive role to play in African forms of healing, they are marginal to Western discussions of musical healing. Within this discourse emphasis has traditionally been placed on harmony (i.e. intervallic relationships) as a means of procuring mental and emotional stability, and stringed instruments are seen as particularly effective tools for achieving equilibrium. The lute, for example, is given privileged status in the 'spiritual medicine' described by Burnett, and is the preferred vehicle for John Dowland's songs of melancholy despair. Other stringed instruments have similar long-standing associations with reason and goodness: Apollo's lyre and David's harp are among the best-known exemplars of this tradition. By contrast, wind instruments are identified with the passions and excess: Dionysus' aulos and Pan's pipes notoriously lead to sensuous abandon and loss of control.[22] These complex webs of associations are not only made by the ear, which discerns the sonorous qualities of individual instruments, but also the eye, which discerns the symbolic meaning carried by actual instruments or their representations.

The associations which particular instruments evoke inevitably affect how they are used therapeutically, and indeed if they are used for such purposes at all. Drums, for example, are not usually considered as having healing properties within the dualistic system just described because they arouse, rather than calm, the passions, and also have strong connections with war. Of course the precise associations any instrument may conjure up varies enormously according to the context in which it is heard or seen. Thus while wind instruments as a general category have been conventionally associated with earthly passions, in particular settings their tonal qualities may elicit more ethereal sensibilities. In their 1971 song 'Stairway to Heaven', for example, the acid rock group Led Zeppelin used a recorder consort and acoustic guitar to evoke feelings of 'unworldliness', nostalgia and simplicity (see Chapter 7). Music therapists also use a wide range of instruments from all over the world in their clinical work, at the same time as conducting research into their different sound qualities and perceived effects on clients. It is clear that within our broad remit of musical healing there is ample scope for exploring the complex ways in which particular instruments, or groups of instruments, have been linked to specific emotions, as well as the effects that new technologies (e.g. electronics) have had on established patterns of response.

Conceptualizing the non-verbal

All our chapters show that there is something about musical healing in its various manifestations which makes it hard to analyse. Not only are the origins and locations of the ailments it works on elusive, but so too are its effects. Measuring the difference that is made by listening to a soothing melodious voice is just as difficult as analysing what 'really' takes place among the participants in a session of Tumbukan trance dancing. Such processes involve inner transformations which are hard to quantify or verbalize, and therefore elude rational, scientific explanations as these are conventionally understood. A similar difficulty is experienced by professional therapists, who have found it hard to establish a research methodology which will produce consistent and generalizable results.[23]

One explanation why non-Western forms of musical healing might resist translation into scientific terms, at least, is given by Janzen.[24] He observes that the application of one form of totalized discourse (for example, Western disciplinary knowledge) to a different totalized system (in this case, African ngoma) necessarily leads to incommensurability. It is clear that the curative potential of 'music' is culturally negotiated, both in terms of what it can actually do and how its effects on people are explained. Whether it may legitimately form part of the interaction between healers and their patients depends on a society's world-view, a broader system of relationships and beliefs through which all bodies, cosmic as well as human, are defined and understood. Since Western medicine is apparently based on a completely different system than non-Western, 'traditional' forms of healing, it is perhaps not surprising that its expectations and explanations of what music can do is correspondingly different.

The Western biomedical world-view is normally portrayed as dualistic, based on the post-Cartesian division between body and mind. Although there is debate about how far mental functioning can be ascribed to bodily mechanisms, and whether it is really possible ever completely to separate physiology from psychology, the basic twofold model is not really in question. The doctor's role is to understand how the bodily system works, and to apply specialized techniques for its repair and maintenance. Another distinctive feature of this tradition is its reliance on germ theory. Laboratory medicine identifies diseases as distinct entities, whose causes can be explained in terms of microorganisms attacking the body. Again, the role of the doctor is to identify specific diseases, and to discover methods of counteracting their effects on the body. This characterization is obviously too simplistic, and fails to take account of specific disciplines such as psychotherapy, where mind–body interaction is taken as given. However, my point is that this 'medicalized' conception of the individual human body as a composite, material entity whose structure and function are amenable to analysis is strongly promoted as the dominant model in Western culture. Within this conceptual framework there is apparently no space for the soul, or any other invisible and intangible entities whose existence cannot be detected through conventional scientific techniques. If it is true that there is a 'certain congruence between available forms of music therapy and the extant configuration of soul in a given cultural situation', as Kramer claims in Chapter 8, there are bound to be difficulties in using conventional biomedicine to explain what is going on in the healing process.

The mechanistic model just described appears to contrast markedly with the understandings of the body which inform the non-Western healing practices described in this volume. Take, for example, the world-view shared by the Andean community Stobart describes. To these people, the earth and heavens are animated, and like humans and all other living things are imbued with *animu* or energy. Most illnesses are attributed to malevolent forces which are derived from other social groups, sorcerers or spirits. Human health not only depends upon maintaining an equilibrium within the body itself, but is also contingent on the balancing of forces beyond its physical boundaries. Sickness is usually regarded as a symptom of imbalance within a much broader system of social and cosmic relationships rather than as simply bodily malfunction. At the same time, however, all forms of disorder in the environment are themselves manifested in bodily terms.

It is within this framework of an animated cosmos that music, or more precisely sound energy, plays a fundamental part in shaping and rebalancing the forces at work in nature. Because sound is considered a form of *animu* which is equivalent to life itself, certain kinds of sound play an important role in ritual healing: those produced by whistles, llama bells and dynamite are among the examples he offers. At the same time, music (i.e. comprising singing, dancing and playing instruments) is crucial to the maintenance of bodily and community health. Each musical genre and instrument type is linked with specific activities or seasons, and in the course of the year their performance is designed to bring about desirable transformations in the climate through control of *animu*.

By most accounts, this kind of magical, animistic thinking has been absent from Western society since the Enlightenment. Since then, we are told, the various kinds of immaterial entities which supposedly interact with humans – gods, demons, ancestral spirits, fairies and the like – have gradually been pushed outside the boundaries of scientific medicine, whose self-proclaimed remit is the natural, rather than the supernatural word, an invisible and possibly non-existent realm best left to priests, poets and dreamers rather than serious medical scientists. The seventeenth-century Scientific Revolution is typically seen as a watershed in European culture, marking the point at which natural philosophers began to develop mathematical and experimental methods for generating reliable scientific knowledge about the material universe, while at the same time distancing themselves from animistic and superstitious beliefs.[25]

Yet the concept of an animated, ensouled cosmos in which 'music' acts as both a generative and regulatory force throughout nature is familiar (to those who work in the humanities, at any rate) as a form of Platonism, or more precisely Neoplatonism, a philosophical system dating from the fourth century AD. Elements of this doctrine were always familiar to the Latin West, but it was not until Ficino published his editions of Plato, Plotinus and Iamblichus in the late fifteenth century that the entire metaphysical system underpinning Neoplatonic magic began to be known in Europe. In the century or so which followed Ficino's intellectual labours, this magical tradition was widely recognized as a stimulating, albeit controversial, approach to philosophical and theological thinking. Yet in the wake of Tommaso Campanella's (1568–1639) life imprisonment for heresy – which involved a practical revival of Ficino's magic – Neoplatonism has remained on the margins of Western thought.[26] Nevertheless its core principles, including vitalism, have continued to exert their influence on the natural sciences as well as on fictional literature and the arts.

We have already noted that it was also Ficino who first elaborated on the principles underlying al-Kindī's 'spiritual medicine', which used music sympathetically to draw down planetary influences as a cure for melancholy and other passions of the mind. Ficino presented his form of spiritual healing in terms of harnessing an impersonal *spiritus mundi* or *pneuma* which suffuses the entire cosmos (the concept of *pneuma* was originally Stoic in origin). Via the ear, this extremely fine and active substance can mingle directly with the human *spiritus*, another vital substance which serves as the intermediary between the human body and soul, and indeed is the latter's chief instrument.

The resemblance between Stoic *pneuma*, Ficino's *spiritus* and the Bolivian notion of *animu* – a foreign term which was taken from their Spanish conquerers – is certainly striking. Yet as Walker has explained, the kind of musical healing Ficino advocated was potentially idolatrous and therefore extremely dangerous. Designed to recreate the powers of Orpheus (who brought the dead to life as well as enchanting beasts through music), his magical songs could be regarded as form of theurgy, in other words incantations designed to invoke demons that could act directly on another's soul.[27] Indeed, Ficino described the matter of song itself as 'in a manner living, made up of articulated limbs, like an animal, not only bearing movement and emotion, but even signification, like a mind, so that it can be said to be, as it were, a kind of aerial and rational animal'. Within this magical cosmos musically moved air is alive, and therefore has the most powerful effect on the hearer's spirit.[28] This description of a living entity instantiated through music bears a strong resemblance to the spirits that are made present through the drums in Tumbukan trance dancing. The idea that music can 'really' be used to achieve such effects, however, seems antithetical to modern scientific thought, belonging more to the realm of fantasy and imagination.

For reasons I have explained elsewhere, Ficino's musico-magical doctrines first achieved prominence in the late sixteenth and early seventeenth centuries, a period when élite interest in magic was at its peak.[29] The potential to summon demons through particular kinds of song was clearly incompatible with orthodox Christianity, and it is not suprising that no one publicly admitted to such practices. What did become acceptable, however, was the literary representation of Orpheus as a mythological expression of universal harmony, a symbol of the power of music to realign the social order with the natural and divine order. It was also acceptable to imitate the effects of his magical songs on the stage through state-of-the-art technology, and to describe successful songwriters as the 'second Orpheus' (Henry Purcell, the so-called 'English Orpheus', being an obvious case in point).[30]

During this period of extraordinary political and social upheaval a whole series of court masques and entertainments based on a Christianized form of Neoplatonism ritually enacted the healing and transformative power of movement and song.[31] Although debates raged across Europe about the legitimacy of such practices in public worship, it was possible to express them in secular entertainments, where magic was allowed to play a central role. Since the seventeenth century public theatres, opera houses and concert halls have continued to function as the main Western institutions where both the language and practice of magic are licensed. Words like ravishment and enchantment, for example, are terms of approval in places where audiences willingly submit to such powers.

It was also in the late sixteenth century that the Neoplatonic concept of 'sympathy' as a means of explaining hidden forces operating within and between bodies first became part of everyday language. As Austern graphically illustrates in her discussion of melancholic songs, the way one musical string could be touched and thereby set in motion another untouched string (i.e. sympathetic resonance) was a potent image of this occult power.[32] A lute's physical properties served as a concrete metaphor for attraction between lovers, elucidated the connections between body and soul, explained how music could alter moods, and at the same time instantiated the harmony between God and his creation. In short, this musical technology provided a visible as well as aural model of unseen realms.[33]

The way that musical symbols have been deployed metaphorically in Western art and literature since the Renaissance is well known.[34] Less well appreciated are the ways in which the same musical models have informed and transformed Western science – or rather natural philosophy – over the precisely same period. In the late seventeenth century, for example, the lute's mechanism came to serve as a model for the inner ear, an inaccessible organ which by means of resonance communicates sound vibrations to the brain via the nerves.[35] At exactly the same time, Newton successfully demonstrated in his *Mathematical Principles of Natural Philosophy* (1687) that the behaviour of musical strings, wave dynamics and the hidden laws of gravity were all governed by the same harmonic principles.[36] Yet since Newton himself did not take musical practice seriously, and publicly rejected magic as a viable mode of understanding the world, the central role that music played in his new system of mathematical physics became overlooked.

The way that magical belief in correspondences and sympathy have been systematically excluded from Western science since Newton is a familiar story among academics and the general public alike. On the one hand, this exclusion is sometimes treated in a positive light, notably by individuals who comprehensively dismiss magic as charlatanism or ignorance, and regard science as a distinctive and progressive tool of human advancement. On the other, the same story of the decline of magic may be treated in a wholly negative fashion, especially by those who consider Western science as a major source of the world's ills. Rather than judging the merits of these contrasting positions, our purpose here is to show how they are inextricably bound up with each other, and are contingent on the circumstances being described and the author's point of view. Whatever their truth value, these tales of Western disenchantment, of the loss of soul in a increasingly materialistic world, of how modern dualism contrasts with the holism of traditional societies, epitomise the problems academics (and also therapists) face when they struggle to frame music's effects in acceptably scientific terms. Terminology associated with mysticism or magic is by definition excluded, so what resources can legitimately be used to understand how music and healing interconnect?

Kramer's chapter reminds us that what might constitute an acceptably 'scientific' explanation for their interaction has actually varied considerably even over the last hundred years. It also challenges the notion that 'soul' has been excluded from Western science since the Enlightenment by showing its role in nineteenth-century medical thought. The therapeutic regime practised in the asylum at Illenau was associated with a peculiarly German model of psychology, in which the *Gemüth* (comprising body and soul, and referring to the essence of a person or community) constituted the central organ of experience. As Kramer explains, the Illenau physicians used gymnastics as a means of imposing a musical order on the bodily movements of their patients. Together with the community which they served, these experts believed that both music and gymnastics could be used as therapies to redress disharmony between body and soul, between the individual and the community. However, this reorganization of the *Gemüth* was not achieved through immersing an audience in a shared experience of a performance. Instead it came about through the arousal of shared visceral sensations, bodily movements that instantiate meaning rather than than merely acting as carriers of a belief structure. Only in a community which associated mental health, collective action and the visceral power of aesthetic sensations as mutually reinforcing registers of experience could the energy released in gymnastic exercises have the power to reorganize the *Gemüth* in the way Kramer describes. In other words, the curative potential of music and gymnastics at Illenau resided precisely in the cultural beliefs which legitimated their medical use in the first place.

Friedson offers his readers a comparable strategy for trying to grasp how trance dancing 'works' for the Tumbuka community, an approach which is also based on a distinctively German philosophy. He suggests that trance dancing (like the gymnastic exercises at Illenau) is not something to be witnessed by an observing subject, but is, to paraphrase

Heidegger's words, a way of being-in-the-world shared by those who participate in its enactment. In this mode of being, 'music' is not an object to be encountered, nor is it peripheral to the healing process: such formulations are embedded in a visualist metaphysics where to *see* is to know, and to *know* is to see. Friedson instead invites us to 'hear' what dancing the disease entails, to imagine a clinical reality where the 'music' of trance dancing is not subordinate or peripheral to some other kind of process, but *is* the activity which at once constitutes the disease and the diagnosis.

For the communities which Friedson and Kramer are describing, the only viable way of grasping the connection between music and healing is through embodied knowledge; that is, a way of knowing expressed through bodily actions rather than discursive speech. Long accepted in anthropological discourse, this performative dimension of human understanding has recently come to the attention of sociologists and historians interested in the 'tacit' skills which are constitutive of scientific and medical knowledge.[37] In trying to analyse such skills, they are confronting exactly the same problem encountered with musical healing: that is, the struggle to translate non-verbal and embodied practices into suitably academic language.[38] As scientists themselves probe ever further into deep space and explore the fabric of the human body in ever more detail, they too are beginning to accept the limits of rational analysis and seek alternative models of understanding. And while few go so far as to claim the need for a God, the existence of a spiritual, non-material dimension to life and the universe is taken for granted.[39]

Faced with the growing acceptance of the limits to conventional scientific methods, our focus on musical healing as a site of investigation seems particularly timely. In this Introduction I have suggested that the kinds of scientific explanations that can be offered by modern Western disciplines are located within a particular world-view, but one which is by no means shared throughout the world. Some glimpses of alternative, and explicitly non-Western, cosmologies are offered here, especially in Chapters 2 to 4 by Stobart, Janzen and Friedson, but also Schumaker in Chapter 9. The process by which such cosmologies have been made known to, and to a certain extent assimilated by, Western scholars is the theme of Burnett's Chapter 5. Although there is a great deal more to learn about how other cultures use music as part of the healing process, the importance of these different traditions for expressing alternative cosmologies is already manifest.

What does seem necessary to emphasize, however, are the alternatives which are available to Western scholars within their *own* cultural traditions. We have already noted that what constitutes scientific knowledge has changed considerably over time, and other scholars have pointed to marked national and even regional differences in scientific styles. It is also important, however, to recognize that 'science', however construed, has only represented a fraction of the explanatory resources available to people. Just because music's effects elude scientific explanation does not mean they do not exist, nor that they cannot be communicated. Indeed, as Rousseau, Austern and Kramer in particular make clear in Chapters 6 to 8, it is precisely *because* music communicates so powerfully that it is used as a metaphor for, and expression of, other forms of human experience. Especially in the domains of religion, art and the humanities, the power of music to restore balance within oneself and with the world, to connect with the spiritual realm, is taken as given. Only in the realm of the 'sciences' do music's powers seem altogether harder to deal with. By way of conclusion to this volume, I show in Chapter 10 just how localized this particular conception of 'science' really is – that is within modern secular universities – and suggest we can look beyond the academy for alternative modes of understanding.

There is, it seems, an inescapable relationship between the way we configure our inner and outer worlds, not only as individuals but as larger communities and even nations. 'Music' (and all the activities this term may encompass) is itself a powerful expression of that configuration, as well as a means of altering it. Yet although music's cathartic and transformative powers may be universal, the ways such powers are harnessed and directed appear to be culturally specific. Indeed, the forms musical healing may take within a given community are determined by how its members conceive of health and illness, as well as their relationship to the material and spiritual realms. These essays start to explore some of the social and conceptual landscapes where music has been identified as part of the healing process, and begin to map out some possible routes across this largely unexplored terrain. In the end, however, the metaphor we will learn most from is more complex than a simple road map. The skills of a choreographer rather than a cartographer are required for recording the kind of complex patterns and dynamic interactions that are touched on in these pages. Our only hope of understanding them is to abandon prejudices and formulas, plunge in, and join the dance ourselves.[40]

Notes

1. For comments on earlier drafts of this chapter I would like to thank Fenela Childs, Rachel Ecclestone, Peregrine Horden and an anonymous reader for Ashgate.
2. For recent music, dance and arts therapy literature, see for example Chodorow (1991); Davis, Gfeller and Thaut (1992); Heal and Wigram

(1993); Payne (1993); Bunt (1994); Pavlicevic (1998). On music in relation to psychology, psychiatry and the neurosciences, see for example Critchley and Henson (1977); Sloboda (1985); Storr (1992). For a discussion of cultural and historical studies of music, healing and medicine, see below and Chapter 10.

3. Coincidentally, Peregrine Horden began to organize a meeting around the same time on 'Music and Medicine: The History of Music Therapy since Antiquity' (London, 24–5 April). For papers on this occasion, see Horden (2000).
4. For further discussion of the definition of 'music therapy' within the profession, see Bunt (1994), 5–8.
5. Ansdell (1997). See also Ansdell (1995) and Aldridge (1996).
6. See the works cited in notes 2, 4 and 5 above.
7. For an overview, see Maranto (1993).
8. The introduction to Horden (2000) discusses Kümmel's work in more detail.
9. Boethius (1989), Siraisi (1973, 1975).
10. Horden (2000).
11. See articles by Gentilcore, Leon and Lüdtke in Horden (2000), also Sigerist (1948).
12. Articles by Voss, Gouk and Heather in Horden (2000).
13. Kessler (1995), 81, n. 7.
14. On music-therapy courses the historical emergence of the 'music therapist' as a distinct category is typically explained in terms of combining these two quite different kinds of identity. I owe this observation to Rachel Ecclestone.
15. See Ficino (1989) and Gouk (2000).
16. See also 'Becoming a Healer' in Roseman (1991), 52–79.
17. As discussed, for example, in Hankins and Silverman (1995).
18. Ibid., 113–47: 'Science since Babel: graphs, recording devices and the universal language of instruments'; see also Kassler (1984 and 1995).
19. For further discussion of these issues, see Burnett et al. (1991) and Classen (1993b).
20. See also Austern's article in Horden (2000).
21. The implications of this cultural relativism for music therapists has been recognized; see Bright (1993).
22. See chapter 12 in Winternitz (1979), 'The Curse of Pallas Athena'.
23. For accounts of this difficulty see Bunt (1994), Aldridge (1996) and Edwards (1993).
24. See below, pp. 62–5.
25. For the classic exposition of this process, see Thomas (1971/1980), and for a more recent interpretation see Henry (1997), especially chapter 3, 'Magic and the origins of modern science'.
26. Walker (1958), 203–36.
27. Ibid.; see also 'The Astral Body in Renaissance Medicine', in *Journal of the Warburg and Courtauld Institutes*, 21 (1958), 119–33, repr. in Walker (1985).
28. Ficino, *Three Books on Life*, III, xxi, quoted in Walker (1958), 10.
29. Gouk (1999), 11–14, 68–72, 263–4.
30. King David was another renowned musician who was able to control spirits: 'And it came to pass, when the evil spirit from God was upon

Saul, that David took an harp, and played with his hand: so Saul was refreshed, and was well, and the evil spirit departed from him.' 1 Sam. 16: 23.

31. Yates (1947), 77–94.
32. See Chapter 7 below, and also Gouk (1999), 169–70.
33. This phenomenon is known to music therapists as entrainment, 'a process in physics whereby two objects vibrating at similar frequencies will tend to cause mutual sympathetic resonance ... music has the potential to "entrain" the heart via the pulse, or "entrain" breathing through its rhythm'. Maranto (1993), 159.
34. E.g. Winternitz (1979) and Finney (1962).
35. First described by the French anatomist Joseph-Guichard Du Verney in his *Traité de l'organe de l'ouïe* (Paris, 1683); see Gouk (1999), 271–2.
36. Ibid., chapter 7.
37. See, for example, the essays in Button (1991) and also Sibum (1994).
38. For a therapist's response to this problem, see chapter 2 of Aldridge (1996), 'Health as Performance', which adopts a phenomenological approach.
39. See, for example, Capra (1996).
40. I take this particularly apt metaphor from the concluding sentence of Grafton (1988), 74.

CHAPTER TWO

Bodies of sound and landscapes of music: a view from the Bolivian Andes

Henry Stobart

Music is widely thought to possess healing powers in Amerindian cultures and countless ethnographies describe the use of song, rattle, drum or other sound-making instruments in medicine. However, it is sound, and its control and shaping, which is the critical element in both music and healing. As Lawrence Sullivan has observed in his study of South American religions: 'because it is a symptom of all-pervasive energy, sound can orchestrate different orders in ways that are startlingly complex'.[1] It is this view of sound as energy, or as the animating quality of living things and of the cosmos, that I shall explore in this chapter.

In approaching the issues of music and medicine in Amerindian cultures it is necessary to reconsider what is meant by illness. Is illness simply the result of bodily malfunction? Can a patient be treated as a physical entity or object independent of the social, economic and spiritual environment which he or she inhabits? For many Amerindian peoples sickness is principally seen as a penalty for spiritual offence.[2] Such an approach demands that the environment be understood as animated by spiritual beings whose feelings may be offended and upon sacrifices to whom human well-being is dependent.

In this chapter I shall address the use of sound in healing in an Andean community and demonstrate how, 'as a symptom of all-pervasive energy', it is seen to animate bodies and is shaped in music. Although the people I shall discuss are among the most traditional and 'Indian' groups of the Andes, they cannot be described as truly 'native' South American.[3] Since the Spanish invasion of the 1530s, and a continued history of political and economic domination, Andean peoples have appropriated numerous aspects of European culture and beliefs – often reshaping them to their own purposes and contexts.[4]

Background

This chapter is based on several years of fieldwork, spread over the last decade, in a rural hamlet of *ayllu* Macha, northern Potosí, Bolivia. In this harsh highland environment (altitude 4100 m) most families live by herding sheep and llamas, and growing potatoes and fodder barley, with some wheat, oca and quinoa in lower-altitude fields. Several men also periodically travel to the larger towns to work as builders' labourers or porters. The inhabitants of this hamlet are monolingual Quechua speakers, and in many ways their lifestyle is highly traditional; for example, dried llama dung remains the main fuel for cooking, water is collected by hand from the water hole, huts are made from local materials (mud bricks or stones, thatched with mountain grasses) and there is no electricity.

Music is of immense importance, but rarely heard outside the context of major social gatherings, such as fiestas or weddings, which amount to a total of about 30 days a year.[5] On these days music, singing and dancing are almost constant. Young women are the principal singers and men exclusively the instrumentalists, most knowing how to play at least four types of instrument. Music is intimately associated with agricultural production and each instrument, genre and dance form is linked with specific activities or times of year. New melodies are collected each year, their origin attributed to magical spirit beings called *sirinus* ('sirens'). These sources of musical creation are linked with the creation of new food crops – as assurance of good health – but inappropriate contact with such musical beings may lead to illness, madness or death. Appropriate music played in the correct contexts, as 'consolation' (*kunswilu*) for the forces which oversee the fortunes of the community, may be seen as directly related to the maintenance of bodily health. However, although sound is an important dimension in ritual healing, to my knowledge music is not performed in a clinical context.[6]

Western European medicine is available from two small health outposts, some two and four hours' walk from the hamlet, and a hospital – at a distance of some eight hours' walk. In practice my hosts were extremely wary of these institutions, and tended to treat the hospital as a last resort. This serves to reconfirm the local belief that people only go to hospital to die. However, it is not so much Western medicine that is avoided as the hospital staff, who inhabit a different social sphere and rarely demonstrate respect for peasant people or their beliefs. For example, I received constant requests for medicines or medical assistance from my hosts, alongside warnings about the dangers of the *llik'ichiris* or 'fat stealers' from the hospital and local towns. These evil beings, I was told, use special 'machines' to extract human fat which is used to grease (Western-style) machinery or in the production of, for example, medicines and communion wafers. The victim is said to acquire a wasting disease, often leading to death.[7] Indeed, the majority of illnesses I encountered – even accidents – were attributed to malevolent or resentful forces, derived from other social groups, sorcerers, or spirits of the ancestors or landscape.

From this perspective, illness is not simply bodily malfunction but rather a symptom of deterioration or imbalance in a much broader series of relationships. Diagnoses supplied by ritual specialists typically involve reading coca leaves to discover the extra-bodily cause of illness and appropriate action, rather than examining the patient's body itself. For example, certain illnesses were attributed to the anger (*phiña*) of mountain spirits (*jurq'us*) or ancestors resulting from failure to supply them with appropriate ritual offerings. It was explained that this revenge may take the form of evil substances entering the victim's body, while asleep outside on the mountain, or of wild predators sent to devastate the animal herds. Illness is thus primarily viewed as one of a number of potential misfortunes, resulting from unbalanced relations with the forces of nature or other social networks.

The animated landscape

Not only is the health of the human body seen to depend upon the balancing of forces from beyond its physical boundaries, but the landscape itself is understood as animated, like a living body. This has been reported widely in ethnographies of the Andes:

> To Andean Indians nature is animated, and persons and nature form an intricately organized unity. They are bound together through common origins, and they reciprocate with one another. This unity depends on a balance in the forces of nature and a complementary balance in social activities. These reciprocations are clearly visible in rituals such as those concerned with birth, death, marriage, misfortune, agriculture and healing.[8]

My hosts regularly attributed human-like emotions to the mountains. For example, I was told that, besides being resentful when improperly treated, the mountains become sexually excited at full moon. Apparently, at these times their mating noises can be heard resounding from the peaks, and sound like those of bulls or llamas. I also attended a ceremony, which prepares for the rainy growing season, in which the mountain (*qullu*) was 'married' to the *wirjin* (lit. 'virgin'), a ritual name for fertile agricultural land. Just like human weddings, marriage music was constantly played during the ceremony.

In the same way as humans, cosmological bodies are also subject to illness. For example, on two occasions I have witnessed eclipses of the moon in my host hamlet, where the moon was said to have become 'sick' (*unquy*). If the moon were to die, it was explained, the earth would then become submerged in water, thus also bringing an end to human and other terrestrial life. The terror experienced by my hosts was astonishing, especially considering that lunar eclipses are by no means rare. The combined effect of women's wailing, crying children and strange unearthly cries from the chickens was very powerful, and after it had continued for several hours I even found myself infected by the mass hysteria. In order to resuscitate the moon, large stretches of dried grasses were set alight on the hillsides, dozens of sticks of dynamite were exploded, and on one occasion an ox-horn trumpet (*pututu*) was sounded. The sound of this trumpet was said to be rich in *animu*, a word I shall discuss in detail, serving to resuscitate the moon or in other contexts to inspire warriors with courage and energy in territorial battles (*chajwa*) (see Figure 2.1).

Following the pioneering work of Mary Douglas in particular, the metaphor of the human body – as a way of understanding social process – has now been recognized in many societies.[9] In her book *Inca Cosmology and the Human Body*, Constance Classen also identifies the Inka's use of the body as a central metaphor for understanding, organizing and experiencing their world. However, Classen suggests that Inka cosmology was not simply 'inscribed' on the passive physical body, as the work of Douglas would imply, but rather that it 'was *lived* and *thought* through the very entrails' of the body. Thus, according to Classen, for the Inkas 'the body was a presentation, not just a representation of the cosmos'. Furthermore, the bodies of the Inka nobility and their subjects were 'not only inserted in the structure of the Inca state, they manifested that structure within themselves'.[10] From this perspective disorder, whether cosmological, natural or social, would be likely to manifest itself as bodily malfunction.

Indeed, shortly after the European invasion of 1532, the indigenous *taqui oncoy* or 'dancing sickness' cult developed in many parts of the Andes (1565). This was one of several responses to the collapse of the Inka empire.[11] The cult's preachers prophesied the end of Spanish domination through restoration of the powers of local indigenous deities or *wak'as*, demanding the avoidance of Spanish dress, food and religion. Andean people expressed the social, cosmological and physical disorder brought about by the conquest – including European diseases and hunger – through their bodies as dancing. According to Sara Castro-Klarén, the *taqui oncoy* acted as 'a space of transition that divided the voyage of sickness to health'.[12]

2.1 Young men with a form of ***pututu*** trumpet and ***kitarilla***, a rainy season guitar decorated with images of growing crops. The sound of both of these instruments is noted for its *animu*.

This notion of transition from sickness to health is both central to indigenous healing practices in the Andes today and characterizes most rural music performance during fiestas. Music serves, in part, to mark passage from one state to another, where the unfolding of the year is understood in terms of the stages of bodily transformation.

Animu – sounding bodies

Despite the abundance of vocabulary for musical genres, instruments and sound qualities, my Andean hosts have no equivalent for the all-encompassing English concepts of 'music' or 'sound'. It appears to be the quality and context of the sound that is important, so that generalized categories such as 'music' or 'sound' are hardly significant. However, I was often told, what all musics and sounds do have in common is *animu* ('animation' or 'energy').

Animu is attributed to all living things, including the sap-filled stems of plants and the seeds of food crops – which are said to 'weep like babies' if not cared for appropriately. Certain rocks, such as the bell stones, *wak'as* and *illas* on the mountain peaks, which are said to ring or emit mating noises like domestic animals during the full moon, are also considered to contain animu. Similarly, the earth itself – with its body-like transformations, hydraulic movements and winds – is thought to be full of animu, as are bright celestial bodies such as the sun, moon, stars and lightning. Animu, as energy, is expressed as sound, movement, light, scent or autoresonance. From this perspective, sound is equivalent to life and its shaping in music may be seen as the shaping of life.

The word animu has been borrowed into Quechua from Spanish; the Spanish *ánimo* is typically translated into English as 'soul' or 'spirit'. Today's word animu seems to build on the existing Quechua word *kama* (*cama*), which has been discussed in detail by Gerald Taylor (1976). He has pointed out a passage by the early colonial writer Garcilaso de la Vega (1539–1616), a native Quechua speaker, whose description of *cama* is highly suggestive of my hosts' use of the word animu. Also, a direct analogy is once again drawn between the animation of the body and the cosmos:

> *cama*, which is to give energy; the verb is arrived at from the noun *cama*, which is spirit: *Pachacamac* means he/she who gives spirit to the entire universe, and in its true and whole meaning, it means he/she who does with the universe like what the spirit does with the body.[13]

While today's use of the stem *kama* focuses on the creation and control of life (and, as a suffix, to a defined period of time or space),[14] animu is used more specifically to refer to the substance of animation, whether enclosed in a body or manifested as light, sound or movement. The concept animu thus appears to be a hybrid which has roots in both Andean and European cultures, and serves to develop rather than simply displace the indigenous concept *kama* (*cama*).

According to my host, each body is endowed with and contains a given amount of animu, which should not change during the course of life. This animu denotes the character of the body. Thus, for example, men have six (identical) animus and women three. Hence, it was explained, men are stronger than women. In turn mountains (*jurq'us*), which are immensely powerful, were said to possess twelve animus – a number which, in ritual arrangements, is considered particularly strong and is widely used to convey a sense of 'abundance and fulfilment'.[15] All the above numbers are multiples of three, and it is this number in particular which is associated with animu.[16]

The colour white, perhaps evoking the energy of light, is especially linked with animu. For example, the white ruff of feathers on a condor's neck, which stands out vividly against its black body, was referred to as animu. Similarly, the white central stripe of *kustala* (Sp. *costale*) sacks used for carrying grains between the valleys and highlands on the backs of llamas is especially associated with animu and referred to as *sunqu* ('heart/viscera').The liver (rather than the organ the 'heart') is generally seen as the core of the body and the source of animu, and sometimes music. Indeed, on several occasions people spoke of 'twisting' (*q'iwishan*) powerful new melodies from the liver (*q'iwicha*). From this perspective sources of bodily animation are equated with sources of music.

From animu to *alma*

At death, the energizing animu contained in the body during life is said to pass out of the body to become *alma*. This is a Spanish loan word meaning 'soul', which my hosts exclusively associate with the dead. As one friend put it: 'the person's animu transforms to *alma*' (*animullataq almaman tukupun runaqta*). This was vividly brought home to me when discussing the terminal illness of an elderly friend, whose lower body was paralysed. It was explained that this inability to move his limbs meant that part of his animu had already gone to *alma llajta* – the 'land of the souls'. This hidden realm is said to lie to the west, just out of sight. It is constantly green, with many weeping willow trees, and, although inaudible to the living, the souls constantly sing and dance the *wayñu* music of the rainy growing season. There is a sense, confirmed in several conversations, that the animu enclosed within a living body also takes the form of music – bodies are animated from their core by music.

Apparently, the fortunes of deceased souls are looked after by *santa animas*, in precisely the same way as those of the living are overseen by the *sapiri* – the unique local mountain spirit which takes the form of a condor. Thus, when an *aysiri* (shaman) was called to help my elderly paralysed friend, he called upon *santa animas*. The aysiri tapped three times on the patient's chest, 'as though knocking on a door', for the animu to return from the sound-filled land of the souls and re-enter the body.

It is immensely dangerous to lose animu from the body permanently, and many illnesses are attributed to its loss. This category of illness is usually called *susto* (lit. 'fright, sudden terror') in Spanish, translated into English as 'soul loss', and attributed to unexpected shock.[17] 'Soul loss' is recognized as an illness category in many other cultures, for example the Temiar of Malaysia.[18] The owl (*juqu*) and a small bird called the *ch'iki* are both associated with 'cutting' or pecking away a person's animu and are considered especially malevolent. The ch'ik ch'ik call of the ch'iki bird is directly associated with the sound of animu being cut from the body. This same ch'ik ch'ik sound is also associated with curses and sorcery and locally referred to as *runa simi*, literally 'people mouth', meaning 'language'. Could this imply an antithetic relationship between speech and sound, as suggested by Lawrence Sullivan in his survey of South American religions?: 'Sound is always meaningful and whole. Speech threatens that integrity by fracturing the sound so that the meaning is parcelled out one syllable, one word, one sentence, or one spoken idea at a time.'[19]

The ch'ik ch'ik sound, with its staccato and percussive ejective, richly evokes such an image of fracturing or cutting. I have already noted that my hosts appear to view the animu enclosed within a body as sound, musically orchestrated from the body's core. Any threat to the integrity of this sound may presumably be understood as a danger to the body. Cures for loss of animu, from sorcery, include drinking blood from a black cockerel, dog or sheep, or a man should drink some of his wife's blood.

Dreams, whistles and llama bells – communicating energy

Although animu must not be lost from the body during life, a person's animu is expected to travel outside the confines of the body during sleep, on journeys experienced as dreams.[20] A living person's animu was said to travel 'forward' during life whereas the *alma* of the dead travel 'backwards'.[21] Indeed the souls of the dead were often described as a back-to-front or inside-out version of the living, or as *lluq'i* ('left'), because they travel to the left, whereas the living travel to the right. Accordingly, when my young godson put his boots on the wrong feet his parents jokingly described him as '*lluq'i* like an *alma*'. As this reciprocal balancing of orientation between the dead and living implies, the dead are believed to take an active role in the fortunes of the living. This is again emphasized in the ritual name for the dead: *mañaq ruway*, meaning approximately 'the lenders that create'.

The idea of the body as a receptacle containing and potentially releasing sound is vividly evoked by my hosts' use of small globular whistles called *wislulu*. These resemble hollow oak apples (1–1.5 cm in diameter) with a small orifice which may be blown across, in the manner of a panpipe, to create a high-pitched whistling sound. I was told that wislulu grow on *q'ara ñanta* trees in the temperate valley regions and, in the windy month of August, are sometimes blown up to the highlands. Globular wislulu whistles may also be purchased, throughout the Potosí region, from market stalls specializing in ritual goods. They are widely used, alongside other ingredients, in rituals to cure loss of animu.

In my host community, where infant mortality rates are distressingly high, I saw a wislulu attached to the knitted hat of newborn baby.[22] The mother explained that the wislulu would encourage the child to be healthy and grow well. Older people also sometimes carry wislulu around with them to bring luck, and to help remember the words and melodies of songs. It was explained that wislulu contain animu and their size should relate to the person who uses them; for example, as I am much bigger than my hosts it was explained that I would need a particularly large size. I was also told that if I sounded a wislulu and thought of someone, even on the other side of the world, I would turn up in the person's dreams and they could be attracted towards me. This form of communication was compared to a telephone (of which my hosts had no actual experience).

The idea of the wislulu as a vessel in which animu is contained, like a fluid, and matures is also suggested by the use of the word as the ritual name for fermentation vessels, used in corn beer preparation. These large earthenware vessels are identical in shape to the tiny wislulu whistles, and their name *puñu* may be literally translated as 'sleep'. The *puñu* enclose and protect the beer as it 'ferments' or 'grows', the Quechua word *puqu-* incorporating both these meanings. There is a sense that animu – like the fluid modalities of sound and corn beer in wislulus – 'grows' or develops its potential whilst enclosed in the body. When it has reached this potential, like fermented beer, the animu emerges and transforms to alma and its power is then shared out to others to bring renewal. Corn beer and music are vital ingredients to any major feast. Their release as drinking, ritual spilling, and sound is surrounded with immense symbolic import, and is in many ways equivalent to a sacrificial act. Indeed, fiesta music is widely referred to as *kunswilu* ('consolation'), a response to sacrifice.

The musical associations of animu are also emphasized in the use of llama bells, worn by leading male llamas on trading journeys to the valleys. During the cold winter months of June and July countless highland herders drive their caravans of male llamas to the warm valleys to exchange highland salt, or other exchange items, for maize, wheat, wood and other valley products. On the journey downwards with salt the llamas walk in silence, but as they return to the highlands, carrying maize, *sinsiru* (Sp. *cencerro*) bells are tied around the necks of the leading llamas. The sound of the bells is said to enchant the animu of the maize back to the herders' highland homes in precisely the same way as a young man plays his mandolin-like *charango* to attract a girl back to his (patrilocal) hamlet to become his wife.[23] It is thus through the medium of (musical) sound, and its influence on the animu contained in bodies, that intensely powerful emotions are communicated and transformations or actions brought about. As in many other Amerindian cultures, my hosts had no doubt of music's power to generate transformations.

Celestial power and knowledge

In the animated landscape of my host hamlet, the bright flashes of light sometimes seen in the night sky are referred to as *luriya* (Sp. *gloria*). The various celestial bodies are considered especially powerful sources of animu and follow a hierarchy which channels power and knowledge from the most distant, powerful and dangerous levels to more localized and accessible ones. The hierarchy may be summarized as follows:

Tiusninchis ('god of all of us' = the sun)[24]
Luriya (Sp. *Gloria*, 'Glory')[25]
Santiyaku (Sp. Santiago, 'St James') and consort Santa Warawara ('St Barbara')
Tata Pumpuri and Tata Wañuma ('sons of Santiago')
Sapiri (local mountain spirit, takes form of condor)

Tiusninchis is the common local name for the Christian god, which my hosts equate with the sun. This name combines the Spanish *dios* ('god') with the Quechua first person plural inclusive marker (*-nchis*), emphasizing the universality of god's realm and influence. *Luriya* not only evokes the idea of god's 'glory' but also seems to be understood in terms of a celestial sea of animu.

Santiago is the lightning god and is said to perform god's punishments (*castigos*). Locally his name is often pronounced *santi yaku*, emphasizing the Spanish *sant-*, 'saint' and Quechua *yaku*, 'water'. Indeed, the arrival of rain in this part of the Andes is almost always preceded by electrical storms with thunder and lightning. Santiago has served as a powerful emblem for Spanish domination in the Andes, and in this capacity the associations of – often arbitrary – destruction, conquest, coercion, hierarchy but also guardianship fused with those of the pre-Hispanic lightning god Illapa.[26] Accounts from as early as the seventeenth century tell of Santiago appearing in the Andes as the local mountain god in a ceremony in which music forms an integral part:

> when an indigenous healer from another central highland village appealed to his mountain god for help, it was Santiago who appeared: 'Resplendent, shining, and he would burn [anyone who could] look at him ... and he entered [the room], making a noise like the sound of spurs ... and they began to sing and chant to him: you who are dressed in gold, dressed in yellow, now you come crossing mountains, plains and valleys.[27]

St Barbara is also associated with lightning and said to be Santiago's consort.[28] Tata Pumpuri and Tata Wañuma, who are said to be the sons of Santiago and celebrate their feasts on the same day (25 August), are important local saints with shrines within Macha territory. The shrine to the 'elder brother' Pumpuri (Bombori), which is especially associated with shamanistic and curing practices, is located in the highlands and the shrine of the 'younger brother' Wañuma in the valleys.

Finally, the sapiri is the most localized source of celestial power and knowledge and is said to reside in a mountain peak, less that one kilometre from my host hamlet. Local *yatiris* and aysiris call upon the sapiri in shamanic sessions to ask the causes or remedies for illnesses, disputes or other misfortunes in the community. The sapiri is said to arrive at these occasional late night sessions in the form of a condor, invisible due to the complete darkness. His presence is often marked by the constant jingling of metal, evoking the sound of flapping wings. He answers questions through the medium of a shaman, but is said to speak in a language from outside the community such as Spanish, or even English, but not Quechua, the local language. In practice Quechua is often used but the reference to foreign languages may serve to heighten the distant and inaccessible quality of the sapiri's knowledge and power, which is channelled to the human world from higher sources.

Lightning-bolt whistles

In order to become a *yatiri* or *aysiri* (shaman) it is usually seen as necessary to have been marked out as different from other people in some way. This may take the form of, for example, a physical deformity. However, the most common way in which ritual specialists are seen to be marked out, or their powers confirmed, is through being struck by lightning. Indeed, Francisco,[29] a close friend from my host hamlet, told me how he had been struck by lightning several years earlier. Since that time he has been learning to become a yatiri, both through practice as a healer and guidance from more experienced yatiris. According to Tomás Huanca, it is through death, from a lightning strike, and gradual revival to life that yatiris acquire their special powers.[30]

In explaining how lightning had struck him, Francisco referred to the lightning bolt or *wala* (Sp. *bala* 'bullet, shot'), which has often been compared with the deadly shot fired from a gun. As the wala flies through the air, he said, it sounds: *lluq, lluq, lluq* and as it hits the ground: ***kururun, kururun, kururun.*** Despite the popular association between lightning bolts and gunfire, Tomás Huanca notes that walas are actually created through the fusion of the metal contents of rocks struck by lightning. He also observes that some walas acquire anthromorphic forms and are said to speak to people.[31] Francisco equated the lightning bolt with the brass globular whistle which he uses to summon the sapiri 'to speak'. This is identical in shape with the wooden wislulu and sometimes referred to with the same name. However, I was warned that it would be highly dangerous for anyone other than a yatiri to sound the brass wala. Its sound would cause the sapiri or Santiago to arrive, with fatal consequences for an ordinary person.

The distinction between the wooden wislulu and the shaman's brass wala seems to highlight the temporality and fragility of human bodily existence in relation to the immense power, durability and permanence of the animated cosmos. It is also perhaps significant that wislulu are said to be blown up from the valleys during the windy month of August, a time associated with bodily growth, whereas wala arrive during the electrical storms of the rains, a period associated with death and regeneration.[32] However, both are represented as vessels which enclose animu and take the form of sound-making instruments – globular whistles. In the next section I shall describe how both these whistles, the *sinsiru* bell and dynamite were used in a specific healing ritual.

Exchanging the animu: a healing ritual

On a few occasions I accompanied my yatiri friend Francisco to healing rituals, acting as his assistant. My presence did not seem to pose a problem, rather my exoticism and alternative spheres of knowledge seemed to add prestige to my friend's powers and reputation. I shall now focus on a single healing ceremony held at the patient's house, some two hours' walk from my host hamlet. The patient, an elderly lady, had apparently been struck by lightning over a year before and been blind since that time. My immediate reaction on seeing the lady was that neither a curing ritual nor Western medicine could possibly cure her blindness. However, Francisco approached the task as he would any other by first reading coca leaves to find the cause of illness and appropriate action to take. He eventually decided that *q'ara alma* (lit. 'naked soul') had entered inside the patient which must be exorcized and replaced in order to cure her.

The healing ritual was performed on Monday evening and continued until dawn on Tuesday morning. Monday is the day of the *almas* (souls of the dead) so the passage from death to life, it was explained, was important to the effectiveness of the ritual. Having decided the form the cure would take from reading coca leaves, a wide variety of ritual offerings was prepared. Several hours later, a young dog was collected and the patient was whipped to cause the corrupted animu to pass out of her body and into the dog. Shortly before midnight the dog was taken down to the river, a fire made, ritual offerings burnt in the embers, and – much to my distress – the dog's throat cut. The dog's body was left near the river and the party returned to the patient.[33]

Shortly after midnight, now Tuesday morning and a day associated with life, a wooden wislulu whistle and a piece of *animu siwayru* were placed in the patient's homespun coca bag (*ch'uspa*) around her neck. *Animu siwayru* is used to cure loss of animu; it takes the form of a round blue chalk pellet, and is widely available from market stores specializing in ritual goods. After various other preparations, the yatiri and assistants set off to a place just above the hamlet where the blind lady had apparently been struck by lightning. A fire was made and a knife was stuck into the earth beside a flat rock where the lightning had struck. Next to the knife was placed the patient's coca bag (enclosing the wislulu and *animu siwayru*) and above this Francisco's wala whistle (see Figure 2.2).

When these preparations were complete Francisco rang a *sinsiru* bell, using it to prescribe a circle around the knife as he sounded it. He then took the knife, scored the shape of a cross in the earth and cut several pieces of soil from the centre of the cross, placing them carefully on a cloth. To this he added three small pebbles. Ritual offerings were then quickly burnt in the embers of the fire. The rock which had been struck by lightning was dramatically whipped, whilst demanding it to release and return to the patient the animu it contained. Finally, the coca bag and wala were collected up, a piece of dynamite put in their place, the fuse was lit, and we all sprinted to safety.

Following the explosion, the party returned to the patient's house where Francisco stirred the soil, three pebbles, and a few scrapings of

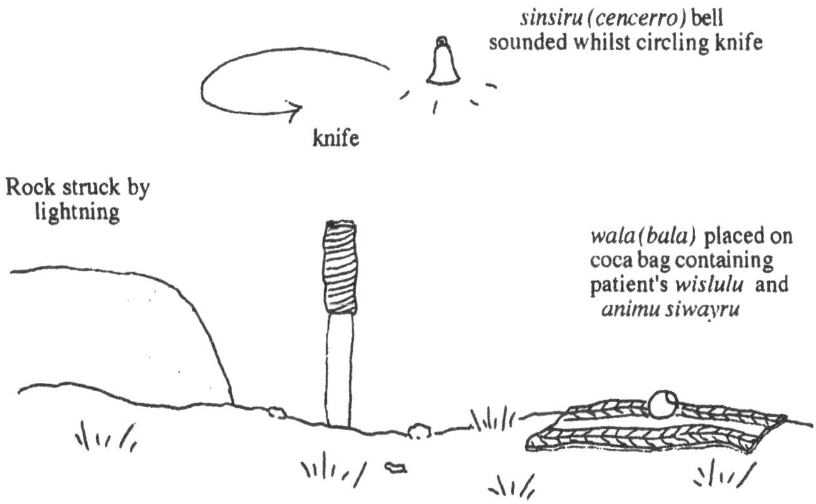

2.2 Placing of knife, coca bag and *wala*.

animu siwayru into a mug of water from which the patient was instructed to drink. A few scrapings of *animu siwayru* were also placed inside the wislulu, together with a tiny piece of *sirka* wood. The *sirka* would act as a boundary, it was later explained, thereby containing the animu so than none is lost. In this image, the wislulu vividly represented the patient's body in which animu must be placed and not allowed to escape. Finally, a chicken was collected and killed – causing its animu to enter the patient – after which the bird was plucked, cooked and eaten and libations continued until dawn.

Despite my ethical problems with this particular ritual, which failed to improve the patient's sight or provide significant therapeutic help, the importance of animu and its relation to sound and health was clearly expressed. The ceremony vividly evoked images of death and regeneration, symbolizing a bridge from illness to health, through the passage of the night. The association of Monday with the dead and the killing of the dog containing the patient's corrupted animu just before midnight were powerful images of death and exorcism. After midnight, alternative animu was placed inside the patient's body in preparation for dawn – symbolizing rebirth with the rise of the sun. The timing of the ritual was crucial and directly related the daily renewal of the sun, as the ultimate source of animu, with the symbolic transition of the body from illness, via death, to health.[34] Similar imagery is found in African ngoma healing, where songs commonly incorporate the phrase 'may darkness be replaced by light'.[35] The process may be schematized as follows:

	dusk (Monday)	*midnight* |	*dawn* (Tuesday)
SUN	----- decline ----	nadir ---- rise -----	
BODY	illness	death	health

Cosmic animu collected from the place in the landscape where the patient had been struck by lightning was crucial to the ritual. To collect it the patient's coca bag – containing her wislulu – was placed alongside the yatiri's own brass wala. The wala served to communicate with the powerful celestial sources of cosmic animu, which it represents, and the wislulu evoked the containment of bodily animu. This animu was attracted for placement in the patient's body using the sounds of a *sinsiru* bell – a sound used elsewhere to attract the animu of maize. Finally, sound was used in the violent explosion of dynamite – a sound used in other contexts to mark or bring about reversals, such as the transformation of the moon's sickness to health during a lunar eclipse.

Landscapes of music

How, if at all, do my hosts' uses and understandings of sound in healing relate to musical practices? I wish to suggest that, although 'music' is not used in a clinical context (to my knowledge), an understanding of the body and the role of animu are fundamental to musical performance. Furthermore, music is intimately linked with agricultural production and thus occupies a crucial position in the maintenance of bodily and community health.

The seasonal alternation of musical instruments, genres and tunings is particularly remarkable in the high Andes. My hosts play two types of panpipes and the small strummed mandolin-like *charango* during the dry winter months (April–October). The sounds of these instruments are said to attract the frosts and winds associated with this time of year. In the rainy growing season, these instruments are exchanged for *pinkillu* flutes, which resemble recorders and are played in consorts of four to six sizes, and the strummed *kitarra*, a local guitar decorated with colourful images of growing crops and the sun. The rainy season instruments are widely said to attract the rain and to help the crops to grow (see Figure 2.3).

A literal association between these instruments and the body is suggested in the report from the nearby Jalq'as, that if a woman were to play a *thurumi* (pinkillu) flute – an exclusively male preserve – she would be likely to experience menstrual problems.[36] However, I wish to

2.3 Young men with wooden *pinkillu* flutes, during the feast of Carnival.

focus on the imagery of musical instruments as body-like vessels which enclose and shape animu during life, and release it to become *alma* at death. These contrasted images of containment and release are vividly evoked in the distinction between the panpipes of the dry winter months and the pinkillu flutes of the rains.

The *jula-jula* panpipes of the dry harvest season of May are usually played in consorts of five or six sizes, tuned at octave intervals.[37] The male *jula-jula* players perform in a long snaking dance, called *link'u-link'u*, in which a mature man plays the largest instrument at the head of the snake and a young boy the smallest size at its tail.[38] The snaking shape of this dance is explicitly compared with a snake (*katari*) and snakes are said to be immortal – the dance suggesting an image of perpetual life. In the arrangement of the players, from a boy at the tail to the mature man at the head, is symbolized the growth cycle from childhood to adulthood. This image of bodily growth is also evoked in the structure of the melody which, in this region, always begins on the smallest and highest-pitched tube and ends on one double its size, an octave lower in pitch. The instruments are held with the smallest tubes on the player's left and progressively longer tubes to his right. Melodies are always said to go 'to the right' (*pañaman*), the direction associated with the living, in contrast to the *almas* (souls of the dead) who travel 'to the left' (*lluq'iman*).

The construction of dry-season panpipes with their progressively larger tubes, from left to right, are a vivid representation of bodily growth, suggesting health and accumulation of mass. Yet, as noted above, the animu contained in a body should remain constant throughout life, suggesting that it is not animu which is accumulated in these progressively expanding tubes but bodily mass. Animu seems to be understood as more concentrated in younger, immature bodies which have yet to grow to their full size; hence children are more 'animated' than adults. Indeed, in the *link'u-link'u* dance it is the boy at the tail, with the tiny *wiswi* or *ch'ili* size instrument, who is called upon to initiate the melody. This high-pitched sound can be heard clearly above the other instruments as its melody impels the dance forward.

As containers of animu, the construction of panpipes resembles the wislulu, where size is also related to bodily mass. In contrast, the recorder-like pinkillu flute, which is played to attract rain and promote plant growth in the rainy season, was said to be 'full of holes', evoking the idea of animu escaping to become *alma*. Indeed, the sounds of pinkillu flutes are explicitly related to the *almas* who, I noted, constantly sing and dance to the music of these instruments in the land of the souls (*alma llajta*). Thus, pinkillu flutes evoke bodily death and are even played outside the cemetery at the start of the rains, when the souls of the dead are invited back to the world of the living.

Such seasonal approaches to music draw both on understandings of bodily and vegetative cycles. In part, panpipes are approached in terms of the seed crops and tubers which must be stored carefully over the dry, winter months so that they mature and their integrity, as containers of animu, is maintained. Their welfare is of critical importance both as a source of food and seed for future years. However, during the rainy growing season, the planted seeds or potato tubers sprout and their integrity is destroyed as they 'die' in the creation of the next generation of fruits. Thus, musical performance, and the control of animu it entails, is seen actively to influence the annual transformation of the landscape. Similar imagery was adopted in the curing ritual described above, where death was invoked to bring renewal as health.

Conclusion

In the first part of this chapter I described local approaches to illness and descriptions of the qualities of the animating substance animu, which is often expressed as sound. Later I showed how animu was manipulated in the context of a healing ritual, using various sound-making instruments which, in Western terms, would not usually be classified as 'musical'. Finally, I demonstrated how animu is alternately contained and then released through seasonally contrasted forms of musical performance, to bring about the annual transformation of the landscape. Although music is not used in a clinical context for healing practices, I hope to have demonstrated a variety of parallel approaches between the use of sound to influence the landscape in music and the body in healing.

The powerful sounds used in shamanic curing practices – such as the wislulu and wala whistles and the *sinsiru* bell – are neither acoustically complex nor considered aesthetically beautiful. Yet, such sounds, which a musicologist might be tempted to overlook, are often thought to have the power to motivate transformations and appear to contain or represent many more complex potential sounds and musics. Accordingly, in musical performance, it is the small, shrill and high-pitched instruments of a consort which tend to be classified as the leaders and are said to motivate the ensemble, rather than the larger sizes.[39] For example, the small *q'iwita* flute which leads the pinkillu flute ensemble is sometimes equated with the *sunqu* ('heart/viscera')[40] and said to be the 'principal motor' of the ensemble. Perhaps we might approach the shrill sounds used in healing, with their 'all-pervasive energy' to motivate transformations, in a similar way.

A number of patterns emerge from the approaches to sound I have described. However, it would be a mistake to interpret the meaning of such sounds in a rigid way, as some form of neat local system disconnected from the multiplicity of external influences, experiences and personal idiosyncrasies which make both music and healing such immensely creative media. For example, for my hosts, traditional healing practices exist in relation to rather than independently of Western medicine. This adds economic and political dimensions to such practices – choosing one rather than the other is both a statement about identity and an economic consideration. Also, as more children attend the local school, knowledge about the body and the landscape begins to change. For example, drawing on local symbolic knowledge, my host and his brother independently insisted that the human body contains a single bone in the left forearm and a pair in the right. Other people maintained that each forearm contains two bones. They knew this, it was explained, because they had learned it at school.

In a similar vein, the seasonal performance of music, which remains strong in my host hamlet, has been abandoned in many places. It is now common to see rainy- and dry-season instruments played side by side and hear beliefs about the effects of music on the climate ridiculed as anacronistic superstition. But with such modernization new elements also creep into ritual healing and musical practices, and traditions continue to be invented. Who knows, perhaps next time I visit my Bolivian hosts I will discover musical performance to have become a central feature of healing rituals – which to the innocent anthropologist might appear as age-old 'indigenous' tradition.

Notes

1. L. Sullivan (1988), 280.
2. Keeling (1992), 49.
3. Abercrombie (1991), 96.
4. See also Stobart (1996b).
5. However, string instruments and *pinkillu* flutes are often played by lone young men 'as companionship' as they walk to the fields. *Pinkillu* flutes may also be played regularly during periods of drought to attract the rain.
6. Music is used by healers in certain other Andean regions. For example, see Giese (1996) on the use of song by healers in northern Peru.
7. Also see Gose (1986), 296, Taussig (1987), 238.
8. Taussig (1980), 155.
9. Douglas (1966/1994 and 1970).
10. Classen (1993a), 145.
11. Taussig (1980), 171–3, Castro-Klarén (1993).
12. Ibid., 171.
13. Harrison (1989), 77.
14. The suffix *-kama* is also a relational suffix meaning 'until' or 'as far as'.
15. Armstrong (1988), 39.
16. Among many other associations, the link between three and animu may relate to its tendency to articulate from a central point, leading to active balancing and latent instability, or in the case of three stripes the enclosure of a central one (see also Harris 1986). It is difficult to gauge to what extent such associations draw on indigenous Andean or European associations, such as the Holy Trinity or the Pythagorean notion of three as expressive of beginning, middle and end (Hulme 1909, 10), suggesting life itself.
17. Joralemon and Sharon (1993), 235–6.

18. Roseman (1991), 165.
19. L. Sullivan (1988), 284.
20. This is very similar to descriptions of soul substance by the Temiar of Malaysia; see Roseman (1991), 25.
21. *Wañuqtin qhipanpi purin. Kay kawsayta animu ñaypaqpi.* 'In death it walks backwards. In this life this *animu* goes forward.'
22. This particular wislulu was of a slightly different shape and species, but I was assured that the standard globular whistle wislulu may equally be used to encourage babies to grow well.
23. An identical description has been recorded by Cassandra Torrico, working in neighbouring Tomaycuri (pers. comm.).
24. The moon is the sun's consort, and sometimes referred to as 'hanging gloria'.
25. *Luriya*'s position in this hierarchy is unclear as it is also referred to as the sapiris 'elder brother'.
26. Silverblatt (1988), 178.
27. Ibid., 184.
28. Locally St Barbara's name is pronounced *warawara*, which in the other local indigenous language, Aymara, means 'star'.
29. Due to fear of sorcery false names are often given to strangers. This is the false name given to me on my original arrival.
30. Huanca (1989), 61.
31. Ibid., 114.
32. See Harris (1982).
33. I was very disturbed by – what I saw to be – the unnecessary slaughter of the dog. I later asked Francisco whether he truly believed the curing ceremony would cure the blind lady and questioned whether he could possibly justify the action of killing the dog. He was sympathetic to my criticism, but we clearly held very different values in this respect.
34. Cf. Armstrong (1988), 88.
35. See below, Chapter 3.
36. Beaudet and Martinez (1994), 14.
37. *Jula-julas* use an anhemitonic pentatonic scale with seven pitches ranged over a compass of a ninth. This is divided between four- and three-tube instruments, which – for all but the smaller sizes – are played using interlocking technique by paired players.
38. The position of the small boy at the 'tail' is confirmed in conversation and found at moments of critical ritual importance; however, in other contexts it may be taken by an adult man.
39. Stobart (1996a).
40. Among the nearby Laymi ethnic group this instrument is called the *chuyma*, an Aymara word meaning heart/viscera.

CHAPTER THREE

Theories of music in African ngoma healing

John M. Janzen

Music in 'ngoma': definitions and challenges

The subject of this chapter is a widespread type of ritual in central and southern Africa that entails divination, song-dance, percussive rhythm, counselling and support during a lengthy therapeutic initiation in which the sufferer-novice often develops an identity-in-song and may eventually become a healer.[1] This widespread and varied institution is often identified with the word *ngoma*, which is translated variously as 'drum', 'drum of affliction', or 'rite of affliction', or more inclusive definitions.[2] I use the African term in my work because of the frequency with which it is used to describe the core sequence of activities in therapy: a sung, danced, healing ritual around a particular song/call-response set, usually focused on a particular person at a time, within a larger setting of a group of healers, their patients/novices, and sometimes their families and other community members. This set of activities is often directed by African medicine specialists known across the sub-continent by the general term *ganga*, 'doctor of medicine', although it is hyphenated to, or substituted by, more specialized titles such as that widespread in southern Africa where the practitioner of ngoma is simply called *i-sa-ngoma*, one who does ngoma. Both 'ngoma' and 'ganga' are probably several thousand years old, and belong to the foundation of historic cultures which spread from West Africa southward and eastward across the continent.[3] Some of the features common to the entire region of ngoma distribution are likely to be as old as the word. We are thus dealing with an ancient, classical African ritual therapeutic process in which music is central.[4] Some of the features of ngoma have spread to other regions, especially in the New World, where they have joined local or Western musical traditions.

Yet, in its therapeutic applications, the 'music' of central and southern African ngoma meets a conceptual chasm when it is placed alongside current Western dictionary definitions of music:

> ... the science or art of ordering tones or sounds in succession, in combination, and in temporal relationships to produce a

> composition having unity and continuity; 1b: vocal, instrumental, or mechanical sounds having rhythm, melody, or harmony; 2a: an agreeable sound; 2b: musical quality; 3: a musical accompaniment (as in a play set to ~; 4: the score of a musical composition set down on paper; 5: a distinctive type or category of music.[5]

Ngoma may not even qualify as music by these criteria, since dance and physical movement are absent from the definition. Dance, in the same dictionary, is defined as 'a series of rhythmic and patterned bodily movements usually performed to music'.[6] If, plausibly, an ngoma could be based on rhythmic movement without sound, it would in the Western definition be 'dance' without being 'music'. Such a definitional paradox has resulted in ngoma being commonly referred to as 'song-dance'. Yet even this hyphenated identification excludes another essential feature of ngoma, the spirits who are brought into – or evoked within – the ritual setting by the song-dance. The point is that the Western definition of music suggests performers or players before an audience, rather than music emanating from amongst the participants for whom the rhythm, bodily movement, sound and words are a conversation that grows in intensity and fullness and movement as it progresses.

This combination of song, dance and catharsis evocation does not make ngoma any less technically 'therapeutic' than technical approaches to Western music therapy. Although I am sure there would be a diversity of opinion amongst the thousands of ngoma healers across the sub-continent, were they ever to meet, those with whom I have spoken emphasize the therapeutic nature of ngoma. Muslim waganga in East Africa, and Christian sangoma in southern Africa, stress that ngoma is 'medicine' rather than 'religion', even though its therapeutic work is to discern the appropriate spirits in the music.

Indeed, this stance is reminiscent of that of some Western music therapists who look for resonance between the particular sound and the physiological effect it produces, as when a music therapist suggests that her clients prefer Mozart to all other music because it relaxes them best; or other researchers monitor brain-wave action of those listening to music so that they can discern with electronic instruments the difference produced by Vivaldi and Heino.[7] Granted, not all Western music therapy is so focused on the physiological effects of music and music-making. Other music therapists stress the relational, or contextual, quality of the clinical setting and the music that is a part of it. Yet the chasm I have mentioned still affects the stance in musicological writing towards African music, or the lack thereof. Of the 75 dissertations produced in music therapy in the decade from 1989 to 1998, not a single one was devoted to African musical therapy.[8] An exhaustive new bibliography of African music has no entries under 'music and healing', 'music and medicine', or 'music and therapy'.[9] The only category close to this is 'music and trance/possession', suggesting that researchers and bibliographers equate music and healing in Africa with trance behaviour. Recent music-therapy writing in South Africa, about which more will be said later, continues this avoidance of African musical therapy as a tradition in its own right, while at the same time opening a conceptual bridge to it.[10]

In an effort to correct several of these misleading distortions about the nature and role of music and therapy in central Africa, this chapter offers: first, a focused ethnographic sketch of 'doing ngoma' as I witnessed it in Capetown in 1982, so as to have before us a concrete basis of discussion; secondly, a presentation and discussion of several theories that may apply to this material as a 'musical' event, and more particularly, as African musical therapy; thirdly, because ngoma is so different, as a social phenomenon, from what is usually presented as music in the Western academic world, the chapter closes with a brief discussion of the implications of ngoma research for comparative scholarship on music therapy.

'Doing ngoma' at a 'washing of the beads' in Guguleto, Capetown

The setting is Guguleto, one of the black townships of Greater Capetown in 1982, over a decade before the demise of apartheid in South Africa. Guguleto was often the scene of violence in those years as police raided illegal residents, broke up suspected resistance activities, and generally harrassed the population. Guguleto's residents included both legal and illegal immigrants who had come from the homelands to work in the thriving industrial economy of the western Cape, and one of South Africa's three capitals. In the endless monotony of government houses with four rooms facing a street and a small back yard, the sessions of ngoma took place mostly on weekends to accommodate the work weeks of the participants. They would usually gather as a number of senior healers, their novice/patients, together with the family and friends of the person featured in the day's events. At least one all-night song-dance session was the centrepiece of the gathering, during which senior healers and apprentice/sufferers would sing/dance in a sequence of many ngoma units, each doing their song/dance in turn, with the others helping as a choir. This gathered community of thirty to fifty persons would also usually eat together at the close of their weekend together, following the sacrifice of a goat, rarely a cow or bull, offered for the healing or cleansing of the individual for whom the event had been staged (see Figure 3.1).

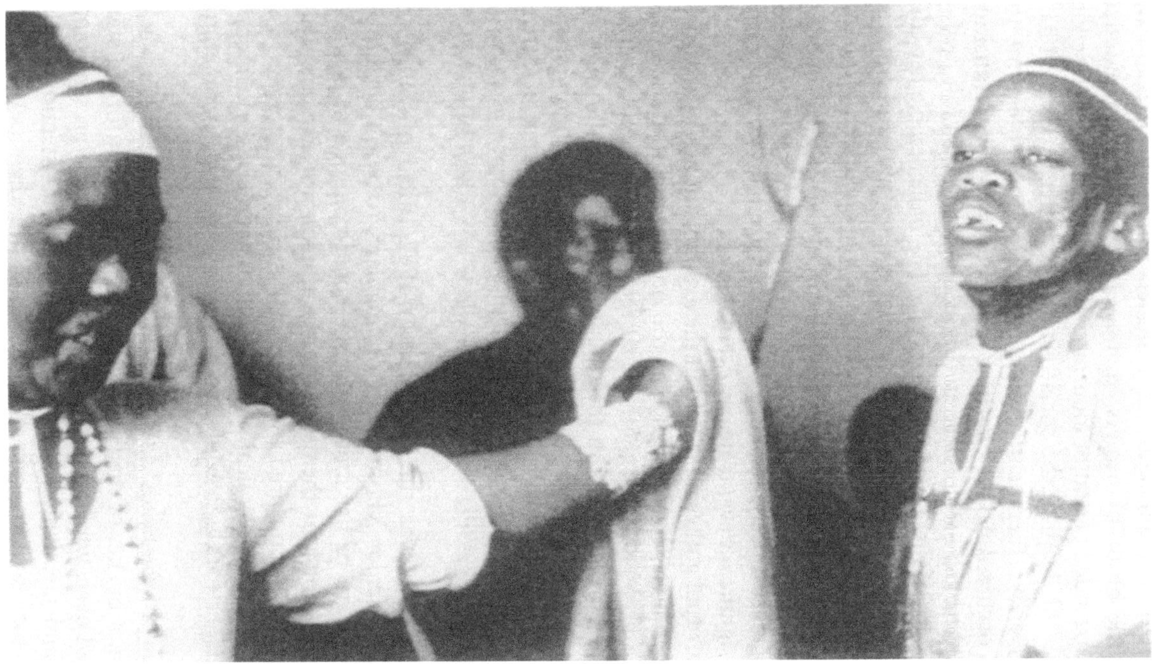

3.1 Two novices participate in ngoma session in Guguleto, Capetown, South Africa. They are part of a close circle of novices who are 'presenting themselves' in call-and-response performance led by a senior healer. White beads mark the liminal status of these sufferer/initiates. Eventually, as graduating healers, they will acquire elaborate and colourful costumes in expression of their more expansive selves. Family members, other healers and their patient/initiates and the general public participate in the room.

The ngoma calendar in this setting is typically occasioned by a few types of significant events in the lives of those in the network around the senior healers and their apprentices and clientele: the formal entry of a sufferer into apprenticeship with a senior healer; the 'graduation' of a novice to full qualification as a healed sufferer/healer; and the cleansing of the beads of healers, that is, their re-entry to practice, following an extended period of mourning after the death of a close kin. The 'pollution' of death in the social vicinity of a healer (as well as a novice) stops active therapeutic work in that person's life until the cleansing has occurred. So the 'washing of the beads' is also a transition in the life of the healer from grief and mourning back into full professional status. Each of these event/nodes (*nthlombe*) in the flexible network of healers (*igqira*, *amagqira* in Xhosa, *isangoma* in Zulu) and sufferer/ novices (*nkwetha*, *amakwetha*) in a locale such as Guguleto, offers the occasion for 'doing ngoma' (*sa ngoma*). In a cell of one of these ngoma communities, in the informal network of healers, a few senior healers who work together loosely, each having five to fifteen novices, may find occasion for significant events nearly every weekend.

The ngoma ritual gathering is held in the available houses, yards, and streets of those involved, in particular the one for whom the event is staged. In the urban settings these sites become 'situationally sacred'. That is, the pivotal locations in the rituals are given definition by the actions and words of the participants, but immediately following the event the sites return to their conventional use and meaning. Particularly the evocation of the ancestors through song, incense or sacrifice creates an aura of sacrality in a particular place at a given time, however fleetingly.

Such an occasion was the *nthlombe* in 1982 called on behalf of Adelheid Ndika, senior Xhosa healer of Guguleto, to 'wash her beads' following the death of her mother, so she could continue in practice. Since healers do not heal themselves in the thinking of African medicine, the event was sponsored by one of her 'sisters' in ngoma.[11] The event was attended by a typically cosmopolitan southern African community of persons of Xhosa, Zulu, Sotho, Swazi, and 'Coloured' ethnic categories.

The 'washing of the beads' for Adelheid was done early in the weekend. To begin, a bucket of medicine was stirred up with a forked stick until it frothed over, while the presiding healer and those present sang. The stirring and the singing were intended to get the attention of the ancestors so they would grace the occasion with their benediction. Adelheid's mother was amongst these spirits, and was expected to now be content in her new status as ancestor. Likewise, the event was also a transition for her, or the relationship between mother and daughter, between freshly arrived ancestor and continuing-in-life daughter-healer. As usual, the 'dirt' of pollution was ceremonially 'thrown out' onto the public street (alternatively it would be taken to the Indian Ocean), so that 'darkness could be replaced by light'. This motif occurs in some of the song texts recorded at this event, especially among the senior healers. Among the sufferer/novices, the songs are more commonly about personal matters. After the purification early on Saturday, and throughout the night from Saturday to Sunday, gathered healers and novice/sufferers turned their attention to doing ngoma therapeutic song-dance.

One of the senior healers led the session of doing ngoma in the main room of the house, together with the gathered sufferer/novices and occasionally others who were 'in therapy' with one of the senior healers but had not yet formally been accepted as novices. This group of a dozen or so individuals was surrounded by other novices, healers, family, friends and the general public who stood and sat alongside the four walls of the room. One of these individuals was the drummer, and the drum, typical in Capetown, was a cylindrical half of an oil barrel, with leather membranes stretched over both ends. One or two drumsticks were then used to beat out the rhythm. Others used metal shakers soldered together containing pebbles or seeds. Yet others joined in with hand-clapping. But the main initiators of the song-dance and the only ones who sang were those gathered in a tight circle in the centre of the room.

From a cultural historical perspective the ngoma of the western Cape is not entirely typical in the vast region of central and southern Africa. The metal drum as described is not part of the historical paraphernalia of ngoma. In South Nguni society (Zulu, Xhosa, etc.) of the pre-colonial, pre-conquest era, there is no record of the typical long, hollow, single membrane wooden ngoma drum that is abundant northward of the Venda, Shangan, perhaps Swazi, and across central Africa. In the Nguni south there is mention by early ethnographers of flat leather membranes stretched on wooden frames, or of no drums at all in association with 'doing ngoma'. The metal cylinder drum is an urban innovation, perhaps modelled after European drums. Not suprisingly, this new-style drum is not called ngoma. That classical term is reserved in this setting for the song-dance, indicative of its central status at the core of the institution.

Ngoma is done in this tight circle, with one individual, as we say, 'being it'. This individual, often in a kneeling position, begins to speak about whatever is on his or her heart. This is called the ***ukunqula***, a kind of 'self-presentation' that is sometimes called 'confessing dreams'.[12] It is a prelude to the second part of the unit, which is the ngoma proper. The two parts of the ngoma unit are one, yet they are very different.

The first is spoken, the second is sung. The first is done with everyone standing still or kneeling; the second is a demonstration of animated bodily motion and rhythm. The first has no instrumental accompaniment, the second is joined by whatever instruments or rhythm are at hand, including hand-clapping, shaking rattles, or the booming drum. (See Table 3.1.)

Table 3.1 The two parts of the ngoma unit

ukunqula (self-presentation)	*ngoma* (song-dance)
spoken	sung
individual	collective
motionless	song-dance, rhythm, instrumentation
'call'	'response'
suffering, confessing dreams	healing

This stark contrast within each unit of 'doing ngoma' represents a dynamic tension within the therapeutic performance that lends a great deal of power to the ability of this institution in all its fluidity to transform the individual who is willing to open up innermost thoughts and dreams to his or her peers.

These evocations that open each ngoma unit were done with great intensity, in a voice often filled with pain and passion, as if spoken by an individual wanting to get a weight off of his or her shoulders by telling it to those gathered. The ukunqula is sometimes about dreams, but other themes are evoked as in this out-pouring by the senior healer for whom the 'washing of the beads' was held, here addressing her mother: 'Ukunqula: ... I'm praying to Mama. We'll leave having washed each other ... We survive because of each other ... while we say we came to "heal".'[13]

The response was either initiated by the self-presenter, or it was initiated by someone in the gathered group of other healers and novices, with this short phrase which was repeated many times: '*Ngoma*: ... mama died ...'.

Regardless of who introduces the ngoma, as soon as it is intoned the circle begins to move in a counter-clockwise direction in a pattern characteristic of African group dance. The dancers' legs and bodies move in seemingly spontaneous yet concerted energy. If the dancers also have rattles in hand, they now begin to shake them in correspondence with their dance step and the singing. Shortly the drum joins the rhythm, but never before the vocal and smaller individual shakers and clappers have begun. The rhythm is thus initiated not by the drum, but by the energized group singing-dancing in a tight circle within the small room. The choreographer, who is singing-dancing in the circle, signals the end of the unit, which comes abruptly. The 'ngoma' is then 'passed on' to another individual who waits for everyone to become quiet, before he or she kneels and 'confesses'. Here is another self-presentation of a senior healer at the session held in connection with the washing of the beads just mentioned. This time the confession is not a dream or a prayer to an ancestor, it is a lament of the stress of working in apartheid South Africa.[14]

> *Ukunqula*: You would have thought that the night 'war' [ref. to the ceremony] would have calmed down this [igqira]. But no, it doesn't. I'm in it, always facing a white person [at work], and maybe that's why I'm 'on edge'.
>
> *Ngoma*: The ancestors are sleeping at the top of the mountains of Ulundi ...

This response by the group is a reference to the Zulu ancestors in faraway Natal province to the east where some of their ancestors come from, or perhaps the ancestors of this particular individual. It is a form of comfort to help her keep her orientation in an otherwise disorienting life situation, especially her work situation.

Later in the early evening another ngoma session is convened, this time for the sufferer/novices. The physical staging and the instrumentation was identical to the earlier session for the senior healers. The choreographer was a recently graduated healer. The self-presentation confessions and the ngoma song-dances were now even more clearly a reflection of the everyday suffering of the novices.[15]

> *Ukunqula*: I am hard-pressed by rental fees and many other things.
> I had to take from my children, asked them to give me some soap,
> for the young women here to smell good.
> *Ngoma*: Blessed be the name of the Lord [in English].
> *Ngoma*: Be strong because it's hard here on earth ...

In this urban setting Xhosa, Sotho, Afrikaans and English languages are mixed together in a polyglot environment mirrored in the call and response of ngoma structures, offering a minimal sense of togetherness amidst the fragmentation of South African society.

In another set, a young man or boy is severely tortured and can barely announce anything, except a cry to his ancestors:[16]

> *Ukunqula*: ... ah Ka Ngwane, hear me ...
> *Ngoma*: ... Sing and clap for the crab next to the river ...
> *Ngoma*: ... He Majola, come out of jail ... I have news of your house ...

The response by the encircled other novices is a double ngoma. The first is an allusion to the crab, a widespread central and southern

African symbol of mediation between the human and the spirit world. The crab, Na Nkala, is seen as a figure who scuttles back and forth between the water and the land, and between the visible world of the beach and the invisible world beneath the sands. In the second ngoma response, the gathered fellow sufferer/novices urge the young man to come out of his jail, out of himself, they have news for him. Such a reference to being boxed in, to being hidden within oneself, is a common metaphor for sickness. The cure, of course, is to speak, to dance, to produce words.

Again, when this ngoma unit comes to an end, one of the voices is heard to say 'we are giving the song (ngoma) over to you, Mama'. Imagine an entire night of such self-presentation, confessions, and affirming counter-singings, in which you are able to pour out your anxieties, dreams and hidden frustrations to your ancestors, to God, and those gathered about you. They, in turn, respond directly to your suffering. Additionally, as a sufferer, you are involved in helping others with their suffering. As a common phrase in the songs puts this process, 'may darkness be replaced by light!'

This scene, and this set of ngoma sessions, within one event occasioned by the end-of-mourning purification of an igqira healer in Guguleto, Capetown, in 1982, is informative not just for what it shows, but for what is missing from the ethnographic sketch. There is no trance, in the conventional sense of that term. Listening to the tapes, one hears very little polyrhythm – it is not entirely absent, but it is minimal. The absence of trance suggests, at the very least, that it is quite possible to have ancestor and spirit presence – what I call an 'ideology of possession', or a 'spirit hypothesis'[17] – represented only in incense, medicine, blood sacrifice and song. The absence of trance or any other 'technology' carries over into divination/counselling by the sangomas in the Capetown setting. They just sit down and talk with their clients, foregoing the instruments of African divination so common elsewhere.

Elsewhere one might have found polyrhythms and trance. In Swaziland a spirit medium was so bizarre that he was beyond being named. He entered the divinatory chamber with dishevelled hair and wild-looking clothing, bellowing like a mad animal, to give a declaration incomprehensible to the presiding diviner. The subdued hypothetical possession in Capetown tells us that the premise of the ancestors or spirit presence is more fundamental than the form taken by possession or ancestor spirit recognition. The music that carries the spirit communication is important less for its instrumental gymnastics than for the support community that listens to, and responds with, encouraging sung solace. Thus trance and polyrhythm, often touted as the hallmarks of African therapeutic music, are optional expressions of the more fundamental features of a gathered community of fellow sufferers, a call-and-response format which is like a spoken and sung conversation; the complementarity of the spoken word and the sung, danced, response: an identification of the spirits or circumstances of the shared agony.

Theoretical directions in ngoma African music

Before one can speak of theories of music in connection with ngoma performance and healing, it is useful to identify more precisely the structure of the social context within which it occurs. This setting is not that of a performer and an audience. It is rather an elaboration around the healer/patient dyad that can further unfold into several constellations: healer with sufferers among themselves; healers among themselves; sufferer, healer and others; elements of the sufferer's kin group; and spirits and humans.[18]

As was seen in the foregoing ethnographic sketch of ngoma in Capetown, the structure of the music is first and foremost an enhanced conversation between two or more interlocutors between whom the spoken word gives way to, or is alternated by, call-and-response song-dance. Instruments enter the conversation as a further enhancement or accompaniment only after the basic conversation has begun. The form of this call-and-response conversation is of course the pattern that generates the unique structure of rhythm in African music that has been so widely noted.[19] The two or more voices of the conversation resonate to become separate but linked rhythms within a polyrhythm. This polyvocal chorus of rhythms and voices echoes in an underlying pulsating beat widely identified as a unique and powerful feature of African music.[20] Multiple levels of body, instrument and voice can amplify and adumbrate this multivocality and polyrhythmicity so that any two or more points can evoke the hidden beat that drives and sustains the whole.

This general structure or pattern of sub-Saharan 'music', grounded as it is in the 'conversation' between voices, is highly dependent upon the social setting, subject to the whims, creative changes and artistic bursts of the conversations between the participants, far more than it is a predetermined score that must be followed. The salient questions about the organizing ideas or theories surrounding African music are not so much 'what is African music in healing?' as 'what triggers the enhancement of the basic spoken dialogue so that speech (*ukamba*) gives way to song (*yimba*), or 'doing ngoma'?

Ritualization of experience

A first line of interpretation to illuminate this question has been offered by ritualization theory, as it grew out of communications theory. Prevalent in the 1960s, this line of inquiry sought to understand ritualization in animal and human behaviour. Communications were thought of as messages flowing through channels, each organized by a code and expressed in a medium. Under certain conditions such a channel could became blocked, or filled with static, necessitating the addition of alternative channels, other mediums, so as to assure the transmission of the message from one point or participant to another. A certain amount of redundancy was seen to enhance communication, explaining the common practice of recourse to multiple channels both in human and in animal communication.[21] Thus, as an illustration, to overcome the effect of the wind that carries away the sound of a voice, one waves one's hand to catch the other person's attention. Bateson and Leach applied this type of communications theory to ritualization with some success. They emphasized that humans even more than animals engage in hidden or non-verbal messages as well as contradictory messages. Whereas dogs will growl and bark to express their fear at the same time as they warn of their threat to attack, we humans are the only species to tell lies with our words, while perhaps betraying the truth of our feelings with our blushes. Symbolic language, suggests Bateson, is almost always accompanied by gesture, body language, and other kinds of non-verbal communication. Repressed thoughts, social messages too dangerous to speak or act out bluntly, are veiled in other idioms such as mime, metaphor, myths, dreams and drama. Particularly the rituals of aggression and healing are known to divert emotions into channels other than explicit language. Thus, music, trance behaviour and non-verbal symbols may become necessary for the survival of life in human society. There may indeed be healing in such communication that releases aggression, or expresses contradiction, rather than engaging the conflicting parties directly in violent confrontation. Thus surely ngoma ritualizes the word.

Metaphors of 'difficult experience' and symbols of emotion

But to call music or song-dance 'ritual' hardly seems adequate. Music, like ritual, bypasses contradictions and blockages of whatever kind, in addition to which music plumbs the depths of emotion. It evokes its own distinctive essence that cannot be reduced to, or explained by, any other principle or word. Nietzsche, in his *Birth of Tragedy*, alludes to music's ability to capture the profoundness of emotion:

> Myth [word] shields us from music while at the same time giving music its maximum freedom. In exchange, music endows the tragic myth with a convincing metaphysical significance, which the unsupported word and image could never achieve, and, moreover, assures the spectator of a supreme delight – though the way passes through annihilation and negation, so that he is made to feel that the very womb of things speaks audibly to him.[22]

Anthropologists of healing and art have discovered clever ways of studying metaphor, narrative and symbol in order to witness the emotional content of a practice or expression. Metaphor creates a parallel image, full of its own concrete signification, that is then associated with the person's unique experience. In suffering and in vague and difficult-to-comprehend changes, the 'metaphorization' process brings clarity through the appropriate mirror-like image that is associated with it. Without specifically tying this process to music, in my work on rituals of affliction I interpreted the fuller, historical operation of the ngoma-type movements in central Africa as the 'articulation of metaphors of difficult experience'.[23] The rise of a particular idiom of ngoma could often be traced to earlier chronic dilemmas such as reproductive difficulties, hunting bad luck, or to more recent sociocultural stress-points such as economic dislocation associated with trade (including slavery), the introduction of diseases like tuberculosis, and the modern urbanization process that began in late colonialism and continued unabated in the national era. Some scholars have worked with particular ngoma idioms for a number of decades and have realized that they continue to evolve through time, with ever changing metaphors as self-mirrors of experience.[24] It is true that rarely did the individual symptoms of suffering in ngoma, or even the generalized metaphors of difficult experience, capture the source of pandemic dislocation, or politically or economically created oppression the way we would think of these forces today. Reproduction-enhancement ngomas of the southern savannah did not link the chronic infertility and fetal wastage they channelled into their ritual gatherings to the sexually transmitted diseases resulting from the coastal trade and migrant labour.

Metaphor made suffering meaningful by connecting it to ancestors, and through them, embraced those who were afflicted. Sometimes, perhaps very widely, true solutions were found to offset the disease or misfortune. The fertility-enhancement ngomas of the southern savannah included a regimen of therapeutic isolation under a midwife's care for women with endangered pregnancies so that they had the maximum opportunity to deliver healthy children.

The ngoma process reformulates into an image or metaphor the power of the experience of suffering. The songs that individual sufferers compose in their novitiate concretely embody their experience. Metaphorization creates an emotionally charged experience that commands attention in society. If such powerful metaphors of suffering are captured by a peer group, and disseminated to the public, other resources are brought together on behalf of the sufferers. Music becomes the vehicle of metaphor creation, whether in words, non-verbal symbols and substances, or movements and dance steps.

Throughout much of sub-Saharan Africa the spirits are an important source of the power and imagery of music therapy. Very often they are associated with particular drums, rhythms and dance steps. In regions where multiple ngoma orders thrive, the names of these groups are usually the names of spirits, or spirit categories. Those who belong to the groups are those who have been divined to have been possessed by those spirits, or visited in suffering. The spirits are part of the 'metaphorization of difficult experience'.

Words, music, and spirits: the wisdom of indigenous theories

Scholars of African healing, however, debate the relative importance of the spoken word in song narratives, such as those given earlier in the cases from Capetown, and the non-verbal features of the music and dance. Early student of ritual symbolism Victor Turner was not interested much in the narratives, nor in the music, but dwelt at great length on the deeply packaged symbolism of the rituals.[25] Following Turner, some students of such therapeutic rituals continue to minimize the place of narrative while they hold high the non-verbal aspects of ritual symbol and dance.[26] However, others have identified the song texts as being part of the consciousness of the sufferers, of their ability to articulate the nature and sources of their suffering and of its alleviation.[27] It is interesting that one such as the musicologist Steven Friedson, who highlights the music as the active agent in healing, does not attribute to the participants a conscious theory of healing, nor does he show much interest in the song texts. Historians Leroy Vail and Landeg White, on the other hand, who have nothing to say about the music of the *vimbuza* rite in Tumbuka society of Malawi, emphasize the changing consciousness of suffering and healing that is evident in *vimbuza* song texts recovered from successive decades.

In my research on ngoma, I asked healers for their understandings of how, whether and why the music worked in healing. Most could not offer a theory or rationale, suggesting that they operated as they had been taught by their master-healers. However, a few ngoma healers had quite clear ideas, and could talk about the relationship of spirits, words and music in their work. Here are the views of the Hassan brothers, two Muslim ngoma healers I met in Dar es Salaam who were heads of one of the major healers' associations in Tanzania. The comments were given in Swahili and translated into English for me by Emmanuel Makala of the National Ministry of Culture.

> The aim of healing ngomas is to make the patient talk, to *heighten emotions*. If that fails, you go to the forest for roots, give them medicine. Either way, talking is important. The purpose of the *drumming is to know the particular spirit*, so it *speaks out in the patient*, so the healer knows how many, which, where they come from, what they want. When the patient speaks, it's the *spirit speaking*. Spirit and person are one and the same. After medicine is taken, and ngoma is played, the patient must *sing in increasing tempo*, the song of the particular spirit. It's thus the patient *who directs the healer* on the type of treatment.[28]

> The spirits like the music, so they may make themselves manifest, so they may talk [through the sufferer]. A specific type of music is for a specific type of spirit; only this way will each spirit reveal ways of releasing the patient. Once the healer has established the type of spirit before him, in the person, he begins the corresponding type of music. The lyrics are the healer's [or the sufferer's] own. It is impossible to give lyrics of a particular ngoma because there is so much improvisation and variation, so much depends on the individual case. How then does an ngoma help a person? The *music enchants the sufferer* so he can express himself better, and reveal the spirit.[29]

These comments hint at the conceptions and emphases at work in ngoma therapy and its relation to music. Talking is critical to identifying the particular spirit that is in the person, especially since the person's talking is identified here with the spirit talking ('one and the same thing'). Both music and medicine appear to be used in the work of getting the patient to talk to reveal the spirit. But once the spirit has been identified, its particular music (rhythm, tone) is engaged to achieve the 'release' of that person from the spirit. In coastal Tanzania the term 'exorcism' has been much used by scholars and Tanzanians alike to speak of this goal of trance healing. However, the Swahili term (*pungwa*, from *punga*, dancing, drumming and healing) has other probably more significant connotations, including the accommodation of the spirit in a longer-term relationship of inspiration and mediumship.[30]

The prescription for the patient to sing the appropriate songs in increasing tempo to achieve treatment comments on the musical intensity involved in ngoma healing. The sustained pitch and 'increase' of ngoma song-dancing, as well as this feature in central African music in general, often is used to achieve a kind of climax that other scholars have commented on as well.[31] But the Hassan brothers clearly do not dismiss, or diminish, the place of the word in this type of therapy. Rather, both word and music are essential though complementary facets of a complex ritual of healing. For them the spoken word seems to be an individual aspect of healing, whereas the singing is collective, a view that confirms the analysis of ngoma in Capetown above. What is striking in the Hassan brothers' comments about spirits, however, is that they are seen as an aspect of the patient's psyche as much as they are independent objective entities. This is why I referred to the 'spirit hypothesis' in my writing on ngoma and to possession as an ideology of healing.[32]

Musicologists look at music and ngoma therapeutic efficacy

Of the many musicologists who have studied African music, only a very few have looked specifically at the place of music in healing as we find it in ngoma. One of the most promising projects on music and healing in central Africa was a systematic programme of recording and field study undertaken several decades ago by the National Museum of Zaire. Unfortunately, the political turmoil of that country and the sad fate of its national institutions of culture hampered its completion.[33] Of most musicologists' work in Africa, it is as Steven Friedson has said: those scholars who have looked at music have usually ignored healing, and those who have looked at healing have not discussed the musical dimension.[34]

This judgement may not apply to our first writer, South African music therapist Mercedes Pavlicevic, who has lived and worked close to African music, in Johannesburg. Pavlicevic's major recent work, *Music Therapy in Context: Music, Meaning and Relationship*, sketches – in far greater detail than can be summarized here – a perspective that appears to be compatible with ngoma as musical therapy.[35] However, because of either her training or for reasons of cultural distinctiveness, her programme ultimately leads her to steer clear of the ngoma healing which exists all around her. Although her approach to music therapy is social and contextual, and although she has even worked with African clients using their music, and even mentions that some of her patients go to sangomas, she holds back from recognizing the music-therapeutic tradition out there, on its own terms. In fact, she has some rather ambivalent words to say about her difficulty in getting South African patients to separate from their 'highly ritualized and socially ubiquitous' music, that it makes her feel 'out of focus' as a therapist. She argues that a 'shift must be made from "social music" ... to "clinical music"'. Furthermore, 'this "social" music may ... detract from bringing the group's dynamic into a sharper focus'.[36] In effect, although her theory of music therapy emphasizes contextual and relational sources of meaning in healing, she cannot bring herself to work with African musical therapy.

Steven Friedson and John Blacking, musicologists interested in music and healing although not music therapists in the full sense as Pavlicevic, face head on the musical forms and dynamics of healing in the musical traditions – and variants of ngoma – that each examines. Friedson studies the music and healing in the vimbuza rite of the Malawian Tumbuka – a rite that utilizes the ngoma drum and most of the features I have been describing here. Blacking (d. 1990) is recognized as the foremost musicologist of southern African music, especially that of the Venda of the northern Transvaal in South Africa. These two authors offer a promise of the directions research and analysis could take in the musicology of African healing.

Friedson sets his study within a phenomenological perspective in order to render insights true to the music which is not an epiphenomenon of something else. The phenomenon he studies includes 'the sound of the ngoma drum invoking the rhythmic mode particular to a spirit, the clapping of the choir, the call and response singing, the sound of trance dancing, the jangle of tin belts and iron anklets ...'.[37] Friedson's ethnography is rich with detail of the ceremonies he attended in the vimbuza rites of Malawi. These rites contain syntheses of local agrarian culture, conquest Ngoni (Zulu-derived) pastoral/warrior culture from the nineteenth century, and missionary-derived Christianity. As one might expect of an ethnomusicologist, his description of the musical dimension of vimbuza is more detailed, and technical, than other ethnographies of healing so informed. His analysis of the dynamic in vimbuza music that is at the core of the transformative rites of healing, indeed is the healing itself, finds description in the very structure and process of the music. This is a process or framework Friedson calls 'the ontology of energy'.[38] The spirits are not merely symbols of the wind, they are the wind in this phenomenology of African rhythm and cosmology. Likewise, the drumming and dancing is not just symbolic or metaphoric of something, it is that something. Thus the song-dance is within the body of the subject, creating a single 'self-actualizing' process.[39] But the musical essence of this self-actualizing process, the 'ontology of energy', is embodied most fully in the polymetric framework of the rhythms that are drummed. As the polyrhythms are shifted from time to time by the drummers, they capture the creative power attributed to the spirits, and to the boundaries between spirits. In vimbuza the ancestors and the nature spirits represent the play of increasingly powerful energy fields. The ancestors expect respect, the nature spirits demand blood. Thus contrasting as well as extending energies of the spirits are represented in the 'polyrhythmic and polykinetic' energies.[40] Twos and threes are the basic forms that are matched one against another. They play not only at the boundaries of their own sound and motion spaces, they are the boundaries between spirit categories of ancestors and nature (see below, Figure 4.3). This is not far from the African expression that 'the drums are the voices of the spirits', as sometimes depicted by a face on the side of a drum.

Friedson's analysis of ngoma in vimbuza comes very close to musical reductionism. Trance induction is called a technology – the Tumbuka apparently speak of spirit as electric energy! But Friedson's phenomenological perspective saves him from going over the reductionist edge. He argues also that however powerful the pulsating underlying beats of the two against the three may be, they are still 'culturally mediated', and this is the particular musical way 'worlds are mediated, revealed, and constituted'.[41] In other words, one has to be socialized into such music for it to put one into a trance, for its 'spirits' to have their workings, for it to heal in its way. If the pulsation of the ngoma drums were truly effective directly upon the neurological synapses, as some writers have suggested of percussion or polyrhythm,[42] it would induce trance regardless of who hears it in whatever circumstance, which is obviously not the case. Also, Friedson recalls that the 'two against three' polyrhythm was represented in ancient Greek musical writing. Marina Roseman's study on music and healing in the Malaysian rainforest world of the Temiar also describes pulsating rhythms of pounded bamboo tubes as the effective musical medium of healing.[43] Rene Devisch's recent monograph on the Khita reproduction-enhancement rite among the Yaka of the southern savannah offers a non-musicologist's but nevertheless very rich account of the role of music in the therapeutic rituals.[44] He stresses the physicality of the dance and describes its polyrhythmic capacity. He suggests, as does Friedson, that the drumming leads the song-dance, and that the doers of ngoma 'sing the drum'.[45]

I am left, however, with a concern in the face of Friedson's analysis of vimbuza music's enabling energy, and the placement of trance at centre stage in African healing. What about the tranceless use of music? What about the importance of words in healing as suggested by the Hassan brothers?

'Totalizing experience' in Venda music

John Blacking's work on the music of the Venda of the northern Transvaal is an important corrective for Friedson's and others' exclusive focus on trance and rhythm as the be-all and end-all of African healing music. Blacking situates ngoma song-dance within the larger framework of all types of Venda music and their social structures.[46] This 'inventory' of Venda music includes 'genres' as well as institutional settings such as the music of the mission churches, the schools and the separatist independent churches, as well as the music of the court, the cult, initiations, playground and hearth. This strategy of inclusiveness establishes a picture of the relationship of these musics to their contexts of power, ranging from that which is most serious and sacred (therefore subject to control) to music of play and amusement (which is not subject to control).[47] *Ngoma dza midzimu* (ngoma of the ancestor spirits), as a genre with a particular kind of instrument, is, next to Venda traditional royal ritual settings, the most sacred and serious music and is therefore sponsored or permitted at the pleasure of the elders. The healing that occurs within ngoma, however it is defined, is therefore related to power and social control.

In his later work Blacking considers carefully the character of the music that is performed in the various genres in these several contexts. The analysis is complex and not easily summarized here. However, for present argument, the gist of what he has to say is that neither form nor instrumentation gives the music its significance, or its efficacy in healing. To illustrate, one could have polyrhythms within a given setting, but if the context is defined as play or entertainment, and the participants are receptive to the predisposing moods, the effect of the music will be entertainment or play.

In order to sketch the critical contextual variable that gives ngoma and some of the other forms their power, as power in healing, Blacking lays out the contrast between what he calls 'segmentary' and 'holistic' events, or phases within events in Venda performance and ritual.[48] Segmentary communication or events are propositional and discursive, whereas holistic events are performative and expressive. The former are often laced with individual language, whereas the latter are more devoted to movement in concert. The former is often the setting of learning, whereas the latter is deeply expressive and transcendent, folding that learning into the culture's deeply held sacred values.[49] Blacking brings a wide literature on dance and other forms of cultural communication into his analysis. He notes the importance of play and mime in learning the more serious cultural forms. In his application of this dichotomy of 'segmentary' and 'holistic' musical modes, some types of events fall mainly into the one, and others into the other. But most intriguing are those events which display both modes, or a progression from the segmentary to the holistic. Blacking situates ngoma fully within the holistic, sacred type of event. However, to the extent that there is an individual verbal component to ngoma, it has a segmentary, discursive prelude, as we have seen. The sequence of the ukunqula/ngoma parts in Capetown corresponds exactly to this distinction made by Blacking, and to the progressive transition from the one to the other.

Blacking speaks of the 'holistic' mode of music in which seriousness, sacredness, and the collective unison of social values are the markers. I would like to paraphrase this musical mode as 'totalistic', by which I mean that it engulfs all of the various learnings and teachings a society has to offer. It integrates and incorporates the diverse techniques of healing and cultural sophistication into an officially sanctioned presentation. It brings together and synthesizes that which Western scholarship and institutional order analytically separates. Such totalizing integration is essential for the efficacy of African healing. The discursive analysis of the ukunqula is necessary in order to identify the nature of the affliction. But the ngoma is required to embrace the affliction with solace and the transcendence of the ancestors.

Without the medicine, the discursive presentation and the rational skills of healers in society, the heightening of emotion in music does not achieve healing. After all, emotional heightening of infertility does not solve infertility. The expression of suffering in South African apartheid does not bring to an end apartheid and labour discrimination. Hunting difficulties are not resolved by singing about being a bad hunter. Thus, as the Hassan brothers emphasized, words, medicines and song-dance are equally important, along with discursive analysis of life's situations.

Scholarship on African healing music: implications for academic disciplines

I have suggested that in the ngoma institution as it has been studied and seen across central and southern Africa, a range of elements come together, including song-dance, that are more than the sum of their parts. Because of its 'totalistic' character, this ancient institution has been able to adapt to a myriad of local historical situations and challenges.

Scholarship of all kinds must resist the temptation to characterize as 'primitive' an institution such as this because it appears to be undifferentiated. Ngoma-type institutions and rituals historically took shape in a range of situations, including the consolidation of state-like power. On the other hand, they could take form around adversity and marginality. When we thus look at this supple institutional form through a 'music therapy' lens we capture only one dimension of a many-dimensional process. Indeed, to call ngoma 'therapy' is probably already a distortion.

I have addressed these issues as 'Scholarly blinders and the ontology of a unique institution'.[50] It seems that the modern state cannot easily accommodate a totalizing institution such as ngoma. Rather, it is usually segmented into functions along the lines of national institutional functions based on the Western colonial and post-colonial models. In Tanzania, for example, the Ministry of Culture, Music Division, organizes ngoma dance competitions. The Traditional Medicine Research Unit at the national hospital is interested in the use of medicinal herbs. The political party in power is most interested in the healers' organizations as a potential power base to capture. No one in the state bureaucry seems to be aware of, or able to accommodate, ngoma's totalizing character.

Thus, as scholars who are affiliated with the specializations of the modern university and its disciplines, we are as prone to segment our analysis as the bureaucratic functionaries to dissect aspects of the non-Western institutions with which they come in contact. Ngoma has become 'music' or 'dance' or 'theatre' for the humanities, 'medicine' for the health scholars, and a marginal aspect of power and authority for the sociologists and political scientists. Thus, if we are to restore our picture of a music like ngoma to its integrative classical fullness, at least in our scholarship, we will have to step outside the disciplinary constraints of the modern university to behold it for what it is, a valid tradition of musical healing in its own right.

Notes

1. This chapter is largely based on research in Zaire, Tanzania, Swaziland and South Africa in 1982, as well as earlier fieldwork in Western Equatorial Africa among the BaKongo people (Janzen 1982 and 1992). Since then I have had the opportunity to witness ngoma and related rituals in Rwanda, Burundi, Eastern Congo, and on the Swahili coast of East Africa.
2. Turner (1968).
3. Although some of the hypotheses about the classifications and historical linkages of these languages as a set family have been cast in doubt, the documentation of their distribution across the broad central and southern African region by Guthrie's work (1967–71) remains valid.
4. Janzen (1992).
5. *Webster's Collegiate Dictionary.*
6. Ibid., 324. For dance therapy definitions of 'dance', see Chodorow (1991) and Exiner and Kelynack (1994).
7. Grosse (1997).
8. On-line Dissertation Abstracts (1999).
9. Gray (1991).
10. Pavlicevic (1998).

11. This account will necessarily be elliptical compared with that which is given in Janzen (1992), 110–18.
12. Janzen (1995).
13. Janzen (1992), 110–18.
14. Ibid., 111.
15. Ibid., 116.
16. Ibid., 114.
17. Ibid., 26, 134, 135–6, 149–52.
18. Ibid., 122.
19. Arom (1985).
20. Chernoff (1979), 51.
21. Bateson (1958, 1972); Leach (1966, 1976).
22. Nietzsche (1965 [1870–71]), 448.
23. Janzen (1992), 145 ff.
24. Devisch (1993).
25. Turner (1968).
26. Friedson (1996); Devisch (1993).
27. Vail and White (1991), 231–77.
28. Omari Hassan, in Janzen (1992), 143.
29. Isa Hassan, ibid., 143.
30. Moore (1998).
31. Friedson (1996), 167–9; Blacking (1985), 78–9.
32. Janzen (1992), 149–52.
33. Researchers working on this project included Querson, Boilo, Malutshi, Gansemans and Esole of the Institut des Musées Nationales de Zaire, Kinshasa.
34. Friedson (1996).
35. Pavlicevic (1998).
36. Ibid., 145.
37. Friedson (1996), xvi.
38. Ibid., 163–9.
39. Ibid., 168.
40. Ibid., 169.
41. Ibid. See also Chapter 4 following.
42. Neher (1962); Needham (1967).
43. Roseman (1991).
44. Devisch (1993), 259–64.
45. Ibid., 259.
46. Blacking (1973), 77; (1985), 64–91.
47. Blacking (1973), 77.
48. Blacking (1985), 77–80.
49. Ibid., 73–7.
50. Janzen (1992), 80–83.

CHAPTER FOUR

Dancing the disease: music and trance in Tumbuka healing

Steven M. Friedson

Shout for help at the dry season gardens
A lion has caught the child
Vimbuza song recorded at *Nchimi* Mseka, 10 October 1987

The women with small children ran out of the temple first. It was about one o'clock in the morning and Mseka had unexpectedly become possessed by *nkharamu*, the lion. When this spirit comes in a fierce way, as it had that night, it may attack people, especially small children, and, true to its nature, wants to eat them. Though it was highly unlikely that things would actually turn cannibalistic, mothers, nevertheless, were not about to take any chances.

The night had begun in typical fashion: drums were tuned over the fire and brought into the *thempli* (temple), and Christian prayers and hymns were invoked. The Free Church of Scotland had done its work well. Virtually all Tumbuka are professed Christians, including the most traditional of healers. *Nchimi* healers, in fact, see themselves in a direct line from the Old Testament prophets. After the hymns and prayers, the drums began to sound the rhythmic mode of the lion.

This wasn't the first time Mseka had lost control of his divinatory trance, nor was he the only *nchimi* (lit. 'prophet') who had experienced *nkharamu* in this way. Nevertheless, it was still a fairly rare occurrence. Usually, when the lion comes, Mseka divines the cause of illness and misfortune in those who seek his help. But what had started as a divination session – why the mothers were there in the first place – quickly turned into the possibility of a situation spinning out of control. Mseka struggled with *nkharamu* that night but, in the end, the lion decided to dance – a decidedly human thing to do – and through the dance was tamed.

Dancing the question

What do we make of such an ethnographic thread? What does it mean to become possessed by a lion, or, as the Tumbuka would put it, 'dance a disease' (*kuvina nthenda*), to be there and not there at the same time? How do we understand bodies that can become so radically other and, in the process, so potentially dangerous? For ethnographers attempting to interpret such phenomena, our received notions of the religious and the medical, the sacred and the profane, body and mind are brought into question. For Mseka and his patients, trance-dancing disrupts the boundaries between spirit and human, self and other, subjects and objects.

At one time this kind of scenario would have become part of an evolutionary discourse of otherness – Africans beating drums, dancing wildly into an exceedingly dark African night. Add the element of cannibalism and the stereotype would be complete. This was everything the West was not – the irrational in all its chaos, the opposite of *animal rationale*. Trance-dancing was read as the locus of an earlier mentality that was fragile. This temporal positioning situated African consciousness as a contested site susceptible to exotic transformations. Lost in a *participation mystique*, the boundary between real and hallucinatory phenomena was fluid, evolutionarily prior.

It was thus to be expected that indigenous health-care systems would be infected with such phantasmagories as possessing spirits supported by the Dionysian excess of African music and dance, itself a categorical assumption not applicable to such situations. After all, what could be more primal than the physical and aural cacophony of drummed spirits and dancing prophets? Musical complexity and bodily movement were interpreted as rhythmic saturation, aligned with race, sexuality, and the over-exuberant nature of primitive mentality.

Ethnographic inquiry, of course, has come a long way since trance-dancing was invoked in the construction of a social Darwinism. Spirit possession has become the subject of a growing body of work whose constructions are more sensitive to cultural nuance and textured meaning.[1] Yet, in many ways, music has not kept pace with these developments; in fact, it seems to have lost ground. Few studies take into serious consideration what I have called elsewhere 'the musical construction of clinical reality'.[2]

At least when music was being foregrounded as a cipher for the primitive, we had a sense of its prominence in clinical contexts. It may have been heard as musical 'noise', but it *was* heard. Music is now usually consigned to the status of epiphenomenon, something accompanying other more important ritual activities.[3] It seems to be difficult for researchers to shed their 'ethnocentric ear plugs' to overcome a cultural bias that relegates music to 'the secondary realms of "art", "entertainment", and occasional "religious music"'.[4] Through this marginalization, music has effectively been silenced, a silence that, none the less, haunts the discourse on African healing.

How then do we understand a health-care system where musical experience is a defining feature of medical praxis, where therapeutics and diagnostics are danced? At its very core, this clinical reality carries a structured ambiguity resistant to synthetic analysis. The quest to rationalize and categorize, to capture in certainty this virtuosic experience of life, obscures more than it reveals. Trance-dancing is not something at hand, present to an observing subject. Rather, dancing a disease is a way of being-in-the-world, and ways of being can never be reduced to things embedded in chains of causality. We may indeed postulate and, not surprisingly, find such linkages, but the moment such an analysis appears it loses contact with the essence of the phenomenon under investigation. What is needed is an approach that does not seek to overcome ambiguity, but rather embraces it.

My concern here – why I have chosen this particular episode about a night of divination gone wrong, one that foregrounds disruption – is to bring out this ambiguity in all its specificity, not to reduce it to a semblance of itself, a synthetic analysis of presence. Of course we may describe in detail the cultural specifics of trance – the types of spirits, indigenous theories of possession, the social matrix of trance-dancers, and so on – but to understand ontologically we must engage a double movement: 'to let that which shows itself be seen from itself in the very way in which it shows itself from itself'.[5] If we move away from the metaphysics of sight embedded in this formula, we may 'hear' rather than 'see' that which is given first and foremost in these situations. In what follows, I want to give Mseka's struggle an onto-musicological hearing, to understand dancing a disease as a musical way of being-in-the-world, a way of being-there which is a being-away.

Dancing prophets and medical missionaries

The Tumbuka are a Bantu-speaking people who live in the northern region of Malawi. They are, for the most part, subsistence farmers, living in extended family compounds of patrilineally related kin. The north is often referred to by Malawians as the 'dead north' because of its lack of economic development since independence in 1964. Most Tumbuka struggle to make ends meet, usually selling what little surplus they grow to pay for such things as school fees and store-bought staples. In a country that has one of the lowest per capita incomes in Africa, the Tumbuka are some of the poorest amongst the poor.

As in all African countries, the Tumbuka have access to both Western and traditional health care. Government hospitals and clinics, complemented by a private system supported by various Christian groups, deliver Western-style health care with varying degrees of success. Virtually all Tumbuka have had contact with Western medicine in some capacity, whether it be for vaccinations or more specialized procedures such as surgery.

Parallel with the Western health-care system are older, more longstanding, indigenous medical traditions that, contrary to the predictions of missionaries and colonial officials, did not disappear under the Western gaze. In the late nineteenth century, medical missionaries from the Free Church of Scotland, following David Livingstone's example, brought 'Commerce and Christianity' to the Tumbuka through what they believed to be the proselytizing effect of Western medicine. Once the natives experienced the healing power of this science, the rationale went, they would surely abandon their superstitious beliefs, an ideology sustained by the uncritical acceptance of the efficacy of magic and witchcraft. And once they opened themselves to the wonders of Western medicine, then their hearts would be open to the healing message of the Church.

While medical missionaries were extremely successful in introducing Christianity to the Tumbuka, indigenous healing did not evaporate as predicted. Western medical practitioners might be able to set bones, perform life-saving operations, and cure various other 'God-caused' diseases – the Tumbuka classification for naturally occurring illnesses – but they could not treat 'African diseases' such as those caused by witchcraft and spirits. Only the traditional health-care sector could deal with these kinds of afflictions. Today, Tumbuka utilize both forms of health care, choosing which system to access according to the initial presentation of symptoms, the trajectory of the illness episode, and other such considerations.

In the traditional health-care system, there are two kinds of healers: *nchimi*, dancing prophets who divine the cause of illness and on the basis of these prophetic diagnoses treat their patients; and *sing'anga*, herbalists who, for the most part, do not practise divination but dispense medicine (*mankhwala*) according to the presentation of symptoms. *Sing'anga* employ a kind of local knowledge, usually acquired through handed-down family traditions or by apprenticing themselves to older, more experienced practitioners. Both kinds of healers use an extensive pharmacopoeia to treat a wide range of illnesses, but only *nchimi* can directly access the world of spirits. *Sing'anga* neither dance nor employ music to any significant degree; on the other hand, the medical praxis of an *nchimi* is musically inspired. *Nchimi* are called to their vocation through a special form of spirit affliction called *nthenda ya uchimi*, 'the disease of the prophets'. Once afflicted, the only cure is to dance the disease and enter the world of prophet healers. If this initiatory call is not heeded then the result is madness and eventually death.

These dancing prophets are the diagnosticians nonpareil in Tumbuka healing. As with many indigenous African health-care systems, in Tumbuka medical praxis etiology drives therapy. It does no good to treat malaria if it is caused by a witch, nor will anti-witchcraft medicine work if the affliction is caused by the spirits. The symptoms may be the same – fever, headaches, general body malaise – but the treatment differs according to what caused the affliction. This is why the divinatory trance is so crucial to clinical efficacy. While entranced, *nchimi* access a wider and deeper world where causality is not sequential but simultaneously linked; it is the time when healers name the disease, and through the name produce a therapeutic. And this was precisely why women had brought their babies to Mseka's temple that night.

Sometimes, however, the specialized techniques of divinatory trance fail: taboos are broken, spirits get overheated, divination breaks down. When this happens, as it had that night with Mseka, the health-care system temporarily ceases to function. Patients don't get their needs met and healers run the risk of being lost in chaos.

The man who laughs with children

Mseka was well known for his ability to 'dance the question' (to borrow from Evans-Pritchard's description of Azande 'witch-doctors'); in other words, to divine the cause of illness and misfortune in those who sought his help.[6] He was particularly noted for his diagnostic skill in treating women with fertility problems. Many of the women who were there that night to see Mseka were having trouble either getting pregnant or carrying the pregnancy to full term. Other women who were present had previously been helped by him and were now mothers who had brought their sick children to be diagnosed. All wanted to find out who or what had caused their troubles. Was it a matter of God's will, or was the misfortune human-made (i.e., witchcraft)? Were they under attack from the jealousy of others, or was the affliction caused by the spirits? Only an *nchimi*, someone who could dance the question, could ascertain the answer with certainty.

One young mother, however, had brought her newborn baby not because the child was sick, but to present to Mseka, to show the spirits the good work they had done. She had come to his *chipatala* (hospital) some ten months earlier because she had suffered several miscarriages. Such reproductive problems in the strong patrilineal society of the Tumbuka are serious affairs, especially for a young woman in the peak of her reproductive years. Mseka danced and divined that her co-wife had bewitched her because of jealousy. He gave her special medicines to neutralize the witchcraft inside of her and summoned the co-wife to come to his compound so that he could 'pluck' the bad medicine (*nyanga*) she was using. Shortly thereafter the woman became pregnant, and now was back to show her newborn son to the spirits.

The baby was presented to Mseka while people performed *nkufi*, a special kind of clapping done in a slow steady rhythm with the hands cupped at a 90 degree angle. *Nkufi* is performed for both spirits and chiefs as a sign of respect, a practice found throughout this part of Africa. As Mseka sat on the floor, which is customary in these situations, one of the senior women adepts knelt before him and welcomed the spirits with the traditional greeting:

> *Pepani, pepani, mphepo zinayi*
> Sorry, sorry, [spirits of] the four winds

and continued:

> You should be happy, the *mphepo* (wind) shouldn't disturb you, or bind your feet. A lady has come from Rumphi to show you a baby, so that you see the baby and that you, *nthenda* (disease), say something about the life of the baby. You should tell us how this baby will live.

As is always the case when clapping *nkufi*, she was talking not to 'the body, but the spirits inside'.

As the *ng'oma* drum sounded the mode of the lion and Mseka stood up to dance, the mother handed him the child. Watching Mseka dance with a baby in his hands, energized by the spirit of the lion, was something to see – especially given the fact that the baby slept through the entire experience. Seeing him later that night on the verge of attacking babies was an irony not lost on those who were present, as was the fact that his full *nchimi* name Mseka Mwana means the man who laughs with children. As he danced there was much ululation from the women, patients and their relatives were singing out in full voice, and the energy in the *thempli* raised to a new level. Music was not only heard, but physically felt. People were truly, in Alfred Schutz's fine phrase, 'growing older together making music together'.[7] (See Figure 4.1.)

After Mseka returned the baby to his mother, he began to 'see' (*kuwona*) the remaining patients who had gathered in the temple. As each woman came forward to have the cause of her misfortunes divined, Mseka would dance to heat the spirits inside of him. It is this musical heat that fuels the divination trance; as the Tumbuka put it, 'the drums are the batteries for the spirits'. Tumbuka consider music in these situations to be an important part of medical technology and make explicit metaphoric reference to this technological fact.[8] When he had

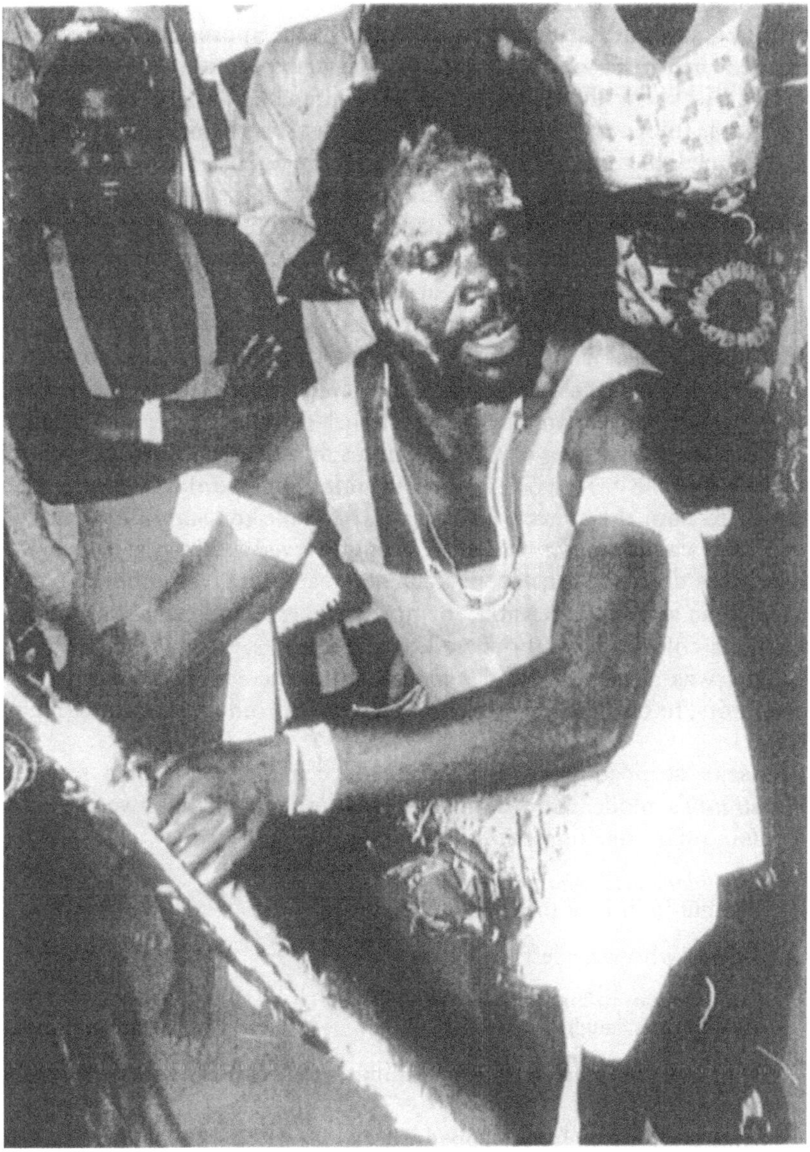

4.1 *Nchimi* Mseka dancing the disease.

finished seeing most of the patients, he sat down to oversee the rest of the proceedings. It was now time for *mutwasa*, new moons, adepts who were in training, to dance.

About an hour had passed and several of the apprentices had already danced their disease when suddenly, and unexpectedly, *nkharamu* possessed Mseka. Without warning, Mseka jumped up and started to circle the dance floor while beating his chest. After several minutes of circling, he stopped in a rigid bent-over position with his arms akimbo. As Mseka held this posture, the drums began to play *nkharamu*'s mode, and his arm muscles began to twitch as a result of a sharply increased muscle tonus that quickly spread to his face, causing his eyelids to flutter, his cheeks to contract, and his eyes to fixate. His visage was threatening, seemingly out of control, and once again he slowly began to circle the temple. This is when people started to become concerned and the women grabbed their babies and rushed out of the temple, leaving only the drummers, the several healers in training, and myself.

His main assistant, a young man in his mid-twenties who had been in training for the past two years, threw maize flour (*ufu*) on Mseka's back to try to cool the spirits. *Ufu* is used to make the staple food, a stiff porridge called *nsima*. If *nsima* is not served with a meal, then a Tumbuka does not consider that s/he has eaten. It is a symbol of hearth and home and, by extension, the ancestors, especially since the flour is white, a colour explicitly related to these spirits. Throwing the *ufu* on Mseka was a move to cool *nkharamu* and increase the power of the ancestors, to bring the possession trance back from its wild state (Figure 4.2).

Mseka stopped once again, and once again the drums renewed *nkharamu*'s mode. Ziloya, one of Mseka's wives who was also an *nchimi*, raised one of *nkharamu*'s songs:

> *Haulane madimba yaye mwe*
> Shout for help at the dry season gardens

And those who were left responded:

> *Nkharamu yakora mwana mwe*
> A lion has caught the child

This song refers both to a lion killing a child and a spirit possessing someone.

While people sang and clapped, Mseka rushed over to a corner of the temple where a large piece of the poisonous candelabra cactus (*mulangali*) was stored and began to eat it, something that he himself says in his normal state would have killed him. But in a way, Mseka was not there at all; it was the lion who was actually doing the eating, and this was

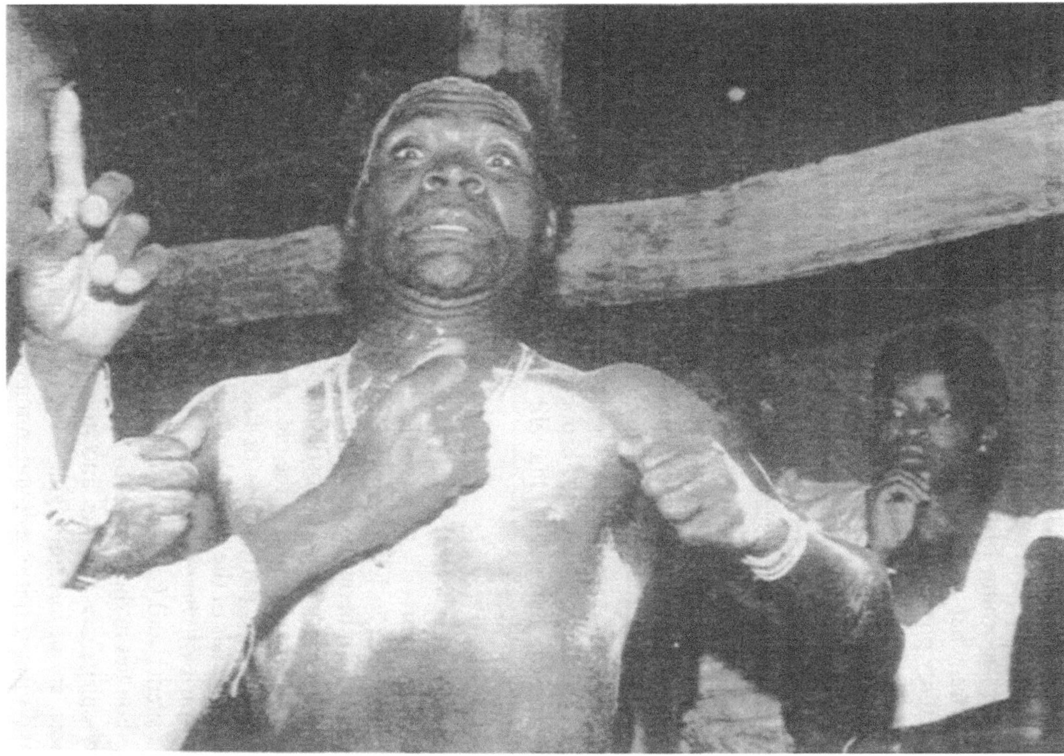

4.2 *Nkharamu* (the lion spirit) possessing *Nchimi* Mseka in a fierce way, resulting in an overheated trance.

precisely the problem. The balance between spirit and healer necessary for divination was disrupted, tipped in the direction of *nkharamu*'s wild nature. But to the relief of those of us who remained, as Mseka ate the cactus *nkharamu* began to dance, bringing its overheated energy into culturally shaped patterns.

The next morning Mseka told me he had gone very 'far out', and wasn't sure what was going to transpire. The reason *nkharamu* had unexpectedly possessed him (he decided) was because the spirit had not been properly informed of the recent death of a relative. His wife's first cousin had died, and the spirits were not formally told of the death, as they should have been, during the *nkufi* clapping. The failure to inform the *vimbuza* spirits – it seems that someone forgot – was why *nkharamu* came with so much pressure. You need to be clear with the spirits at all times, to uphold your obligations, or else you could become seriously ill and run the risk of going completely crazy (*chifusi*).[9]

The last time *nkharamu* had possessed Mseka in this way, he had tried to hurt a mother and her baby, and he was concerned that it might happen again. But instead of attacking someone, *nkharamu* danced and through the dance Mseka was brought back to himself; but it was a self that was now more than himself, the very definition of a dancing prophet.

Of lions and men

Because of its inherently wild nature, many healers have trouble binding *nkharamu*'s energy to diagnostic purposes. But if bound to the task of divination, it can be one of the most powerful *vimbuza* spirits. *Vimbuza* are, for the most part, spirits of foreign ethnic groups (never individuals) and animals of the bush, though some of them may be as ambiguous as the spirit of *singo* (the neck), *mukarachitutu* (the kind of *vimbuza* that is silent), and *kachekuru* (the spirit of old people with stiff joints).

The lion lies in the 'region' of *fumu za pasi*, chiefs of the ground. These chiefly spirits are not the ancestors of the Tumbuka but, like other *vimbuza*, are of foreign origin.[10] The differentiation of spirits into ancestors and foreign spirits is found in many cultures of central and southern Africa, as is the relationship between chiefs and lions. In Zimbabwe the spirits of Shona chiefs after they die are believed to enter lions;[11] among the Venda of South Africa a chiefly ancestor often returns in the form of a lion;[12] Chitimukuru, the hereditary title for the paramount chief of the Bemba of Zambia, is believed to rule with the spirit of a lion in his heart, and the list goes on.[13] But more is going on with this distinction for the Tumbuka than merely the obvious analogy between a king of beasts and a chief. This difference between animal and human produces an ambiguity, a reflexive movement: the spirit of a lion, the spirit of a lion in a chief, the spirit of a lion in a chief who dies and enters a lion who possesses an *nchimi*. *Nkharamu* is all of these things and more; its boundaries are blurred as are Mseka's when he dances.

Vimbuza not only references a category of spirits, but it also names the disease caused by these spirits, the music/dance used to treat the affliction, and, according to some healers, a natural substance found in all human beings. Most lay Tumbuka, however, are not aware of this last explanation, it being the specialized knowledge of certain *nchimi*. These healers assert that *vimbuza* is a part of human physiology, probably located in the blood because it does not show up on X-rays. According to this theory the *vimbuza*, as substance, heats up and this is what attracts *vimbuza* spirits to possess. Sometimes this heating is a result of the *vimbuza* reacting to witchcraft in the body. Other times it may heat up as a result of an extreme emotional state such as can be found at a funeral, and still other times it may heat up for no particular reason at all.

While *vimbuza*, in its substantial form, is always part of the body, only the *vimbuza* in its spiritual form can physically possess someone, can actually enter the body. The *mizimu*, the ancestors, may come in visions or dreams, but they cannot cross the physical boundary of the body. Virtually every people that the Tumbuka have encountered have been transformed into a form of *vimbuza*. This kind of spiritual history of a community does not lie upon a page but is performed. The spirits of Bemba, Ngoni, Swahili, all dance their disease as do those of the lion, the rabbit, and the neck. This engagement of the body by the *vimbuza* spirits is a reality that confirms their existence.

Nchimi, however, need to access both the *vimbuza* and the ancestral *mizimu* in order to divine. According to indigenous exegesis, the *vimbuza* should be 'pushing' the ancestors from 'below'. If the *vimbuza* are 'on top' (i.e., too hot) then the *mizimu* are shut out of the process and divination is blocked. It is only when the correct configuration of spiritual energy is in place that an *nchimi* can dance the question.

Healers are not born into this divinatory trance but must grow into it, have a history with it. The disease (*nthenda*) needs to 'mature' (*kudankha*) as with a fruit ripening. When Mseka first became afflicted with *nthenda ya uchimi*, the disease of the prophets, *nkharamu* would possess him and he would run wild into the bush tearing off his clothes, disappearing for days, a classic case of the primary phase of an initiatory illness.[14] According to Mseka, it was only the sound of the drums that called him 'back-into-place',[15] back from the bush to the parameters of hearth and home.

In the mode of the lion

Each spirit has its own special drumming mode. Only the rhythms of *vyanusi* will heat the spirits of the Ngoni, a people from southern Africa who conquered the Tumbuka in the nineteenth century, and only the sound of *nkharamu*'s drum will call forth the spirit of the lion. The drum that invokes the *vimbuza* modes is known as *ng'oma*, an 'ancient proto-Bantu cognate' of which there is no adequate English gloss.[16] Not only does this word name a musical instrument, it also references an entire healing complex and all that attends to such an institution (see above, Chapter 3).

Although singing and clapping are important to musical experience, it is the drumming that is essential. This is not a matter of exoticizing the rhythmic aspect of African music – of 'inventing it', as Kofi Agawu has argued – but of paying attention to what the Tumbuka do about the matter.[17] Though many songs relate to specific spirits, the same kind of one-to-one relationship found in the drumming modes does not apply. And the Tumbuka are very clear on this point: it is not the songs that heat the *vimbuza* but the drumming. When *nkharamu* finally began to dance that night while eating the cactus, for example, Mseka signalled for the singing to stop so he could enter entirely into the drumming.

I have suggested elsewhere, and will not rehearse the whole argument here, that shifting metrical patterns in the drumming modes, combined with a refined sense of retrieval (what is usually referred to as repetition), are conducive to consciousness-transformations such as those found in Tumbuka medical praxis. These shifting patterns not only are found in the drumming, but also are realized in clapping and, importantly, in the dance itself. *Nchimi* wear metallic idiophones around their waist and ankles when they dance, which contribute an essential element to the musical texture. In other words, the dancing body is as much a musical instrument as are the drums. Separate articulations between movement of the feet and shaking of the hips produce hemiola-type rhythmic relationships that interact with the shifting patterns of the drumming modes. In this context, music and dance are univocal.

The musical mode for the lion, typical of most *vimbuza* music, is based on a twelve-pulse span that articulates a musical space (see Figure 4.3). This is a basic schemata – what Gilbert Rouget calls a musical motto – that is constructed through the manipulation of timbre and subtle shifts in pitch.[18] These rhythmic mottoes cohere to particular *vimbuza* spirits, though sometimes these relationships are polyvalent. For example, the motto for *nkharamu* is also a variant used for *fumu za pasi*, chiefs of the ground, and for the *vimbuza ßaßemba*, an ethnic group from Zambia whose hereditary chief is called Chitimukuru (see

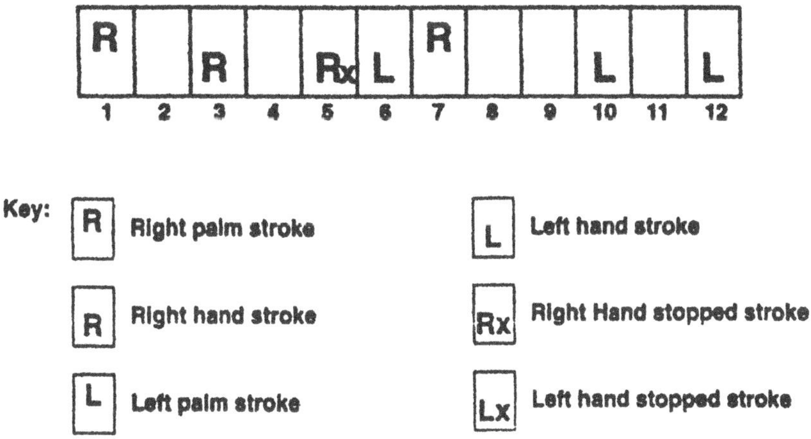

4.3 Rhythmic motto for *nkharamu* (the lion). This example uses a modified form of TUBS (Time Unit Box System) notation (Koetting 1970). Each box represents one pulse. The letters inside the boxes relate to different drum strokes, which produce timbral differences that articulate the structure of the rhythmic motto.

p. 76 above), a musical relationship that points to a historical reality. The musical boundaries of *nkharamu* are blurred, both metrically and spiritually.

The *vimbuza* modes, however, are not static forms, nor are they merely signifiers of spiritual referents. *Nkharamu*'s mode is both much more and much less than this. Through a process of filling-in structural gaps in the motto, drummers open a space between metrical patterns of two and three, which in turn opens a musical space between healer and spirit, creating the necessary distance for divinatory trance. These modes are not simply musical constructs, those favoured objects of theoretical analysis, but ontological, ways of revealing and concealing.

William James, in his discussion of the self-contradictory nature of the 'mystic range of consciousness', remarks that it is music rather than conceptual speech with which 'we are best spoken to by mystical truth' and, thus, 'music gives us ontological messages which non-musical criticism is unable to contradict ...'.[19] The message in *vimbuza* tells us that through drumming, human and spirit acquire a capacity to be in the world musically, an experience that is both a being-there and a being-away. This leads us back to an unacknowledged beginning in this onto-musicological investigation, and thus a question. To paraphrase Martin Heidegger: how must a being be in the first place such that the possibility of the potentiality for trancing can belong to its specific manner of being?[20]

Being-away

Being-away – that 'peculiar manner of being' – is a distinctly human phenomenon.[21] Only human beings can be away because only human beings can be there, can have a world. According to Heidegger, stones have no world (*weltlos*), and animals are poor in world (*weltarm*), restricted to 'disinhibiting rings' of behaviour. Humans, on the other hand, are *weltbildend*, world-forming, comporting themselves in a 'ring of contextuality', attuned in their very being.

Attunement (*Stimmung*) – a particularly apt term for the kind of musical experience under investigation – is not something that accompanies or goes along with human existence, but is fundamental to it. Being-in-the-world always involves some kind of mooded existence, whether it be angst, boredom or, in this case, music. Heidegger, in fact, in one of his few uses of a musical metaphor, relates attunement to a melody:

> An attunement is a way, not merely a form or a mode, but a way – in the sense of a melody that does not merely hover over the so-called proper being at hand of man, but that sets the tone for such being, i.e., attunes and determines the manner and way of his being.[22]

For dancing prophets, mood music may take on a whole new meaning. It does not impart a mood, as music in a film might do, but *is* a mood.

We are not usually aware in everyday life of being attuned, just as fish are not aware of the water they swim in, metaphorically speaking, because only humans have the capacity to be aware of things as such. Attunement is something that needs to be awakened. How then, Heidegger asks, do we awake an attunement, something that has been asleep? This is not a matter of bringing into consciousness something that was unconscious (for that which is asleep can also be conscious, e.g., dreams). Making an attunement conscious, into an object of knowledge, does not awaken it but destroys it, or at the very least weakens and alters it. Attunement is not something at hand to be discovered, but ontological, both revealing and concealing, thus there and not there at the same time. This simultaneous being and not-being contradicts a venerable proposition of traditional metaphysics, which is exactly Heidegger's intent – 'to shatter [metaphysics] in its very foundation'.[23] He does not want to do away with metaphysics but to move us to a different understanding of being, one that includes being-away and, for my purposes here, trance-dancing.

To bring us within the circle of the existential possibility of being-away (*Weg-sein*) Heidegger offers two examples: daydreaming and madness. We all are acquainted with the first; our degree of familiarity with the second may be more circumspect.

As you sit listening to a paper at an academic conference – an experience with which most readers will be familiar – you may occasionally drift, finding yourself occupied with where and what you are going to eat later that night, what happened earlier in the day, and a myriad other things. What took you away probably was not a conscious decision but a spontaneous happening. And just as suddenly you may find yourself pulled back to the talk, by an unexpected loud noise, something interesting that was said, or nothing in particular. You are back 'in' your body, you are once again here. You were displaced, and now you are implaced.[24]

While daydreaming is an everyday example of being-away, madness is, by its very nature, extreme, extra-ordinary. We say the mad person is de-ranged, out of his/her mind. It is no coincidence that possession trance, as an extreme form of being-away, is often read from a Eurocentric viewpoint as a form of madness – a psychological pathology. Within its ring of contextuality, in this instance clinical reality, not only is trance not seen as abnormal by the people who experience it, but it is considered a beneficial part of an indigenous medical technology.[25]

In both daydreaming and madness, being-away cannot be deflated to a distinction between conscious and unconscious. We are conscious in our daydreaming, which can be understood as an almost obsessive awareness, focused and narrowed, and madness often involves a heightening of consciousness – if we follow Aldous Huxley, a kind of hyper-consciousness. How does the conscious/unconscious dyad play with dancing a disease?

The initial stage of *vimbuza* possession trance is a being-away that is, by its very nature, extreme. These initial possessions lead to amnesic experiences. A maxim of spirit possession trance is that it is not the person who dances but the spirit, more precisely the disease (*nthenda*). When questioned, those possessed claim no memory of the trance experience. We might jump to the conclusion that this experience is, of course, unconscious. But is amnesia, the inability to 'tell' of the experience, really equivalent to being unconscious? For example, if spirit trance is a predominantly right-brain experience as has been suggested by many researchers – keeping in mind oversimplistic formations of right-brain/left-brain constructions that have entered popular discourse – then it may be conscious but unable to be linguistically shaped because language is a predominantly left-brain activity.[26] Perhaps trance-dancing is not an unconscious state, but an embodied awareness that eludes textual description. This is to say nothing of the fact that for the spirits trance is always a completely conscious affair. Following indigenous understanding, it can only be such, as spirits do not have an unconscious.

But dancing prophets are trance doublers. It is this ability to remember the trance, to be able to articulate its occurrence, that distinguishes an *nchimi* from other people afflicted by the spirits. *Nchimi* must remember, for, according to them, how else would they know what the diagnosis was and thus how to treat the patient effectively? What Mseka, as with all *nchimi*, seeks in musical experience is a *Verdoppelungerlebnis*.[27] And this is exactly what did not happen when *nkharamu* the lion possessed him that night in such a fierce way.

Nkharamu seized Mseka and filled the psychic space completely; there was no room for anyone else. This negative possession was a retrograde movement in that it recapitulated Mseka's initial encounter with *nkharamu* when he first was afflicted with the disease of the prophets.[28] And as happened during those initiatory possessions, it was ultimately the drums that tamed the lion.[29]

What is a being-away for Mseka, is a being-there for *nkharamu*. This is an inversion: *vimbuza* spirits, in relation to the everyday world, are in a constant flux of being-away just as human beings are in a constant flux of being-there. When the drums sound, they open the possibility for *nkharamu* to be-in-the-world, to be-there. Animals, in their natural state, cannot be-there because they are poor in world, they lack a ring of contextuality. But the spirit of a lion, one that is capable of possessing a person, is neither animal nor human; it is a *trans*formed being. It does not lack a world as does a stone; nor is it poor in world as with an animal; it is not even world-forming as with a human being. Rather, *vimbuza* spirits are world-possessing. They do not manifest themselves in disinhibiting rings of behaviour, nor rings of contextuality, but are realized in *trans*posing rings of existence that during possession trance overlap with the contextual ring of *Dasein*, being-there, revealing *trans*actional ways of being-in-the-world.

For ordinary Tumbuka and newly possessed healers, dancing the disease is a polarization. This is not a drifting in and out of being-there as in daydreaming, but an exponential drift to an extreme being-away that is sustained over long periods of time in an intense musicality. Interestingly, Dilthey has something to say about this kind of musical experience: 'There is no duality of lived experience and music, no double world, no carry-over from one into the other. Genius involves simply living in the tonal sphere as though this sphere alone existed.'[30] Dilthey is discussing here the genius of a 'composer' in the Western art–music tradition, someone like a Mozart, but he might as well be describing the being-away and being-there of trance-dancing, where both human and spirit live in a tonal sphere.

If we take seriously what Tumbuka say about such experiences, then we will begin to understand that music is the very existence of human and spirit during trance-dancing. Musical experience in this situation is, in a sense, a doubling that is doubled: a metrical doubling leads to a spiritual doubling, being-there musically for a spirit and a musical being-away for the trancer, a concealing of the person, and a revealing of spirit. While this is the typical configuration in ordinary *vimbuza* spirit affliction, for prophet healers a still further kind of doubling is needed.

What Mseka, as with all *nchimi*, seeks in the musical is a doubling of experience, a kind of liminality, a being-in-the-world that is a being-in-between. This is what separates dancing the question from dancing the disease. One is amnesic, the other a boundary phenomenon. When Mseka divines, he is possessed and not possessed, the lion and not the lion, both there and not there at the same time. Trance-dancing is a liminal opening, a gathering in the density of being where the fourfold of mortals and spirits, earth and sky meet.

Notes

1. See Boddy (1994) for an overview.
2. Friedson (1996).
3. Some notable exceptions in African ethnography include Stoller's work on the Songhay (1989), Besmer's analysis of *bori* (1983) and Katz's ethnography of Kung healing (1982).
4. Keil (1979), 199, Ellingson (1987), 163.
5. Heidegger (1962), 58.
6. Evans-Pritchard (1937), 178.
7. Schutz (1951).
8. Friedson (1996), 31–7.
9. The Tumbuka make a clear distinction between *chifusi*, a mental illness, and spirit affliction. *Nchimi* state that there is little they can do to cure *chifusi*.
10. Animal spirits are never domestic but always of the bush, and by analogy foreign.
11. Lan (1985), 32–4.
12. Hammond-Tooke (1974), 332.
13. Vansina (1966), 88–9; Wills (1985), 55–7. Chitimukuru is one of the *vimbuza* spirits in the region of *fumu za pasi*.
14. Lewis (1971), Eliade (1964).
15. Casey (1993).
16. Janzen (1992).
17. Agawu (1995).
18. Rouget (1985), 66–7.
19. James (1936/1994), 458–9.
20. Heidegger (1995), 218.

21. Ibid., 65.
22. Ibid., 67.
23. Ibid., 61.
24. To use Edward Casey's (1993) terminology.
25. In Bourguignon's survey of over 488 cultures, 90 per cent of them had some form of institutionalized trance: Bourguignon (1973), 9–11. Its conspicuous lack in Western culture places us in a small minority. This data suggests that trancing is part of the psychobiological makeup of being human. We all have the capacity to engage this way of being-in-the-world regardless of whether the possibility is ever realized. Some cultures promote it, others repress it.
26. Lex (1979), Walker (1972), Peters and Price-Williams (1983).
27. Crapanzano and Garrison (1977).
28. 'Negative possession' is Bourguignon's (1968) term.
29. As Rouget (1985) has pointed out, one of music's main functions is to socialize the trance state.
30. Dilthey (1985), 17.

CHAPTER FIVE

'Spiritual medicine': music and healing in Islam and its influence in Western medicine

Charles Burnett

The intention of this brief chapter is to sketch the theoretical bases for music therapy in the Middle Ages and to explore to what extent this theory was put into practice in Islamic and Christian societies. Most medical theory and practice in medieval Western medicine derives from Arabic medicine, and it is interesting to see in the case of music therapy whether the Arabs contributed anything to Western medicine, and, if not, why not.

In the Middle Ages there were two theoretical bases for the practice of musical therapy, which may be termed the 'ethical' and the 'astrological' respectively. The first was based on the doctrine of ethos and sprang from the observation that music affected the emotions, and therefore had a direct influence over the state of the soul. The best-known illustration of this was in the story of Pythagoras who calmed a drunk adolescent of Taormina by changing the mode of the music he was listening to, in Boethius' preface to his *De musica*, or *Fundamentals of Music*.[1] But many similar stories were transmitted in Antiquity, especially associated with the legend of Orpheus. It found a medical context in the largely lost Greek work of Rufus of Ephesus on curing melancholy, which was known to Arabic and Jewish doctors. For example, Ibn al-Jazzār, the ascetic doctor of Qayrawān (d. 979), in his medical *vade mecum* 'the Guide for the Traveller and the Aid for those who Stay at Home', writes:

> In the case of sickness caused by excessive love, to prevent men from being submerged in excessive brooding, tempered and fragrant wine should be offered, and hearing various kinds of music, speaking with dear friends [etc.] ... Rufus says: 'Sadness is taken away not only by wine drunk in moderation but also by other things like it, such as a temperate bath. Hence it is that when certain people enter a bath, they are inspired to sing. Therefore certain philosophers say that the sound is like the spirit, the wine is like the body, of which the one is aided by the other.' Others say that Orpheus said: 'Emperors invited me to feasts so that they

> might take their pleasure from me, but I am delighted by them, since I can turn their spirits in whatever direction I want to, for example from anger to gentleness, from sadness to happiness, from greed to generosity, from fear to boldness.' This is the application of musical instruments and wine in respect to the health of the soul.[2]

A contemporary of Ibn al-Jazzār called Ibn Hindū described this kind of therapy in somewhat nostalgic terms:

> The science of music also belongs to the medical art in some way or other. Relying on Hippocrates, Theon of Alexandria tells that the philosophers before Hippocrates would cure the sick by melodies and by playing the lyre and the aulos. However, that kind of therapy has decayed and vanished. Even Hippocrates, in spite of all his greatness, did not know it any longer; only those prior to him having practised it. Should we undertake to revive it, it would be regained only after many generations and epochs. Our discussion should, however, be based on the Hippocratic medicine that is still available. So we state the following: It is true that the subtleties and mysteries by means of which those physicians were able to cure, disappeared and are beyond our capacity. However, we still know its major and evident aspects. We know, for example, that there is a mode of melody and rhythm which arouses sadness, one which rouses joy, one relaxing and tranquilizing, another one disquieting and tantalizing, one which keeps awake and one which induces sleep. And whenever we order those who suffer from melancholy to be treated with the respective modes, it helps them. The physician need not himself be a performer of the drum, the aulos or the dance, just as he does not need to be a pharmacist or a phlebotomist, but rather employs these people to aid him in his therapy.[3]

The Greek musical modes expressed different emotions. The Arabic *maqāmāt*, by which both rhythms and melodic patterns were classified, and which were much more numerous than the Greek modes, were said to do this to a much greater extent, and Arabic and Persian literature is full of references to the playing of a particular *maqām* in order to induce a particular emotional effect.

The 'astrological' basis incorporates much of the previous theory. It is based on the analogy between parts of the universe. It is most fully expatiated in the musical treatises of the ninth-century Arabic philosopher al-Kindī, who may have been responsible for its development. He shows how each of four basic rhythms is associated with each of the four strings of a lute, the quarters of the zodiac, the four elements, four winds, four seasons, four quarters of the month, four quarters of the day, four humours, four ages of life, four mental faculties, four faculties of the vegetative soul and four behavioural characteristics. Combinations of lute strings played together result in mixtures like the mixing of the four qualities. The strings which correspond to joy and sadness produce, when played together, the effect of equanimity in the actions of the soul.[4] In another treatise, al-Kindī assigns the seven notes to the seven planets, the 12 parts of the lute to the 12 signs of the zodiac, and the 30 finger-spans of the length of each string to the 30 degrees of each sign. In a third treatise, al-Kindī develops this idea of analogy even further: the ratios which create musical harmony are said to have correspondences with the aspects the planets form in the heavens.[5] All this is explained as the result of music being the science that creates harmony between the soul and the universe.

Soon 12 of the *maqāmāt* became associated with the 12 signs of the zodiac, which were (as in al-Kindī and generally in astrological works) distributed among the four elements, the four humours, and were alternatively male and female.[6] This theory gave a great deal of scope for the doctor who wished to add music to his therapy. For the doctor would already have a good knowledge of astrology, and would be able to apply the precepts of al-Kindī and his followers quite easily.

The first basis for musical therapy was equally known in the Arabic world and the Latin West. Boethius' well-known tale of Pythagoras was frequently referred to. Typical are the words of Peter Abelard:

> There is nothing that so delights and entices minds (*animos*) with such sweetness as melody. Nothing is so apt to compose minds or move them, or placate them, since philosophers know, according to that saying in the first chapter of Boethius' *De musica*, 'that the whole binding of our soul and body is joined by a musical bond', to such an extent that philosophers notice and bring about that anger and madness are quelled by melody, and the pains of the most serious illnesses are cured.[7]

The *Guide for the Traveller* of Ibn al-Jazzār was translated by Constantine the African at the end of the eleventh century. He also translated an Arabic text specifically on melancholy, by Isḥāq ibn ᶜImrān, which prescribed listening to music as a therapy, and in his popular *Pantegni* Constantine incorporated Ibn al-Jazzār's prescriptions.[8] It must be noted, however, that in all these cases, the use of music is described only in general terms, alongside other pleasant activities such as drinking wine and walking in beautiful gardens. Texts discussing the use of particular *maqāmāt* for inducing particular psychological states were not translated into Latin, partly, I suppose, because the technical terminology was impossible to translate. One would expect much more specific information from the astrologers.

What one finds, however, is that, in spite of the importance of a knowledge of astrology for doctors in the Latin Middle Ages, the use of astrology in music therapy is, as far as I have discovered, not found in the Middle Ages. This must be partly because astrological theory was brought into texts on music and not vice versa. The relevant Arabic musical texts were simply not translated into Latin. In the highly developed astrological literature of the Arabs the planets and the signs of the zodiac are assigned to the different elements, humours, seasons of the year and ages of man. But in none of these classifications are the rhythms or the *maqāmāt* mentioned.[9] Thus, in Western scientific astrology, which is based entirely on translations from Arabic, musical modes are not distributed amongst the planets or signs of the zodiac. There are musical elements in this literature, such as that Venus and the sign of Virgo are particularly relevant for the playing of and listening to musical instruments and that, if you want your child to learn a musical instrument, you should make sure that Venus is in one of her 'dignities' and that the Moon is in a sign appropriate to the kind of instrument your child is learning.[10] There is also, of course, the tradition of cosmic harmonies, including the pitches of the planets and the intervals between them (which predates Arabic influence),[11] and the analogy of the planetary movements and the lute strings; and the comparison of the aspects between the planets (as in al-Kindī) is found in Latin sources.[12] Nevertheless, beyond the general acceptance of the essential Platonic idea that the movements of the soul must be in harmony with the movements of the universe (from the *Timaeus*),[13] nothing specific is said about bringing about psychological cures through the observation of particular astrological situations. One has to wait until Marsilio Ficino before such a theory is developed.[14]

One can observe, too, on the part of the Latin translators and their patrons (or prospective audiences) a lack of interest in music therapy as such. After Constantine the African's translation of Isḥāq ibn ʿImrān's short text on melancholy, no treatise on 'passions of the mind' was translated. The Arabs had their own term for this genre: 'spiritual medicine' (*al-ṭibb al-rūḥānī*), and several texts were devoted to this subject. For example, al-Rāzī, the foremost Arabic doctor of the tenth century, having completed a book on cures for bodily ailments for his patron, the sultan al-Manṣūr, wrote a 'spiritual medicine' for the same patron, as a complement to the first book.[15] The *Kitāb al-Manṣūrī* was translated, as the *Liber Almansorius*, by the greatest of the medieval translators of works from Arabic into Latin, Gerard of Cremona. But Gerard did not translate the 'spiritual medicine', nor does any other work on the topic feature amongst the large number of Arabic medical works that he translated in the second half of the twelfth century, and that became the staple for doctors in the rest of the Middle Ages. A similar situation can be seen in respect to the very popular *Secret of Secrets*, a manual of health and statecraft allegedly written by Aristotle for King Alexander of Macedon. Two translations of this work were made from Arabic into Latin: the first of the medical section only, the second of the full text. But in both cases the section devoted to 'spiritual medicine' was omitted.[16]

Is this imbalance in the theoretical works in Arabic and Latin respectively reflected in the evidence for the practice of music therapy? I think it is. In spite of the nostalgic words of Ibn Hindū, there are a considerable number of Islamic sources which tell us of the use of music by doctors, both for dietary regimes and curative purposes. The early khalifs – the Umayyads – had a 'wine day' once a week, on which music too could be played for therapeutic reasons. 'Cold' *maqāmāt* refreshed the listeners during the day, and 'hot' *maqāmāt* were used during the evening and at night-time.[17] Al-Kaḥḥāl (d. 1320) tells of therapists taking the patient's pulse and singing to him in a corresponding rhythm.[18] The Shefaʾiyya asylum in Divrigi in Anatolia, completed in 1288, contained 'a wonderful basin in which the melodious sound of falling water-drops was utilized for mental treatment'.[19] Later, the famous Turkish traveller, Evliya Çelebi, tells us that, in 1648, the sultan Bayezit had employed ten musicians for the cure of the ailing, to strengthen the spirit of the mentally ill and to reduce the black bile. Three of them were singers, the rest were instrumentalists who played the flute, violin, flageolet, cymbal, harp and lute:

> They came three times a week and played a piece for the ill, whereupon many of them felt relieved. They understood most of the *maqāmāt* [a list is given]. When the *maqāmāt* Rast, Busalik and Zankula resound, this instils life in the patients. All instruments and all modes provide nourishment for the soul.

Indeed, when one looks up these *maqāmāt* in the theoretical texts mentioned before, one finds that Rast should be played to give pleasure, Busalik strength, and Zankula slumber.[20]

We do not find, as far as I know, examples of practical music therapy like this in Christian Western Europe. Admittedly, Pietro d'Abano considered musical theory to be an essential part of the education of a doctor, and referred specifically to the correlation of the pulse and musical rhythm.[21] Many doctors, too, had a knowledge and interest in music.[22] We may presume, too, that doctors applied the general precepts in Constantine's works. Nowhere, however, to my knowledge, does a systematic attempt to put into practice music therapy seem to have taken place.

This contrast between the two cultures is susceptible of various explanations. The failure to translate texts on 'spiritual medicine' might have been due to religious scruples. The word 'rūḥānī' had overtones of the 'spirits' or 'demons' who inhabited the cosmos and were manipulated by magicians in the science of necromancy.[23] 'Spiritual therapy' in the Christian sense was the prerogative of the Church. But Western doctors were not averse to magic, and often included distinctly heathen recipes alongside Galenic prescriptions both in their translations from Arabic and in their original works.[24] Perhaps of more relevance is the fact that special care for the mentally ill developed in the Islamic world in a much more organized fashion and at a much earlier date than in the medieval West.[25] This development is testified by the existence both of asylums and of medical texts written especially for the care of their patients. The classification of mental diseases and their treatments was as rigorously scientific as that of physical diseases, and it is not, perhaps, surprising if we find that the musical remedies for such diseases are as rigorously classified.

Notes

1. Boethius (1989), 5–6.
2. Ibn al-Jazzār, *The Guide for the Traveller (Viaticum)*, 1, 20; for an edition of the Latin text of this passage see Burnett (1993), 4. See also Wack (1990).
3. Bürgel (1988), 98–9 (adapted); see also Dols (1992), 167–8, and Shiloah (1972).
4. Wiesner (1993), 124.
5. Ibid., 129, Dols (1992), 169.
6. Bürgel (1988), 95.
7. Abelard (1969), 104–5.
8. The text on melancholy is translated and edited in Isḥāq ibn ʿImrān (1977). See also references in Burnett (1993), p. 5.
9. Neither the modes, nor any other musical elements, feature, for example, in the extensive lists of attributions to the planets and signs of the zodiac in al-Bīrūnī (1934), which incorporates much material from the astrological texts of Abū Maʿshar and al-Kindī.
10. Burnett (1993), 5–9.
11. Sullivan (1977).
12. E.g. Hermann of Carinthia (1982), and his translation of Abū Maʿshar's *Greater Introduction to Astrology*, VI, 3, in which the aspect–interval comparison is introduced into a passage which lacks any reference to music in the Arabic original; see Burnett (1993), 12.
13. Compare Hermann of Carinthia (1982), 40–41, also 230–31: '[God ordered man to be] fitted into a certain miniature pattern by the consonant choruses of the Muses – fitted, that is, to the related example of heavenly harmony whose leading movements, by their perpetual guiding, would temper the modes of this related music, as a model for his own double condition' ('... nichilominus in qualibet exigua formula consonantibus Musarum choreis ordinatum, ad cognatum videlicet armonie celestis exemplar, cuius motus previi cognate musice modos, instar gemine habitudinis sue, perpetuo ductu temperarent'). See also Gersh (1996).

14. This development in Ficino has been explored most deeply by Angela Voss (1992 and 1999).
15. al-Rāzī (1950).
16. An English translation of the section on spiritual medicine can be found in Bacon (1915), 217–18. Compare Dols (1992), 168–9, quoting Farmer (1926). The section begins: 'And now that I have finished describing physical remedies, I am going to mention spiritual ones. Know that mental diseases are also amenable to treatment. But their treatment is carried out by means of musical instruments which convey to the soul through the sense of hearing the harmonious sounds which are created by the motions and contacts of the heavenly spheres in their natural motion, which affect the right perceptions ...'.
17. Bürgel (1988), 96–7, quoting al-Muẓaffar, *k. mufarriḥ al-nafs* ('the book of the soul's rejoicer').
18. Neubauer (1990), 230.
19. Bürgel (1988), 100.
20. Ibid.
21. Siraisi (1973), 96–7.
22. See especially Howell (1990). Howell shows, convincingly, that most of the earliest descriptions of stringed keyboard instruments are by doctors and/or are found in manuscripts of astrological material. He does not, however, give any indications from this fact that doctors were using their 'musical research' for medical purposes.
23. There are several Arabic magical texts called *k. fī ʿilm al-rūḥānīyāt* ('on the science of the spirits') and such like, most of which are concerned with talismanic magic, or, to use the medieval Latin equivalent, 'necromancia': see Burnett (1996).
24. The theoretical basis for the use of magic by doctors is discussed in the short text of Qusṭā b. Lūqā, *De physicis ligaturis*, which is lost in Arabic, but was very popular in its Latin translation, which was probably due to Constantine; see Wilcox and Riddle (1995). An example of the use of magical recipes alongside Galenic ones, in respect to the cure of impotence, is mentioned in Green (1994), 140–41.
25. Dols (1992), esp. p. 112. Dols's arguments have been refined by Horden (1993). While stressing that the treatment of the insane in hospitals in the Islamic world may have followed a Byzantine example, Horden admits the 'predominantly secular character and Galenic orientation of Muslim hospitals and the ecclesiastical administration and Christian purpose of Byzantine philanthropic institutions' (p. 190) which resulted in fundamentally different kinds of care between to the two cultures.

CHAPTER SIX

The inflected voice: attraction and curative properties

George Rousseau

She's entranced by his voice – she hasn't seen him yet
Molière, *Le Bourgeois Gentilhomme*, Act III

Voice as problematic for cultural analysis

Our postmodern generation has witnessed a more diverse set of interests in the human body than any other since waves of anatomical discovery in the Renaissance, and obsessive curiosity about the nervous system in the Enlightenment, drove on the quest for corporeal meaning. The 'body movement', viewed as competing acts of interpretation of the body's linguistic and visual representations, has progressed so far that we, perhaps more than any other generation in recent memory, have medicalized virtually all human conditions. Oddly, except for a few studies, the voice has largely been omitted from these discussions.[1] Voice has fared better than *the voice*; that is, the metaphor (voice) has enjoyed a higher profile than its anatomical producing apparatus (the voice), including the tongue and vocal chords, as well as the ears of listeners and their attendant associative and interpretative mechanisms based on what they think they have heard.

My province of concern lies specifically in the cultural history of the functions of *the* voice and in the therapeutic possibilities of the inflected or melodious voice for the broad range of medical, especially psychological, conditions in which traditional remedies fail. That is, (1) the types of voices in relation to their hearers; (2) relations between these speakers or makers of sounds and their listeners, especially on grounds that the latter are as crucial in interpreting the productions of voices; and (3) the healing functions of certain voices compared with others alleged to be less curative. The decoding of these three processes concerns me as much as any conclusions I may be lucky enough to reach. Furthermore, a search for the contexts of these matters persuades me that *the voice* is: (1) the most important quality of our era to be problematized for music therapy; (2) recently the most overlooked

– and possibly even the most neglected – amongst the wide group of innate anatomical attributes; (3) the most neglected domain of human communication and its imaginative and artistic capabilities, despite the brave attempts of such recent theorists of voice as Jean Cocteau ('la voix humaine'), Roland Barthes ('the semiotic voice'), Garret Stewart ('the phonetical voice') and Kaja Silverman ('the acoustical or female voice').[2]

This is admittedly a far-ranging, even sweeping, tripartite affirmation that could form the basis of a lifetime's exploration in various disciplines. At the very least, these contentions require a context, an awareness of the methods used to construct such a context, a clearly iterated agenda about the forms of procedure followed, the crisp presentation of facts as well as fictions to make plain what precisely it is about *the* voice that needs problematizing, and, most of all, proof of its postulated prominence and concurrent neglect. This is a tall order. Surely such a huge task cannot be accomplished here. At best, I take this opportunity to sketch out what such a programme could amount to, and the contexts that would help us understand what is at stake in making such a claim. I am also palpably aware that part of my dilemma entails the lack of any existing discourse, let alone adequate context, into which such a discussion can readily fit or be set; for it transcends the disciplines altogether: methodologically it lies at least within the realms of interdisciplinarity, for the voice *itself* is multidisciplinary. Nor does *the* sounding voice have a readily identifiable history (the metaphor of voice has fared better). The cultural history of *voice*, and *the sounding voice* when we wish to emphasize the essential and enduring biological quality of its heritage, is one culled from all the realms: religious, cosmological, scientific, medical, philosophical.

This claimed, for the purposes of this chapter and in the light of the concept of 'the voice as therapeutically useful', I am specifically concerned with the inflected or melodious voice: that is, musical qualities of particular voices, especially the range of their melodious capabilities, and the repertoire of associations of which these voices are capable; by which I mean especially their effect upon listeners. Such voices obviously exist in degrees: from the barely melodious to the fully so. And the matter is further complicated in that *inflected* or *melodious voices* are such not only by virtue of their range but their tone, pitch, force in terms of both strength and modulation, as well as quality and texture. We cannot proceed very far into this enquiry unless we possess a sense of inflected as distinguished from unmelodious voices. The judgement of the difference lies among those capable of recognizing and even comparing these qualities. Yet who are these discerners and by what authority do they judge? The inflection range of any voice, as in the ordinary speaking voice, is capable of being statistically and decibally measured. Various instruments and devices exist to chart the variety of pitch and hence its degree of melodiousness. Imagine for the sake of simplicity a scale of 1 to 10 in which 10 is the highest degree of inflection. A listener claiming a voice measuring 1 was 'extremely inflected' would be wrong; the voice was not: it merely measured 1. Nevertheless, if the listener awarding it a 1 due to impaired hearing claimed she had been healed by its therapeutic properties (as if it were a 10), we should not challenge her perception. The healing she received did derive from the inflected voice, despite its being much less inflected than she imagined. Actually there is no contradiction here. The statistical measurement in itself is unimportant. What counts much more is the listener's sense (however erroneous) that inflected voices are healing (or its opposite) and, secondly and perhaps more importantly, that even those who cannot discern inflection respond and become healed.

The latter case is perhaps the more widespread. Many people are incapable of hearing melodiousness, yet they themselves claim, in their own language, to have been attracted to particular voices and healed by them. The fact is that many who themselves cannot consciously recognize a melodious voice nevertheless respond to it, enjoy it, and are occasionally healed by it. Tone-deafness in this context is germane to a degree only: it delimits the range of response to voices. In itself, however, not even tone-deafness eliminates those struggling under its constraints from some type of response to inflected voices. That is, in this scenario there is *no* such absolute state as being tone-deaf. The tone-deafness is relevant only in an absolute auricular statistical sense with little applicability to this emotionally charged and essentially affective, non-verbal transaction.

Cultural and historical contexts

One may adjudge, of course, such 'effect' as inconsequential. Or suggest that I cannot logically demonstrate, let alone prove, any of these claims because they are so subjective and incapable of systematization. The caveat is valid. But the whole of history demonstrates the effects melodious voices have had on their listeners. Admittedly, much store has lain in the hearer's ability. Those less able to perceive degrees of inflection have benefited less, and it can be said that the more exquisitely sensitive the listener, the greater the propensity to benefit and (in cases of despair and depression) obtain therapeutic cure. Still, it will be asked: is this not too broad (the sheer *variety* of effects) or personal (the same voice producing entirely *different* effects on different listeners)? It may be so.

Yet it is still worth attempting to problematize the voice in this way in view of its neglect, except among a few sets of specialized experts in fields such as opera criticism (singers' voices), literary criticism (narrators' voices), and music therapy (potential uses of voices for the purposes of healing). Besides, even the internal study of music history demonstrates what particular melodious voices have meant to their listeners. This has been especially so in musical forms that reify grief and suffering, and there has even been agreement about some of these generalized effects on group audiences within specific cultures. The Renaissance song of sorrow, suffering and grief soothed not only the singer, who was often the bereaved sufferer, but also other listeners. This is the tradition of song and suffering, voice and healing, developed by D'India, Caccini, Melli, Rossi, Kapsberger, and perfected by Monteverdi in laments such as 'Se i languidi miei sguardi' and 'Disprezzata Regina'. It continued through Purcell and Handel, although less forcefully, and could be referred to as the 'Rodalinda school of soothing'.[3] The natural voice captured in simple but poignant and passionate melancholic song calms the most turbulent passions. It may not be too fanciful to think that the millions of pounds currently made by CD companies recording Gregorian chants of Benedictine monks and other early music is related, at least in part, to this tradition of voice as healer. Some of the advertisements indicate as much.

Furthermore, along the lines of endowing the matter with significance, voices *with* melody (melodiousness of whatever type) and *without* (flat, monotonous, unmodulated) seem to me to evoke rather different ranges of associations. I refer not merely to the monarch or statesman whose particular quality of voice comes to give rise to specific associations through repeated listening and habituation, but also the voices of ordinary persons who lie outside the public sphere. The more we inflect these voices through melody (as above), the greater potential we have for general human communication as well to use voices for therapeutic purposes. I recognize that the term 'melodious' (melody) is fraught with peril. A battle has raged about its status in relation to rhythm and harmony, especially in the world of Ficino and other Renaissance musical humanists who sought to recover ancient music and its modes. Despite these historical and definitional hazards, I continue to think it valid to distinguish them in this way.

Barthes and company notwithstanding, voice certainly has been neglected in musical realms outside its technical role in areas such as polyphonic voices, instrumental voices, individual singers' voices and so forth. It is the range of these differences I wish to explore here in a preliminary attempt to postulate a music therapy based, in part, on the melodious voice. By music therapy, I indicate a broad range of therapies both professionally certified (music therapists, psychologists) and informal (friends and family). I do not claim originality for the idea itself, but I think the *range* of its associations has been much too narrowly conceived. Nor am I advocating a new music therapy based on some type of isomorphic melody theory, let alone new historical background, which still appears to have no place in the developing praxis. The suggestion rather focuses on the ontological status of the inflected voice and the ways it has been culturally constructed and interpreted in early modern and current societies.

Work of this sort requires a broad-ranging enquiry constantly tempered by concrete examples, all the more so as there is no discourse to contain these ideas, drawn from the diverse contemporary interpretative map. I am unaware of any devices that measure and compare effects on the senses, although history has been riddled with such schemes.[4] The results have often proved ambiguous, casuistic and unclear in the original agenda: the activation of passion in one of the senses compared with activation in another. But I do know from a lifetime's experience that the grating of an *unmelodious* and callous voice exasperates something within us – almost unlike any other bodily attribute: it offends and grates on the ear more so than defect of physique (sight) or unpleasant odour (smell). It may be that those who have been musically trained are predisposed in this example, and that those who have not been will be more offended by visual asymmetry or olfactory disturbance. Or that hypersensitive types (hypersensitive to *all* the senses) will, conversely, be equally disturbed by offence to *any of their senses*. Without proper surveys it is difficult to know. Why is this so and what is the ear and the acoustical sense in comparison with the others, if it is capable of making such fine discriminations of sound?

Historical bearings

To restate the matter in another key (speaking of inflection), let me begin with a rather humorous example cited below and recorded by Sir George Ent in the *Philosophical Transactions* in London in the 1670s, during the peak of English interest in acoustical science.[5] Ent was medically and mathematically trained and maintained a serious interest in the acoustical voice all his life. He thought he had made an amazing discovery in correlating social popularity with the musicality of certain types of inflected voices:

> Sitting in some company, and having been but a little before musical, I chanced to take notice that in ordinary discourse words were spoken in perfect notes; and that some of the company used eighths,

some fifths, some thirds; and that those were most pleasing, whose words, as to their tone, consisted most of concords; and where of discords, of such as constituted harmony; and the same person was the most affable, pleasant and the best natured in the company. And this suggests a reason why many discourses which one hears with much pleasure, when they come to be read scarcely seem the same things.

From this difference of music in speech, we may also conjecture that of [musical] tempers. We know the Doric mood sounds gravity and sobriety; the Lydian freedom; the Aeolic sweet stillness and composure; the Phrygian jollity and youthful levity; the Ionic sooths the storms and disturbances arising from passion. And why may we not reasonably suppose that those whose speech naturally runs into the notes peculiar to any of these moods, are likewise in disposition.

So also from the cliff [clef]; as he that speaks in gamut to be manly; C Fa Ut may show one to be of an ordinary capacity, though good disposition. G Sol Re Ut to be peevish and effeminate, and of a weak and timorous spirit. Sharps an effeminate sadness; flats, a manly or melancholic sadness. He who has a voice in some measure agreeing with all cliffs, seems to be of good parts and fit for variety of employments, yet somewhat of an inconstant nature. Likewise from the times; so semibriefs may bespeak a temper dull and phlegmatic; minims grave and serious; crochets a prompt wit; quavers vehemency of passion, and used by scolds. Semibrief-rest may denote one either stupid or fuller of thoughts than he can utter; minim-rest one that deliberates; crochet-rest, one in a passion; so that from the natural use of mood, note and time, we may collect dispositions.

There are a number of striking aspects about this passage, some intentionally comic. First it shows how music and the passions continued to be related in the late seventeenth century, long after the musical humanism described by D. P. Walker lost momentum.[6] It also reveals the status and enduring significance of the ancient modes (Dorian, Phrygian, Lydian, etc.) at a time when the 'temperaments' (specifically as in the tuning of instruments) and scales were in transition. Furthermore, the passage implies the ways in which temperaments and moods continued to be of primary importance to later theories of melancholy. The most original aspect of Ent's statement lies in his uncanny sense of an 'appropriate musicality' to the voice that embeds the passions. All human credibility (and therefore, Ent suggests, attractiveness) depends upon just mimesis: the right representation of a speech act in an appropriate musical key. This idea touches on all the points I have been promoting about the 'natural voice', even if Ent's approach depends upon the ancient modes and Renaissance temperaments in ways no longer widely understood.

Ent's anecdote, brought before the learned gentlemen of the Royal Society, also underscores how melody and the emotions combine to produce a particular vocal *effect*. This was an issue that continued to be debated throughout the eighteenth century but which was never resolved to the satisfaction of any constituency. This approach suggests a further question about the melody of the human voice in ordinary speech. Despite the rise and development of Enlightenment linguistic theory, this line of inquiry (the voice as curative) was barely studied as an area of linguistic communication in Ent's own time or more recently.[7] The curative voice has been identified in our century by various figures (see below) but was virgin land before then. In our century poets, folklorists and opera composers have turned to it. Janáček, the Czech opera composer, studied it for many years and used its results in *Jenůfa*, the story of a maiden afflicted by jealousy and love, which ends, as in so much opera, in misfortune and tragedy.[8] One strain of the post-Enlightenment melody debates *c.*1800–1900 had been that the melody lies purely in the narrating or singing voice. Another, the one Janáček adopted, concluded that the attraction of the voice lay in a subjective 'truthfulness' when viewed in relation to the psychological and physiological characteristics of the real person lodging behind it. In this second strain, the voice is organic: [a phenomenon] clearly larger than the sum of its parts. The parts are significant, but the composite voice endows them with meaning and an organic wholeness surpassing its individual qualities. The effect of a melodious voice therefore amounted to something more than a measured pitch or force and related to the organic wholeness of that voice.

The relation of written to spoken words was a particular case in point, one which had beguiled philosophers and theologians for centuries. The bishop of Down and Connor, Jeremy Taylor (1613–67), epitomized the matter in one of his most widely read theological works, *The Real Presence*: 'As Aquinas said, in all sciences words signifie things, but it is proper to Theologie, that things themselves signified or expressed by voices should also signifie something *beyond* it.'[9] The 'beyond' forms part of my exploration, although in a less abstruse or philosophical context than this one: that is, the voice endowing all things with further meaning and enabling possible curative effects. Taylor's treatment observes that in the received doctrine of 'real presences' – that is, the things of this world which we know to exist but cannot always see with the naked eye – the gift of language had been God's greatest generosity to humankind. But where was the gift of *voice* in this munificence? The early modern Western world was imbued with the 'correspondences' of words and things: language had not yet broken off from 'things' as it would in the Enlightenment. The 'thing' was itself related to the 'anatomical part' it signified in particular naturalistic ways (*acorns* and *walnuts* in relation to their physical objects, brains, thought to be especially curative through the object resembling the part of the human anatomy). This was an old tradition that endured into the Enlightenment world. Furthermore, *speaking* the word (i.e., uttering the word 'walnuts') did not alter the word's significance in any metaphysical sense, but (and this is the point that has been so often suppressed) made the physical property and hence the anatomical part (walnut resembling brain) more real and concrete than it would have otherwise been. So real and concrete that by about 1700 (to select merely an approximate date to make the point) the word *was* the thing.

This was the spoken and written word in relation to its signs. The divergence or convergence of spoken versus written words is far more complex and, Walter Ong has suggested, raises difficult questions about orality.[10] That is, the word stood for the thing, and was as good as the thing itself; all the more reason for voice to add meaning to its (the word's) new status as a substitution (metonymy). The voice was thus a sign of the word, and the word a sign of the thing. Voices and things thus came into a new set of relationships. This version of the paradigm of the signifying voice greatly simplifies and compresses the matter but does not solve its major riddles, especially the one about the greater curativeness of inflected over uninflected voices.

The Romantics, and others nostalgically and allegorically inclined, excelled in this mode of reasoning. For many Romantics and Victorians, voice – alone among the musical instruments – was divine because it had been so in the ancient world, even more so than music itself. John Ruskin, the prolific Victorian art historian and author of *The Stones of Venice* (1851–3), grasped at an almost Renaissance polyphonic position: 'The Voice is the eternal musical instrument of heaven and earth, from angels down to birds.'[11] In this line of reasoning, God endowed the birds with an innate musical language which they perpetually chirp: ongoing song exceeding in inflected expressiveness even the sublimest poetry. The power of the (birds') singing voices produces more solid and quantifiable effects than that of printed poetry. Hence the voice's *concrete* capability amounts to pure melodiousness without verbal signification. This is the 'language of the birds' celebrated by poets (for example, Keats's legendary nightingale), as well as the divine, non-verbal language of Olivier Messiaen's mystically inspired *oiseaux*. Throughout these debates and positions a stream of questions runs about the knowledge and reflectiveness of the singer, whether bird, animal or human. Does the bird know anything or does it merely sing? The question was usually unanswered, weight given instead to the quality of voice itself and its effect on the hearer. The exaltation of voice as a sound lying beyond the power of all musical instruments was itself an old trope by the time early nineteenth-century thinkers pronounced on these matters.

This point about the Romantics' sense of voice and the language of the birds reminds us (again within the context of these discourses) that the record about voice remains scattered despite its prolificness and profundity. It is not encoded in a single discourse we can label 'a' or 'b'. Schopenhauer, the German philosopher of idealism, thought his listening to polyphonic voices the most sacred experience of his life, and for ever kept voice as a category apart from other musical, and even philosophical, categories.[12] No less original a writer than Marcel Proust carried the penchant further, if for psychological rather than primarily religious reasons. Proust's own anatomic voice was the subject of many comments among his contemporaries, especially for its wide range of musical inflections in precisely the way I am using these terms.[13] But Proust's cult of physical voice exceeds inflection. The memory of his mother's voice came to him in a dream in which he heard her almost hysterically weeping. Its sound haunted him for long periods. The remembrance precipitated a new threshold of memory – the memory of a pain so intensely charged Proust had never experienced anything like it before. The moment of pain was specifically in the act of remembering rather than at the actual time of hearing her voice. Proust remembered many events and voices, of course, but none comparable to his mother's distinctly expressive sounds. He placed a version of this *cries-de-memoir* in *Gourmont* after experiencing her death in 1905, embellishing it with a didactic *psychology of origins* in which the mother's voice is the *first* we hear after birth, for which precedence it assumes terrific consequences for many of us. But what do most of us remember? His mother's is a differentiated *female* voice, whose particular attributes connect with the infant in some basic, almost umbilical, way. A Faber-type *Book of the Voice* requires compilation, demonstrating not merely *first heard voices* and the praises voice has received throughout the ages, but also how inflection and melodiousness have been privileged. Proust's mother's voice apparently had full-throated melody. He even remembered its 'colours' very acutely.

This matter of the privileged status of the inflected voice raises other challenging and contradictory questions. If the voice-as-instrument is compared with violins and flutes, for example, it is not immediately apparent why voice has always been adjudged the more divine. It is voice, not any viol or lute, for instance, which has been considered the 'divine gift' almost from time immemorial. Violins and flutes have been celebrated, but rarely endowed with the sublime range of expressive qualities or soothing capabilities (this latter is the one consistently remarked) of the animal or human voice – the latter poised to command primary place in any proper historical survey. Even the music of the birds was noteworthy for its melodies rather than harmonies peculiar to their avian language or any resemblance to resounding violins or warbling flutes.

A systematic development of these questions (which this preliminary exploration does not pretend to be) about the inflected and melodious voice and the range of its effects, would extend the discussion to our own time; addressing issues, for example, on the connection between the brain and the voice, and the brain's role in creating nuance through an anatomic voice versus through the synapses in the shoulder and hand that permit instrument-playing. Also issues interrogating the role of memory in responding to inflected voices: how do we remember these voices? Do musical sounds achieve anything *more* than firing up the neurons in areas related to memory and habit? The most sophisticated research on the emotions and feelings suggests, not surprisingly, a subjectivity of response to external stimuli; almost as if association and habit count for something intrinsic to the experience.[14] But what is subjective about musical sounds, especially if the inflected voice is isolated as a more or less stable category? And how can we account (beyond early development and musical education) for the fact that we all have different musical tastes? So far neuroscience has revealed little about the brain's perceptions of the voice, especially its mysteries in regard to subjective affect and mood development.[15]

Voice is not, of course, a sense, nor produced by any of the five senses but by the anatomical organs within the throat; nevertheless, such discriminations formed one of the mainstays of the Renaissance 'five senses' debates.[16] The Enlightenment augmented these arguments, especially when the new linguistic theory asserted reasons for priorities in such phrases as *vox populi*: 'giving voice to the other forces in society'.[17] We rarely claim to be 'seeing vision' to these 'forces' (an impossible linguistic construction); if we do we are misunderstood. Yet the difference is no mere accident. In modern English we routinely still invoke phrases such as 'I do not see the world through your eyes', and we would not normally say 'I do not hear the world through your ears'. But since the Renaissance, collective wisdom and social will are said to descend through a 'common voice' rather than a 'common eye'. The collective social psyche was auricular before it was visual, no matter how visual an epoch the Renaissance was, a matter with magisterial effect for the early history of poetry. Notions of common view and shared vision arose later, followed the post-Enlightenment development of local communities and then sentimentalized their alleged communal values. Diverse subtleties are embedded here, to be sure, such as mediated and original voices; and it is still impossible to imagine readings and translations and paraphrases without invocation of 'voice' in some fundamental way. All of which may point to the anatomic tongue itself as more significant than has been thought: a further reason to continue in this vein of problematization of voice. The tongue is a vital organ in the production of language, as well as one of the body's most exquisite concentrations of nervous networks, rivalling only that of the genitals.[18]

Resisting these positions is one exploring whether sight – seeing rather than hearing – has been the priority of Western civilization. It is all well and good to claim to have heard the imagined voice of the deity: e.g., I heard God's voice in a dream. But what about religious visions and schizophrenic sightings? Vision has indeed been powerful but lacking the intensity of sound. Musical sounds rather than paintings were curative to those grieving in the Renaissance, for reasons that are more complex than appears. These cases may appear fanciful to some postmoderns who continue to wish to privilege the visual over the auricular, or whose perception of voice omits the musical (i.e., inflected) dimension, yet there is a case to be made for the voice and it is strengthened by some of the greatest Western poetry and music. Romantic poetry and music, for example, would have found themselves pathetically unable to describe the feeling (*Gefühl*) underpinning them without recourse to a driving vitalistic and pantheistic force called *Stimmung* or voice. This voice exceeded the physical one, amounted to more than the sum of its anatomic parts (tongue, jaw, head, etc.). Robert Schumann and the German poets (their influence on him can never be overestimated) dramatized *Stimmung*, as in Schumann's magnificent Op. 35, 'Kerner Lieder', where voice (*Stimmung*) is elevated to the highest order of musical subject. Here pure human voice, diverse and expressive, combines with mystical vitalistic urge and eventually disappears into the silence of the night. This 'voice' as imagined by Schumann can ultimately no longer perform; consequently now unable to heal the listener or assuage her passions and lingering maladies.[19] Voice – physical and symbolic – has done its work. Now it must sleep, as do all other living and breathing organisms.

The voice and the postmodern conditions of life

The riddle of locating appropriate contexts for the effects of the inflected voice and its curative capabilities for medical conditions where other therapies fail (extreme depression unreceptive to medication, unbearable grief owing to circumstances beyond one's control, bereavement and death, unrequited love) is that – paradoxically – the voice has been theorized in sophisticated ways in our postmodern generation. A broad range of postmoderns ask: who makes this sound and does it matter who speaks? What is the interest and motive of the speaker? Critics divagating on this subject (Jean Cocteau, Roland Barthes, Garret Stewart, Kaja Silverman, all mentioned at the start) concur only to the degree that they privilege voice over vision. The varieties of configuration are many, and extend from problematizing the voice as a *concept* rather than anatomical production, to relating voice to its *non*-musical (i.e., non-inflected) aspects. But they omit the heart and soul, so to speak, of the maker: the tone, texture, inflections and musicality of the narrating voice. Even modernism (the aesthetic movement broadly conceived) assumed that all texts implied voices – especially the looming speaker's voice; and they argued that to appreciate the text's voice(s) poetry should be read aloud in the *original* language for its inflections. Hence poetry's fundamental music. But this 'melody' or inherent musicality of words is of somewhat different order than the *subjective* effect of the speaking voice unless the poem itself is construed as seductive and curative. Romantic and modern poetry have, of course, been said to seduce and heal the reader/listener – one of poetry's main functions – but not on any massive scale. Comparatively speaking, music probably enjoys the greater capability to cajole and cure.

There is another, communal, dilemma facing those trying to create appropriate contexts for considering the curative effects of certain kinds of musical voices. This problem arises from recent changes in the social functions of voice *vis-à-vis* the community through the development of new information technologies. Some sociologists and psychologists (Sherry Turkle) have already proposed that cyberspace and virtual reality are constricting the range of the human voice's expressiveness; others that they are putting an end to natural (i.e., live human) voices altogether.[20] In our epoch of the microchip we hear fewer and fewer living and breathing voices except when playing electronic devices: CD and cassette players, televisions, video recorders. Fax and e-mail are more concise and less personal than telephone conversation, and also less expressive *precisely by virtue of the disappearance of the voice's inflections*. It is undeniable that more people than ever before speak on their mobiles and talk longer because phone rates have dramatically declined; but the mere statistical fact of hours spent is irrelevant to the point about inflection, which is that the melodious range of voice contains the therapeutic capsule, not the presence of voice – any voice – in itself. The day is practically here when 'virtual voices' will be stock features of electronic mail and the internet: voices speaking the message as the reader reads it. Yet what kind of voice is this *vis-à-vis* inflection and melodiousness? A survey of the expressive inflections of electronic voices (of the kind robots now use in prerecorded messages) will produce few inflections compared with the Renaissance and Romantic music discussed above. Furthermore, the English language contains the richest vocabulary of any on earth – now comprising well over two million words – but the ordinary daily vocabulary amounts to just a few hundred and has been almost steadily decreasing. Where is the paradox? Language remains rich, but human speech continues to grow impoverished. The voice itself does not suffer this poverty but is denied a chance to display its expressiveness. The postmodern human voice's expressiveness continues to be constrained.

Has the long decline of song in communal life since the ballad traditions of the eighteenth century also played a part in this narrowing of the expressiveness of the human voice? Some will say that popular music contradicts these claims. They argue that classical music is in decline relative to popular; that the popular is – if anything – expanding expressiveness. Popular music, moreover, centres on the voice and particular vocal styles distinctive for the range of their emotional appeal. All this is true, but will the curative dimension of popular music (vocal or instrumental) rival classical in (let us propose) a generation? It is too early to know – the odds are not great.

Roland Barthes's strictures about voice, always perceptive despite their notorious difficulty, give us pause here for the way they resist these views. Why should Barthes in particular hold them – Barthes the tubercular patient who lingered in pulmonary debility for so much of his life? In an article entitled 'Lesson in writing' discussing *bunraku* (Oriental metaphysical puppet theatre in which man is the puppet, God the manipulator, and assistants the messengers of fate) Barthes claims that:

> The voice is really what is at stake in modernity, the voice as specific substance of language everywhere triumphantly pushed forward. Modern society (as has been repeated often enough) believes itself to be ushering in a civilization of the image, but what it actually establishes overall, and particularly in its leisure activities which are massively spoken, is a civilization of speech.[21]

What can this claim amount to in the light of the questions we are asking about the conjunctions of music and medicine? Is voice merely Barthes's metonymy for music itself? I think not, and it is significant that Barthes-the-perpetual-patient, whose pulmonary health was fragile from the start, should place such a premium on the auricular voice (i.e., a civilization of speech made from the lungs). Barthes never uses the explicit language of healing, nor does he claim close kinship between 'la voix' and 'musique', but he so strongly privileges the inflected, melodious voice over the abstract flat one that he must harbour some therapeutic underpinning. In his autobiography he even claims that

> the voice is always particular; there is no such thing as a general voice in the abstract. This is what opera lovers know when they can differentiate Callas from all the others. Fetishes have developed

> over particular opera singers for identifiable vocal characteristics. Voice is par excellence the symbol of opera despite the importance of drama, setting, costume, movement, etc. The fetish lies explicitly in the voice because in opera voice is destiny. You *are* your voice. Callas *is* her voice above all.[22]

As in opera, so too perhaps in everyday life partaking so routinely of illness and suffering. A systematic search of diaries and memoirs would reveal a mass of material about the soothing (and jolting) effects of just these subjective, personal voices: i.e., 'you *are* your voice'. One might even claim, in a broader cultural sense, that the tropes used to describe *particular* inflected voices should be considered a literary sub-genre. But how far would Barthes proceed? If we 'are' our voices, do we (for example) also fall in love with voices? With the solitary voice apart from its anatomical contexts, as in my opening epigraph?

These and similar approaches, if carried to absurd ends, trivialize the matter and neglect the therapeutical potential. That is, they want empirical (existential) or logical (rational) proof of a phenomenon which is by definition incapable of sustaining such rigour. By analogy the matter resembles the old debate about whether medicine is an art or a science. Proof either way is impossible, yet the debate continues down through the centuries, usually apart from its cultural contexts.[23] In the late nineteenth century such theories of the purely acoustical voice, enacting all its virtuoso feats entirely by neurophysiological processes, were sought out by scientific positivists (usually physiologists) intent on discovering the secret of voice modulation.[24] Many believed that *all* modulation and its effects were the result of the body's anatomy and physiology. Entire books were written by 'professors' of 'vocal science' dedicated to demonstrating that nothing but neurophysiology influenced vocal modulation – neuromechanical bodily processes undergone by the anatomical organs of the body. The idea was that physiology holds the secrets of a 'science of voice', and that the organs of the body must be explored if one wishes to understand how to frame a beautiful singing voice. William Aikin, a Fellow of the Royal College of Surgeons in London, was one such proponent, although nothing in his biography makes it clear why he held such views. His positivistic belief is summed up in a sentence in *The Voice: Its Physiology and Cultivation* (1900): 'This new phase in the science of physiology is in my opinion the only thing that can dispel the error and confusion resulting from the inaccurate knowledge of the vocal instrument commonly displayed in the writings and utterances of the present day.'[25]

The new phase formed part of the late nineteenth-century neo-positivistic moment, when optimism was high that everything about voice production and effect could be ascertained. Even so, it is curious the extent to which it was thought – and continues to be adjudged – that voice *qua* voice (i.e., sound) is the fundamental communicator and that visual signs accompanying it are of a lesser sort or an attachment to it. The American novelist John Updike recently performed an anatomy of 'Car Talk' in which he felt compelled to observe that 'a human being has vocal cords, a tongue, teeth, and, for expressive reinforcement, eyes and hands; a car has nothing but its horn and lights'.[26] It is an imaginative stance in one of America's deftest writers who is sensitive to voice inflection as well as the ravages of sickness and suffering. His approach enhances my melodious-voice theory by taking into account other factors: the eyes, hands and teeth, etc. providing the expressive elements. But for every Updike cunningly delineating the voice's 'repressive reinforcement', there are many others seemingly oblivious to its capability to soothe and heal and cause people to find themselves smitten – falling in love with a pure, unadulterated voice. In Michael Ondaatje's recent novel, *The English Patient*, the 'hero-patient' recounts to his nurse how he was struck in the desert: 'That night I fell in love with a voice. Only a voice. I wanted to hear nothing more. I got up and walked away.'[27]

The voice was entirely sufficient; in fact the patient wishes to 'see nothing more' rather than 'hear nothing more'. Voice itself was sufficient. 'Pure voice' itself is probably not therapeutic in any extended sense, or even affirming that 'falling in love with voices' is, or has ever been, widespread; but I am tapping into a tradition that exalts *sound* above the other senses and identifies voice as containing the largest expressive range of all the classes of sounds. There is nothing new in the claim, which extends back to at least the Greeks, who developed it as part of their theory about music and the inflammation of the passions. The elenchus of reason was this: music was sound – especially voice – encoded in rhythm; music, above all other arts, communicated directly with the passions of the soul without the further intervention of other means; therefore, music, and especially vocal sound, must be the most divine art. Yet if music is essentially 'the expression of voice', as Barthes had argued so vigorously in his various essays, then voice and the passions come into closer relation than is often acknowledged.[28] Perhaps this logic accounts for the metonymies that have been sustained as long as the 'music–passions' argument: that voice is the single representative of self, the most identifiable quality of individual soul, the likeliest human characteristic 'to fall in love with'.

Yet what types of 'voices' are the subjects of these claims? Voices young, old; male, female; trained, natural? The record is usually silent on such differentiation. However, artifice is devalued while the natural voice – untrained, primitive, in its original pristine state – is exalted. *Natural voice*, especially when it stands as a metonymy for the whole person, the entire individual, is the one most prized. And in aesthetic discourse natural voice remains the single category of artistic originality. It can be argued again that the trope (natural voice) is merely a metaphor. Even so, why should voice be the word of choice in domains having little to do with sound, as in literature, philosophy, painting and so forth? Yet natural voice dominates the metaphor market: even more markedly in the categories of the highest forms of genius and creativity, where it gets distinguished from the artificial or crafted voice (artifice again), especially to differentiate a Mozart or Schubert who possessed that 'grace beyond the reach of art' that not even every genius can attain.

My method leaps forward and backward chronologically because I want to show the *longue durée* of voice: the strains of thought that have emerged over time in their richness and the fullness of their diverse sources. If grades of significance can be assigned, a therapeutic claim for voice can be made, perhaps supported by those more knowledgeable than I am in the realms of applied music therapy. 'My therapy' (if I were to have one) would privilege *voice* over other musical instruments, and I am attempting to explain here not only *why voice is privileged*, but why we live in an era delimiting the boundaries of the voice through visual competition, sheer decibel level, and the new information technology which suppresses voice (on the one hand) and permits such complete simulation (on the other) that the originally inflected and expressive natural voice is threatened into extinction. The high and low of this process – extolling and suppressing voice – requires deft untangling of concurrent strains.

Hence ancient shepherds piping their flutes in the fields. Whose attention did they seek to attract? They also sang in their own voices: the natural voice of the shepherd in Nature. Berlioz's creative response to this haunting phenomenon was the idyllic 'Song of the Shepherds' in his *Symphonie fantastique*, a section that has long fascinated musicologists. *Au fond* of their analysis lurks always the idea of pure melody. The notion that the code to crack is the mystery of inflection itself: this is what I continue to mean by natural melody or musical voice. Inflection *is* melody, all its nuance lying in the degree of inflection. Throughout the history of music therapy, the idea of diversion has been a mainstay. Philip Barrough, a Renaissance didacticist who pondered therapy for melancholy, was prescient in intuiting that different musical inflections lead to different moods. Barrough states that in trying to cure a melancholic one should 'Let them be as merry as may be, and heare musicall instruments and singing'.[29] This was the age-old remedy through opposition.

On the advent of the millennium it seems appropriate to develop a therapeutic practice that would teach patients (of all melancholic types broadly construed and especially those, as I have been reiterating, who do not respond to traditional therapies) how to come closer to the 'voices' of those they love. To learn to embrace the voice and be soothed by it, as in a lullaby. To learn to sleep through it, as did Count Goldberg of Bach's 'Goldberg Variations' fame. Nothing else soothed the Count to sleep except music. All else failed. So he commissioned Bach to compose those bejewelled night slumbers conveying him to the Lethe's banks in an age before Xanax and benzedrine and other sleeping tablets.[30] That is, a cult of the expressive voice capable of soothing despair and despondency.

Embracing the inflected voice

In conclusion I want to devote some space to an early work in the history of music therapy which is probably the first *explicit* therapeutic work written in English.[31] This is Dr Richard Browne's *Medicina Musica* (1729), a 'revised and corrected' treatise of 125 pages of which no first edition has ever been found.[32] Browne was a competent practitioner who also wrote other works influenced by the post-Newtonian iatromechanical theories of his day, but his sally into music therapy seems surprising. No biographical information survives (letters, diaries, memoirs, medical case books or the like) that provides a context for his fascinating, if, to us, seemingly naive work, except that he travelled widely in the Balkans and the Levant, collected exotic remedies for medical conditions, and configured a post-Renaissance vision of the 'humane body' described in his now scarce but bizarre treatise *Somatopolitia: or, the City of the Humane Body Artificially defended from the tyranny of Cancers and Gangreens ... how the Humane Body may be called a City ... How it may be compared to a Political City ...* (1702). Browne penned *Medicina Musica* when young ('wrote in the time of my Apprenticeship'); it was thoroughly neglected in his time, having given occasion neither to comment or criticism.[33]

The gist of Browne's approach, which is really a manifesto *pro therapia musica*, is that auricular anatomy and bodily exercise combine to provide music therapy's best options. That is, music therapy occurs in proportion to the ear's sensitivity, as a consequence of which those who are tone deaf will not derive much good.[34] Continuing the ancient line about music and the passions by invoking the soul, Browne reasons that 'Singing communicates a Pleasure to the Soul' afforded by no other activity.[35] He contends that 'in Singing we plainly discover that the Air is expell'd from the whole Capacity of the Lungs, with greater force than in common Expiration ...'.[36] Hence, despite Browne's reason for extolling voice and song in this way (i.e., his ulterior mechanical motive is physiological), he still privileges voice and song above all other forms in his music therapy, marvelling at 'what a vast Influence Singing has over the Mind of Man ...'.[37]

Browne makes grand claims for the exercise of the voice in song. Appealing to acoustics and the physics of sound, he describes how music, especially song, can heal maladies where all other therapies have failed, as in 'Tarantism, where Patients lie in an Apoplexy'.[38] Unlike many other people of the day, including Augustan satirists Pope and Swift, Browne championed Italian opera, 'for the Pleasure of hearing the fine Adagio and Allegro Parts in *Italian* Operas causes cure of gloom and melancholy'.[39] He compares the therapeutic value of music to dance, painting and literature and votes for music for the severest cases, fully aware that the exercise of the lungs of patients with pulmonary disease, as in singing, was deleterious. 'I now come to consider the power of Music in the Cure of Diseases', he writes, and compares music with dance, as was commonplace in the *medicinae gymnasticae* of his day touting exercise and the regulation of the non-naturals (the six areas governing health: air, earth, diet, water, exercise, sleep). Browne's survey compares music with the other mechanical arts and ranks music first, dance second, but gives the ribbon to music in every case of 'difficult to cure conditions'. Browne nowhere mentions musical instruments as an alternative to, or in comparison to, the benefits of singing: either playing or listening to them. Indeed, his whole system centres around the idea of a healthy pulsating pulmonary cavity moving around the animal spirits and other vital fluids so that one set of passions is transformed into another. Take this activity away – the active voice and the listening ear – and the basis of his therapy evaporates.

Browne's early system of music therapy is admittedly inchoate in many ways, and he has not addressed all sorts of questions, or even faced certain logical inconsistencies which seem obvious to us, but he remains original and (in my view) fundamentally correct in intuiting that the effects of the voice can soothe the most pained patients. But our discussion is equally about the passive recipient, even within the context of Browne's music therapy and his relation to the traditions of the voice I have been describing. If his method requires further fine tuning, as it no doubt does, then it is this passivity we should be exploring in relation to health and healing. All along, my suggestion, in contrast to Browne, has been that those *receiving* the pleasure of the voice profit as much as those using their voice; but this is a discrepancy of such magnitude that active singing versus passive listening merits treatment elsewhere if the differences are to be appreciated.

Contemporary academic critic Garrett Stewart's virtuoso analysis in *Reading Voices* implies some of these directions.[40] Stewart discovers himself fast on the track of the 'melodious voice' and its capabilities in a universe bulging with melody and kept harmonious by it. Thinking of poet John Keats in the famous line about 'unheard melodies' in the 'Ode on a Grecian Urn', Stewart posits that 'in texts, as in plastic representation, "melodies" are not less melodious for being "unheard" (Keats, l. 11), for keeping the silence of their unspoken vocalizations'[41] (that is, the 'silence' of texts, as well as the silence within human relations and communications, as for example in the therapeutic encounter). Keats was especially well poised to discriminate among the different voices he thought he heard: still young, trying to write poetry, aiming to live, and to love Fanny Brawne, while in the full knowledge and sorrow of his terminal illness and imminent death. In brief he was a patient: the kind of patient who responds exquisitely to the plenitude of inflected melodious sounds and relates them to his own troubled state of mind even if he cannot be cured by them.

Silence and sound, as Stewart (a literary critic of splendid bravado) suggests indirectly through Keats's resolution, are the final points of this discussion: the types of sounds that are evoked and their ability to calm and soothe troubled minds. The much larger question of silence and sound *throughout* our culture will arise, as will the matter of natural human voices in relation to those artificially or electronically produced. So too will the matter of transcultural changing decibel levels in which diverse local cultures have different tolerations to sound volume. Even the status of melody in a post-electronic musical world is now more controversial than it was in Ficino's Renaissance, or even before the Age of the Computer Chip. But the main issue about the privileging of melodious voices over other types of sound remains constant, and is not a matter one hears much discussed despite the attention being given to 'voice' as a newly invigorated and quasi-stable category. As time moves over the millennial line, and human voices continue to be hurled further into the background, or heard only in Baudrillardean simulacra representation (as copies rather than original voices), I think the voice's therapeutic potential will increase even more. This may be the first time in recent Western cultural history when certain groups will have been unable to tell the difference between soft sounds beneath a certain decibel level, as well as between real and simulated voices. What valence then can remain for the natural expressive human voice whose range is a million times more diverse? Simulated voices are nothing to real ones, just as computer memories (no matter how large in RAM) are nothing to the human brain's range of complexity. The aesthetics of the voice will then change again in an almost post-Foucauldian epistemic sense. Which of these melodious or inflected voices – human, natural, synthesized, virtual – will then have healing powers? Perhaps all, but before we leap in certainty we must know more about the effects of *different kinds of human voices* on different groups of people. This research has not been undertaken and would entail a massive project taking many years. It raises the spectre, once again, of the *terra incognita* this chapter has attempted to enter: the effects of certain types of inflected voices on their listeners. We do not even possess synthetic studies of the effects of voices on their listeners in history, still an uncompiled archive from Herodotus to Hitler.

Notes

1. See the discussion of the tongue and its productions in Hillman and Mazzio (1997), which contains a remarkable chapter on the 'Sins of the Tongue' by Mazzio with some discussion of the voice. By inflected I mean the range, texture and quality of the voice's pitch.
2. Barthes (1977); Cocteau (1930); Silverman (1988); Stewart (1990). For the iconographic figure of the speaking woman see Kahane (1995).
3. Taken from Act III, Handel's *Rodalinda.*
4. From the Enlightenment forward see: Mollet (1752); Bain (1855); Bynum and Porter (1993).
5. Ent (1809), 441–2.
6. For an overview of Walker's work see Walker (1985).
7. Barry (1987).
8. Janáček added much to 'inflect' (in my sense, n. 1 above) Gabriela Preissová's libretto; the introducer of the Deutsche Grammophon CD of *Jenůfa* notes: 'He [Janáček] had for many years been studying folklore which lead him towards systematic research of the melody of human speech – a relatively independent part of language communication.'
9. J. Taylor (1654), 129, emphasis mine.
10. See Ong (1982).
11. Ruskin (1885–1900), vol. 3, 162.
12. Schopenhauer (1974), 434–5.
13. Hayman (1990), 212.
14. Langer (1982).
15. See Harrington (1992).
16. Baker (1947).
17. Boas (1969).
18. See n. 1 above.
19. See Rosen (1995).
20. See Turkle (1995).
21. See Barthes (1977), 175.
22. Ibid., 67.
23. One of the many virtues of Roy Porter's *The Greatest Benefit to Mankind: A Medical History of Humanity* (1997) is insistence on this broad cultural context.
24. See Bach (1880); Bristowe (1880); Bishenden; (1869); Holmes (1879).
25. Aikin (1900), 7.
26. Updike (1997), 108.

27. Ondaatje (1993), 144.
28. Barthes (1977), 70.
29. Barrough (1624), 76; compare Bacon (1683), 128: 'Instrumental Musick and Songs, have the potential to stir the soul from the seat of its depressions and melancholies.' For further discussion of musical modes and human moods, see below, Chapter 7.
30. The cultural history of music and the sleeping psyche remains unwritten; it is one of the richest metaphors throughout the realms of music and literature, especially as the dominant motif of the odes to psyche and sleep; see the very suggestive comments in Winn (1998).
31. Many passages can be found in English prior to 1729 but there is no prior work written in English explicitly devoted to music therapy; see Gouk (2000).
32. Most libraries, including the British Library and the Wellcome Library in London, have copies reading 'the second edition'.
33. Browne (1729), 5. For example, no reference to Browne is found in Brocklesby (1749).
34. Browne (1729), 2–3.
35. Ibid., 6.
36. Ibid., 13.
37. Ibid., 16; an entire section analyses the effects of singing on the blood, solids and fibres, and on man's nervous system.
38. Ibid., 37.
39. Ibid., 39.
40. See Stewart (1990).
41. Ibid., 157.

CHAPTER SEVEN

'No pill's gonna cure my ill': gender, erotic melancholy and traditions of musical healing in the modern West

Linda Phyllis Austern

Love is the Tyrant of the heart, it darkens
Reason, confounds discretion, deafe to counsell:
It runnes a headlong course to desperate madness.
John Ford, *The Lovers Melancholy* (1629)

Musicke restoreth madmen to their wits.
The Praise of Musicke (1586)

In 1979, rock-n-roll sensation Robert Palmer recorded John Moon Martin's song 'Bad Case of Loving You' for his album 'Secrets' (New York: Island Records, Inc.). Shortly thereafter, America's airwaves were vibrating with its infectious melody, its insistent opening tonic chord which drops to the dominant only after eight reiterations, and, above all, its thrice-repeated and doubly syncopated chorus of 'Doctor, doctor, give me the news – / I've got a bad case of lovin' you / No pill's gonna cure my ill / I've got a bad case of lovin' you'. From Henry Playford's *Pills to Purge Melancholy* (1699) to Alanis Morissette's *Jagged Little Pill* (Burbank, Calif. and New York: Maverick-Reprise Records, 1995) almost exactly three hundred years later, and from Robert Burton's massive *Anatomy of Melancholy* (1st edn 1626) to The Smashing Pumpkins' monster hit album *Mellon Collie and the Infinite Sadness* (Beverly Hills, Calif.: Virgin Records America, Inc., 1995), music has been marketed as medication for the self-cure of whatever ails body and soul, most often the pangs and fits of unrequited love (see Figure 7.1). It has been equally clear during the three centuries of the modern era that, just as men and women have been treated differently by philosophers, medical practitioners and marketing experts, they have also been assigned, and have accepted, different sorts of music to alleviate or occasionally emulate erotic ailments.

With the exception of the female love-object's profession and the percussive, electrified sound of the modern rock-band, virtually nothing about Martin's song would have surprised a listener from three hundred

7.1 Smashing Pumpkins, *Mellon Collie and the Infinite Sadness* 1995 album cover illustration by John Craig. © Virgin Records America.

years earlier. Its brief, first-person text presents a love-stricken man yearning for a hard-hearted woman with the 'smile of Judas on [her] lip'. Its music suggests his frenzied desire through its rapid tempo, textually related melodic ascents and descents, sudden if simple harmonic alterations, short pauses between phrases to break intellectual concentration and continuity, and the metrical irregularity of syncopated rhythms at unexpected but textually significant moments. Not only would any listener from the early modern through the postmodern era immediately recognize from his music that he's 'got it bad, and [he's] got it good', as Martin's text explains, but that he's a controlled, self-reliant man singing to rid himself of the distracting pangs of lovesickness. The few brief, descending melismatic flourishes on such pained expressions as the blueness of his agitated heart, or the 'badness' with which the affliction troubles him, return quickly upwards to tonic resolution and stability. Any educated listener from the days of Robert Burton and Claudio Monteverdi onwards would approve, if only subconsciously, of his choice of a simple duple metre, rapid tempo and major mode as 'a roaring-meg against melancholy', obviously caused, in this case, by the unyielding heart of his beloved.[1] The same listener would recognize symptoms of the disease and attempts to overcome it in some of the other particular features of the music. Transported to an earlier era, or left in their own, Martin and Palmer exemplify the self-sufficient man using music as cure for the most common masculine variety of lovesickness.

Melancholy, philosophy and medical theory

Since the days of Aristotle, Western thinkers have most often considered erotic disorders among the psycho-physical depressive ailments traditionally classified as 'melancholia'. Originally, 'melancholy' referred to the bodily humour of black bile, and the gloomy, introspective personality that accompanied an overabundance of the substance. According to the medical and philosophical traditions that dominated Western thought for over two millennia, wellness was, at its simplest, a symmetry between bodily elements, in particular the four humours of blood, phlegm, bile or choler, and black bile or melancholer. Normal, healthy individuals displayed a wide range of proportions between these four humours, endowing each with a unique temperament and constitution that had to remain in proper balance for body, mind and soul to function correctly. The ultimate cause of disease was an imbalance between the four humours, for they controlled both physiological and intellectual functions. Sufferer and healer alike had to remain aware of the characteristic norms and pathologies of the sanguine, phlegmatic, bilious or choleric, and melancholic person while allowing for the full range of individual variation that characterized the human species.[2]

However, neither Western medicine nor underlying epistemologies of mind and body have remained simple, constant or monolithic for the past 2 500 years. Even before its demise at the hands of modern laboratory medicine, humoural theory had coexisted alongside a number of other physical and spiritual systems that also explained disease. Sufferers and healers could select particular elements from any of these as they chose.[3] Melancholy stands as one of the few disorders that has obsessed the minds of poets and physicians, artists and philosophers alike for such a long duration. As such, it has been granted at one time or another a bewildering variety of underlying causes, cures and cultural significances. In addition to the humoural theories codified by Aristotelian–Galenic medical practitioners, melancholy has been linked to the astrological influence of Saturn, the aging process, inborn temperament, diet, the contemplative life, demonic possession, an excess of passion and geographical displacement, among other factors.[4] Its evident manifestations, too, have varied across the entire range of human inventiveness of vision, delusion and desire. Its sufferers have been diagnosed as robust or fragile, manic or withdrawn, frenzied or deluded, depending on time and place of observation. It has been both feared and desired, a sign of madness and of inspired furore, and a distinct indication of class or professional talent. In short, largely because of conflicting systems of healing, it has defied simple codification even within a single era and location.[5] But yet, for such a bewilderingly varied disease, there has been a remarkable consistency of fundamental indicators. In general, and allowing for terminological variation, the disorder has almost invariably been linked with pathological sorrow and severe depression. The list of clinical symptoms compiled in 1970 by neurologist and psychiatrist Mortimer Ostow, MD, would have been recognizable to Aristotle's ancient followers: the sufferer is sad, pessimistic, withdrawn, may speak of death or attempt suicide, and may range from utter inertia to aimless pacing 'in agitation which is distressing to watch'.[6]

By the end of the sixteenth century, 'melancholy' had come to stand for any non-specific malaise, especially characterized by morbid depression, gloominess or generalized sorrow. Even by then, an imbalance of the heavy *humour pessimus* was no longer necessarily a contributing factor. Like other affective disorders of the era, melancholy, including its diagnosis and its treatment, occupied the vast and extremely diverse middle ground between body and soul. Thus the condition belonged to the realm of the humours, passions, and the vital spirits that conveyed messages between occult and manifest aspects of the human entity. As the Elizabethan author and physician Philip Barrough explains, with homage to several conflicting earlier theories,

> Melancholie is an alienation of the mind troubling reason, and waxing foolish, so that one is almost beside himself. It commeth without a fever, and is chiefely engendered of melancholy occupying the minde, and changing the temperature of it... . The most common signes be fearfulnes, sadnes, hatred, & also they that be melancholious, have strange imaginations ... Moreover, they desire death, and do very often behight and determine to kill themselves, and some feare that they should be killed. Many of them do alwaies laugh, and many do weepe, some thinke themselves inspired with the holy Ghost, & do prophecy upon things to come.[7]

This same vague definition of overwhelming, non-specific sorrow has been inherited by our own century, in spite of its almost boundless clinical refinement and fragmentation into hysteria, madness, depression, anxiety and other mental disorders from the later seventeenth century through the Freudian era to the age of Prozac.[8] Each of these has endured to some extent in the popular consciousness under the baleful gaze of its dark, mythic forebear, Melancholia. From the élite language of French psychoanalytic philosophy to the popular accessibility of modern American 'alternative rock' music, melancholy still remains, at the end of the twentieth century, an 'infinite sadness' (see Figure 7.1). It is, says Julia Kristeva in her famous 1987 description, like a black sun whose invisible, lethargic rays strike the sufferer as if from a distant, eerie galaxy, causing, as any early modern physician would recognize, 'a life that is unlivable, heavy with daily sorrows, tears held back or shed, a total despair, scorching at times, then wan and empty. In short, a devitalized existence ... ready at any moment for a plunge into death ... a living death ... absorbed into sorrow'.[9]

From Aristotelian thought to the tortured writings of Kristeva, and especially around 1600, melancholy has remained the élite disease of the solitary intellectual, the visionary, the artist, the mystic and the clairvoyant whose infinite transcendence is tragically disabled by the weight of his dark, earthbound existence. The disorder has exerted particularly strong influence on both the artistic imagination and those prone to susceptibility during periods of violent change in political and religious institutions, or during the sudden replacement of dominant epistemologies by strange new ones, when 'new cosmologies call it all in doubt'.[10] It acheived veritable cult status among Elizabethan and early Stuart courtiers, and engaged the fancy of Freud's darkening Vienna. It has particularly stricken those of the highest social, educational or professional status; lesser individuals have merely suffered common mopiness or mild depression. The melancholic has long been considered the troubled genius whose mind has become weary through too much contemplation. As such, he is perhaps most familiarly seen in image after early modern image as the white-faced man whose hair and beard match the somber blackness of his clothes, thinking or playing the lute alone beneath the unseen shadow of night's black bird.[11] With the exception of variants that border on hysteria and literally arise from the womb, melancholy has traditionally been a male affliction, the distinctive disorder of the contemplative in a culture that associates men mainly with the mind, and women with the body.[12]

Lovesickness and desire

Likewise, melancholy has long been linked to love, both the desire for sublime spiritual union with the Divine, and the earthly hunger for sexual satisfaction. Lovesickness has had many names in Western descriptive and diagnostic literature, but its essential nature as the dark and solitary agony of a lone soul yearning for fulfilment has most often rendered it an adjunct to melancholy. Modern medical literature has defined melancholy as 'a great despairing cry for love', an idea dating back to the early modern era in which 'melancholly' was considered a standard modifier for 'lover'. Born of a fiery longing so intense that body and soul became racked and scourged by feverish tempests and turmoils raised by unfulfilled desire, lovesickness was considered a completely debilitating and potentially deadly disease by pre-modern diagnosticians. It was most appropriately treated by learned physicians. Like all other experiences with both physical and social aspects in Western thought, erotic illness was a set of conditions whose specifics varied by era and location. However, there were a few generalities that consistently defined the ailment. Like the more generalized melancholy to which it was related, lovesickness or erotic melancholy was long considered an especially distinctive disorder of noble men. Its classic and easily recognizable symptoms included listlessness, sleep deprivation, lack of interest in food or drink, and the langorous wasting away of the entire body, except for the eyes, which, according to one tradition, revealed the infection of the sufferer's system through the optic nerve and into the three ventricles of the brain by the phantasmic image of the beloved. The disorder was accompanied by emotional instability, an irregular pulse, and an ambulatory mania born of restlessness; it was often associated with abnormal erotic phenomena and enhanced capacity for sexual performance. The most natural and effective cure, and the one most fervently desired by the sufferer, was union with the beloved.[13] As the reader of any medieval romance or audience member of any Baroque opera realizes, sometimes this was not possible.

Because of its literal auditory harmony and its vast sympathetic vibration with all things visible and unseen, music was the most obvious cure, short of physical consummation, for the '*Dispassionate*, and *Infortunate Sonnes of Love*, thereby to asswage the *turmoyles*, and quiet the *tempests* that were raised in them'.[14] The early modern nobility and ambitious middle class alike took seriously the idea of curing dullness and heaviness of spirit, whatever the cause, with the solitary performance of vocal and instrumental music. To an era that not only held Love 'the first inventor of Physick [and] Musick', but had inherited a stock set of conventions proclaiming music to be both a general '*Antipharmacon* to sorrow' and emulator of secret thoughts, music became the standard vehicle through which erotic melancholy was both relieved and represented.[15] In particular, for pre-modern thinkers for whom the literal and metaphorical, or embodied and spiritual, were not completely separable, Love and Music possessed strikingly similar affective powers and physical pathways to inward reception. Both crossed the vast chasm between the physical and metaphysical worlds, step by step through all the intermediary channels of arousal. Both were introduced to the mind by the senses, gaining easy access into an unguarded body, and finally mingling with the spirits of the blood to produce a state of exquisite ecstasy unlike anything known independently to the separable entities of body and soul. In addition, according to the occult doctrines of the era, both love and music emulated the phantasmic language of the divinely given soul, and bore secret, compelling messages directly from one soul to another.[16] From the conventions of seventeenth-century Dutch painting, to English drama, to Italian opera, we see this idea again and again, a commonplace of the era's medical manuals and philosophical tracts brought to life before audience after audience.

Jan Vermeer's mid-seventeenth-century painting of *A Lady at the Virginals with a Gentleman* vividly unites several of these strains in a classic, if silent, articulation of erotic yearning at once made musical and rich with promise of fulfilment (Figure 7.2). The rich furnishings, sumptuous clothing, and exquisitely decorated instrument instantly position this narrative of secret desire within a world of wealth and privilege – the very one in which melancholy disorders most often originated. The action and placement of the two figures immediately reminds us of the great power attributed by Burton to 'a faire young Gentlewoman' at the virginals to entice men to love and its attendant melancholy.[17] The central figure of the image, the lady of the title, plays her instrument against the wall of a light-filled room. With downcast

7.2 Jan Vermeer, *A Lady at the Virginals with a Gentleman*. The Royal Collection © Her Majesty Queen Elizabeth II.

head turned from the gentleman who gazes at her raptly with parted lips, her hands and face remain demurely hidden from the viewer. Behind her, against the patterned tiles at the bottom centre of the painting, lies a discarded bass viol. Its silenced strings point towards the man, waiting for hand and bow-stroke to give it life and resonant support for the more ephemeral keyboard harmony which decays in an instant. Above the woman hangs a mirror, image and reflector of melancholy in early modern thought. So positioned, it may also serve as a subtle reminder of the extrasensory perception and highly developed phantasmagoric faculty associated with the most inspired forms of melancholy and its ability to confer artistic aptitude.[18] The Renaissance Neoplatonist Marsilio Ficino (whose ideas on magic, melancholy and healing remained constant well into Vermeer's century through such codifiers as Burton) explains that celestial gifts may be won by exposing lower things to higher ones in the same manner in which a mirror reflects the viewer's face, or a wall amplifies sound into an echo; and that the astrological influence of such a planet as Venus, celestial bringer of love, can be called down through the appropriate music just as the string of one instrument will tremble to another similarly tuned.[19] Here, we witness the love-magic of music taking place. For from within the mirror, the coy virginal player gazes downwards towards her listener from another plane, her secret, disembodied self answering his desire. We know equally well that her powerfully reflected music echoes in his ears, and, should he touch the viol that already vibrates in sympathy to her keyboard strings, his melancholy would vanish as Love rendered him musical according to a common saying of the day.[20] The same idea is seen in a contemporaneous emblematic image, reinforcing the precept that just as a mirror reflects the sunlight it receives, so does love reflect its source on the beloved – again, in the form of a well-appointed lady playing to an attentive gentleman (Figure 7.3). Here, there is no doubt of the presence and efficacy of love in such musical matters; it is Cupid himself, mischevious son of the allegorical goddess whose powers remain in the planet bearing her name, who directs radiant beams towards the duo at the virginals. Should we hear their music, it might be the soft, wantonness of Venus, full of the tranquil serenity of erotic dalliance, for 'he that intends copulation ought to be free from turbulent passions of the mind, and vain phantasms'.[21] Vermeer's couple, suffering no longer but rapt in a duo of love fulfilled, might play such serene, simple compositions based on dance melodies and other familiar tunes as those published in *Parthenia In-Violata*, perhaps intended as a royal wedding present for a viol-player and his virginal-playing bride.[22] Or he might continue to drink in her music in his solitary sorrow, suspended in that exquisite liminal space between desire and solace, and the worlds of flesh and spirit, as Vermeer has left him.

Although there was general agreement among early modern thinkers that music was extremely affective and altered bodily and psychic responsive states, there was some debate as to what sorts of music accomplished which results for whom. The English Jesuit Thomas Wright, for example, remained convinced that a particular response to music was both culturally conditioned and based on innate temperament, rather than inherent in sound. Therefore one would only be moved to do what came most naturally, or what one had come to associate with particular

7.3 P. C. Hoofts, Emblem 'Sy blinct en doet blincken' from *Minnezinnebeelden, Sonnetten, en Zangen*, Amsterdam, 1675. National Gallery of Art Library, David K. E. Bruce Fund.

auditory phenomena, no matter what one heard.[23] In contrast, others who considered musical affect and listener response believed in the efficacy of particular musics for precise psycho-physical purposes. According to a number of authors who considered the problem, music to balance the brooding, wasting, introspective disorder of any sort of melancholic should stir the listener's blood, draw his mind away from inner turmoil and attenuate the imbalanced spirits and humours of his listless body.[24] In the synaesthetic imagery of the English physician Timothy Bright, the music to dispel the rapid ups and downs of all melancholy disorders should be quick and cheerful, the auditory equivalent of pleasant pictures and lively colours, acting as a strong magical charm against mental instability and sorrow. It should not be unpredictably abstract or eccentric in form like fantasies, dumps or consort music with their learned imitations and constant variation of rhythm, metre and melody, but instead remain mirthful and bright.[25]

On the other hand, erotic melancholy, like Love itself, was often seen by early modern men, trained as soldiers and statesmen in a gender-separate culture, to be potentially effeminate and effeminating, a pathological state that could ultimately refer back *in extremis* to some sort of intrusive femininity or effeminate frailty. For their more tender sisters, the natural cure was marriage and children. Music, too, with its invasive qualities and ability to alter the spirits of the body or suspend the listener in a state of ecstasy not unlike the most inspired form of melancholy, was not a little suspect to the more conservative thinkers of the era for its very ability to 'effeminate' the susceptible listener.[26] Burton considers music the most powerful cure for the disorder in general, but specifically forbids it to the obsessive, amorous melancholic 'who capers in conceit all day long, and thinks of nothing else, but how to make Jigges, Sonnets, Madrigals, in commendation of his Mistress'. Such a love-struck man, who has obviously lost all sense of masculine perspective and manly rationality, will be driven to complete physical breakdown by music. Lovesick maidens, on the other hand, should be married if at all possible, and sometimes know how to use the charm of music to that end.[27]

Early modern physicians typically describe debilitating melancholy disorders arising from love or from unspecified causes in strongly gendered terms that are remarkably similar to their era's delineation of ornate, florid 'effeminate' music – the music of Venus at its most voluptuous extreme. Music that wavers wantonly, changes direction, flickers teasingly, and is embellished with insubstantial decoration like a lovesick man, or like a woman's most extreme natural condition of pregnancy or hysteria, could only reinforce the illness that arises from unfulfilled love or from reduction to a state more resembling femininity, according to these thinkers.[28] For those such as Bright who recommend music to cure this sort of imbalance in persons of unspecified gender, it is clearly to be the most direct, rational and inspiring styles, such as simple, forward-driving military marches, cheerful secular songs and dances, and bold hymns of holy praise. Many of the era's most diverse manuscript and printed collections of music take on new meaning in this light, from the eclectic lute and keyboard compilations at the beginning of the century through *Cheerful Ayres and Ballads* to the rollicking tunes and lighthearted amorous texts that dominate *Pills to Purge Melancholy*.

The wide variety of early seventeenth-century vocal songs of unfulfilled love demonstrate a further hierarchy of gender, power, self-cure and clever artistry. From antiquity to the present day, melancholy has been perceived either as a privileged state of inspired genius and thus implicitly masculine, or as an unstable pathological state of fragility that borders on the ultimate feminine state of hysteria. At no point has this been more true than in the era during which the Renaissance gave rise to modernity, when the intelligentsia and the fashionable élite regained interest in both melancholy and the ancient powers of music to move body and soul.

Composers and melancholy

Unlike the writers and visual artists who indulged the taste for melancholy and the ancient passions of the soul, early modern composers had no available models to emulate, and were therefore limited to the musical language of their own era and such devices as they could invent within that rigid framework. In keeping with the class associations of the interest in ancient learning and melancholy conditions, those who chose to express or appease affective disorders through music were literate composers of art music, creating for the pleasure of powerful patrons or with an eye towards the increasingly lucrative market for published music. English court composer John Dowland's dark, hypnotic songs of sorrow and his lachrymose instrumental music have recently been reconnected to the early modern cult of melancholy, musical emulations of the inspired state of visionary solitude intended to bestow the distinction of the disease and produce in the hearer what Burton and *The Praise of Musicke* paradoxically consider pleasing melancholy.[29]

Although none of the composer's songs of unattainable love sustains the same clashing dissonances, chains of suspensions, extended temporal displacement and descending melodic motifs as his more famous expressions of more general melancholy, they are far from consistently bright, cheerful, and predictable in the prescribed manner of auditory pills against sorrow.[30] In such brief pieces as 'What if I Never Speede' from his *Third and Last Booke of Songs or Aires* (1603), Dowland instead imitates the particularly manly passion of deliberately unrequited love, in which, since the heyday of *amour courtois*, the careful, controlled and indefinite postponement of longed-for consummation served to ennoble the male sufferer's soul by maintaining it in a state of ecstasy beyond vulgar appeasement.[31] It is no steadily doleful dump, but includes glimpses of light and hope amidst its darker moments.[32] The dark text of despair, sorrow, and wish for solace is fragmented into minute phrases, treated to alternation between upward flashes of steady brightness and mercurial retreat to lower registers, alternating hope and despair, control and lingering desire. As the narrator addresses his beloved, the steady duple pulse becomes displaced through syncopation, the most graphic musical means to indicate indefinite temporal postponement, psychic displacement, and disruption of the steady rhythms of the human interior faculties. The auditor thus comes to identify, and identify with, a love-stricken man whose true inner state of agitation alternates with rigid public control, neither fully yielding to the glories of the disorder as the composer does for pure melancholy, nor depicting a completed and successful healing of the erotic ailment. Only the imaginary beloved could alleviate the narrator's pain, but instead he remains on the eternally orgasmic edge of an ecstasy enabled by 'singing ... to set the more on flote that pensiveness wherewith [he is] perplexed'.[33]

Perhaps the most famous early seventeenth-century auditory image of a love-stricken woman is Claudio Monteverdi's setting of Ottavio Rinuccini's *Lamento della ninfa*, included in his eighth book of madrigals.[34] Considered in the light of the era's medical and philosophical works on love, the virtuoso piece is almost literally a textbook example of feminine erotic melancholy given sound and voice. This familiar piece has been analysed many times and from many perspectives, though its precise medical associations have yet to be drawn. As commentators too numerous to name have noted, it is most strongly marked by the masculine frame placed around the love-stricken nymph, by the relentless, obsessive descending tetrachord that dominates and grounds the instrumental accompaniment to her lamentation like falling tears, and by the affective use of virtually every expressive device available to an early Baroque composer. Monteverdi's extraordinary miniature auditory portrait anticipates and provides early exemplarity of some of the most central musical and music-dramatic trends of succeeding centuries in Western art music.[35] But yet the Lament is founded as much on a backward glance at the understanding and emulation of feminine passion as on the more modern ideas of musical abstraction for which it is best known. Such excessive grief as we see in Monteverdi's madrigal was a topic that preoccupied writers on melancholy throughout Europe during the seventeenth century; and clinical records of women mourning loss emphasize the weeping, aimless wandering, restlessness, fear, solitariness, and (implicit) wish to die that we see in Rinuccini's poem.[36] The pre-modern world particularly held such excessive love to be characteristic of women, but yet 'women's passions' were considered 'natural' and thus incapable of self-healing. Under such circumstances, madness could result from the inability to process increasingly stronger agitations that crossed the permeable boundary between body and soul, for passion was 'a vehement pang' that involved both aspects of the human creature. And the unfulfilled hungers of the womb alone could result in many hysterical conditions.[37]

Even before we meet the hapless title nymph, the manly vocal trio serve as detached, clinical diagnosticians of her condition through text and music. We hear and hear of her listlessness, pallor, ambulatory mania, and complete disruption of her psycho-physical systems as if reading a learned medical or philosophical account such as Burton's description of 'Symptomes of Maides, Nunnes, and Widowes Melancholy' as:

> a kinde of still dotage & grief ... with much solitariness, weeping, distraction, &c ... troublesome sleepe, ... dejection of minde, much discontent, preposterous judgment ... [T]hey pine away, void of councell, apt to weep, and tremble ... fearefull, sad, and out of all hope ... They take delight in nothing for the time, but love to be alone and solitary ... Many of them cannot tell how to expresse themselves in wordes ... you cannot understand them ... they are in despaire.[38]

Through old-fashioned madrigalisms, Monteverdi's musical clinicians particularly emphasize her sorrow, wandering, huge heart-felt sighs and tears with such obvious auditory gestures that the listener feels and empathizes with her condition even before hearing her voice. The seventeenth-century listener would also have been aware that 'costiveness of the womb, little sleepe, troublous and naughty dreames, swemming of the head, and sound in the eares' were not uncommon to such melancholiacs, or that young maidens on the verge of sexual awakening were subject to particularly intense forms of erotic desire.[39] The nymph's own fragmentary utterances, with their unpredictable, fantastical turns of melodic, harmonic, and rhythmic direction, their starts and stops, and the steady, solitary weeping of the *basso continuo* constructs a highly recognizable auditory portrait of the woman driven mad by unfulfilled desire, beyond words, and requiring the constant interpretation and diagnosis of the voyeuristic male chorus. In such a tender, awakening soul, we are told by the era's experts, the force of imagination is very strong, and 'oftentimes supposeth more then really there is', and such a body 'abounds with bloud, seed, and spirits', causing her terrible trauma.[40] As McClary particularly emphasizes, the pitiable creature, whose sexuality has presumably been ignited by the cad who abandoned her, strains at her very limited musical bounds in an ultimately hopeless attempt to exceed what is there.[41] Like Dowland's narrator, there is but one real cure for her; unlike him, she does not redirect her carnal desires towards a state of deliberately controlled, and ultimately sublime, ecstasy. Of that her gender and current state render her incapable, filled as she must be with excessive blood and spirit, forcefully aroused, and awaiting only the conciliatory, healing touch of a man. Like the frame around Vermeer's could-be lovers, the detached narrative quartet restrains Monteverdi's nymph within the fragile psycho-physical realm where fire merges with ice, and desire outweighs its own fulfilment. She is transformed into an imagined object of pathos, forever suffering, beyond even the reach of those male listeners who might, as Burton suggests could happen, fantasize healing of her hurt.

This pathetic and stereotypical representation of classic feminine lovesickness could scarcely contrast more with Barbara Strozzi's solo cantata 'Questa e la nuova'.[42] Here we find another early modern female voice singing of love gone wrong. Unlike her older male antecedents, Dowland and Monteverdi, Strozzi calculatedly and deliberately presents a musical cure to lovers. Her setting of the anonymous first-person narrative of love lost is direct and lyrical, rendering more subtle and personal the sort of musical language used to such striking dramatic effect by Monteverdi.[43] Her soprano voice, neither distanced by manly interpolation, explanation, nor mythological characterization and narrative that position the story into some literary realm of the past, sings directly to the listener. Her steady metre, frequent upward stepwise motion, and bold melodic leaps certainly give us the auditory equivalent of lively colours, as Bright recommends. In addition, her sly extended melisma and excited sequential rise on 'canti', and her treatment of 'canzonetta', remind the listener that yes, indeed, it is song that may cure lovesickness. Even her brief, stereotypical treatment of the pain, tears and torment that necessarily dominate love are humorous and ironic in context, for she dismisses these words with such equal ease that the listener is only aware of their passing in contrast to the predominant musical message of the song. These effects are all the more striking in the light of her favoured mode of expressing the lachrymose suffering of love through music. As the first-person soprano narrator tells the listener through union of text and music, well is she enduring the situation. For the narrator-singer and listener alike, music becomes an 'anti-pharmacon to sorrow', in spite of the contrasts in its text.

The century of Dowland, Monteverdi, Strozzi, and also of Bacon, Descartes, Galileo and Newton, witnessed the coincidental codification of the modern tonal system and the beginnings of modern experimental science and medicine. As has been pointed out, both are founded on the strict rational control of subjects and materials, on a distinct hierarchy of laws and regulatory mechanisms, on formulaic theories, and on the exultation of abstract logic and hyper-rational intellect. Under these systems, the emotional, the sensual and the instinctual became mistrusted, devalued as distractions or as the inferior and useless markers of such hierarchically lower states as wild nature, popular culture or immaturity.[44] Tonal art music, like science, quickly became intent on shaping and subduing recalcitrant materials, purging elements of disorder and keeping potentially dangerous or explosive elements in separable, discrete containers of very finite size. John Shepherd has especially emphasized that tonal music, the music of the industrialized West, maintains much of its effect from the combination of an objectification of the passage of time through strict metrical control, and from the magnetic pull towards a key note or tonal area.[45] We have already seen these precepts used and violated to excellent effect in early articulations of the system he describes. But yet, beyond the realm of artistic creativity and its deliberate containment, the modern disciplines of psychology and psychoanalysis have returned to questions and conceptions of embodied emotionality that would have been recognizable 350 years ago. One strain of twentieth-century thought, partly founded on Nietzschean ideas, has reunited mind and body beyond Cartesian disconnection so that human life again regards passions as carnal, and language or other utterance as bond between flesh and idea. Once again music has come to serve as a scientific language of embodied emotionality, measurable under laboratory conditions by trained neuroscientists.[46] In the words of post-Freudian psychoanalyst Maurice Merleau-Ponty, resonant with faint echoes of pre-modern occult science,

> We touch here the most difficult point, that is, the bond between the flesh and the idea, between the visible and the interior armature which it manifests and which it conceals ... Literature, music, the passions, but also the experience of the visible world are – no less than is the science of Lavoisier and Ampere – the exploration of an invisible and the disclosure of a universe of ideas. The difference is simply that this invisible, these ideas, unlike those of that science, cannot be detached from the sensible appearances and be erected into a second positivity. The musical idea, the literary idea,

> the dialectic of love, and also the articulations of the light, the modes of exhibition of sound, of touch speak to us, have their logic, their coherence, their points of intersection, their concordances, and here also the appearances are the disguise of unknown 'forces' and 'laws'. But it is as though the secrecy wherein they lie, and whence the literary expression draws them were their proper mode of existence. For these truths are not only hidden like a physical reality which we have not been able to discover ... [T]he ideas we are speaking of would not be better known to us if we had no body and no sensibility ... [I]t is that they owe their authority, their fascinating, indestructible power, precisely to the fact that they are in transparency behind the sensible, or in the heart.[47]

Rock music and twentieth-century melancholy

By the middle of the twentieth century, several ostentatiously rebellious movements in the arts and culture had also come to question the dominion of rational precision over all human endeavours. Perhaps none of these stands out as much as the social and cultural phenomena associated with rock music, based from the beginning on carefully constructed liminal protest against staid scientific and social convention. In the milieu around which rock was created and marketed, pre-modern and non-Western thought from astrology to tantrism were suddenly attributed with the keys to alternative means of investigation, understanding and healing; and such highly regulated actions and substances as sex and drugs acquired new contexts, meanings and uses.[48] But, like virtually all products of popular rebellion, the underlying structures of rock music and its cultural affiliates remain conservative, reaching back to the simplicity of earlier eras beneath its new packaging. A great deal of rock music simply foregrounds long-held notions about the close connections between music, gender and erotic ailment, audible for centuries in other such highly artificial and complicated genres as madrigal, opera and *lieder*. As Frank Zappa put it most simply through the whispery narrative voice of the Central Scrutinizer on his 1979 record-album *Joe's Garage* (Chicago: Polygram Distribution), 'As you can see ... girls, music, disease, heartbreak ... they all go together'.

Rock-music scholarship has increasingly emphasized the genre's fragmentation into distinct styles with separable followings, but certain patterns of style and consumption remain evident. Perhaps most importantly, as music scholars are only just beginning to observe, it is the musical languages and musical underpinnings of the texts that both musicians and listeners consider fundamental to meaning, affect and audience following.[49] Theodor Adorno has pointed out that, unlike the art musics that retain a dialectical relationship to their historical forms, 'song hits' and related popular genres rely on patterns of identification, appealing in particular to a lonely crowd, to the immature, to those who cannot express their emotions and experiences, either because of lack of experience or cultural taboo.[50] As any late twentieth-century listener knows, the emotions and experiences expressed by rock music and its lyrics are overwhelmingly and unsubtly sexual, from the forbidden fantasies of the disempowered to articulations of almost universal experience. In the words of Simon Reynolds and Joy Press: 'Rock offers an imaginative space in which you can reaffirm your sexual identity, or stretch and sometimes escape its limits altogether.' As Adorno adds, as if speaking of Dowland's or Strozzi's songs in another context, 'in an imaginary but psychologically emotion-laden domain, the listener who remembers a hit song will turn into the song's ideal subject, into the person for whom the song ideally speaks'.[51] Rock music therefore reinforces and resolves the problems which arise from eros, offering the imaginative listener a sympathetic voice and public expression of his or her own thoughts.

In spite of the rallying cries of 'free love' and the egalitarian unisex attire of many early rock audiences, the genre has remained, like most Western musics, overwhelmingly oriented to heterosexual male tastes. In addition, recent cutting-edge rock has come to be identified more strongly with an educated and privileged élite.[52] As with Western art genres, women's place and voice have either tended to be dictated and circumscribed by male desire, or located in subgenres with smaller circulation and more intimate performance venues. Although rock has long provided a playing-field for gender identity and sly and occasionally subversive experimentation with sexualities and sex roles, it has tended to rely on two distinct sorts of sound, which John Shepherd has identified with the loaded terms 'cock rock' and 'soft rock'. The former is 'an explicit, crude and often aggressive expression of ... sexuality', whose performers emphasize their powers of dominance and control through a hard, rasping vocal timbre produced overwhelmingly in throat and mouth instead of the resonating chambers of chest and head, and with a strident, percussive guitar sound to match. 'Soft rock', in contrast, is the gentler sound of 'top 40' pop, based on the sentimentality of the ballad form with a warm, vulnerable, often highly melodious sound emanating from the resonating chambers of the singer's chest or head, to a softly sythesized or gently electrified guitar accompaniment.[53] Each of these is associated with predictable musical expressions of unfulfilled love in ways that both reinforce and subvert stereotypical notions of gendered sound.

The most common sort of rock homage to what was once known as erotic melancholy would probably be familiar to John Dowland except for its rapid, rasping vocal timbre, harmonic simplicity, and driving, percussive instrumental sound. Like Palmer's 'Bad Case of Loving You', such pieces are dominated by extremely short phrases, unusually insistent use of the tonic into which the dominant or an occasional dominant seventh intrudes unexpectedly before immediate banishment, rising sequential phrases to illustrate mounting desire, and well-placed, sometimes extended use of syncopation. These unsettling devices, however, are ultimately dominated by an invariably rapid tempo, the generic brightness that most often colours hard or 'cock' rock, and lively motion to the final cadence. These boys and girls are clearly unnerved and excited in equal measure by the fickle objects of their fancy, but the state of unresolved desire is ultimately untroubling, more a source of artistic inspiration than soul-wrenching agony. Like the listeners who identify with their state, they'll survive. Classic examples include Cream's 'Sunshine of Your Love' (from *Disraeli Gears*, Los Angeles: RSO, 1968), with its breathy, syncopated sequential ascent to the title state, at which it bursts into a florid melisma of imagined erotic bliss that any early modern composer would envy; and the Rolling Stones' '(I Can't Get No) Satisfaction' (from *Out of Our Heads*, ABKCO records, 1965), with its sly little pauses between the notion of what the singer can't get and the item itself, and its greater excitation to illustrate his attempts rather than to present the object of his desire. As more rockin' women have broken out of the stereotype of utter dejection after rejection that was old long before Monteverdi, this sort of sound has crossed gender barriers with increasing frequency. No longer must women fuse tears with orgasm in a pattern at least one modern neurologist-psychiatrist has observed to be typical of female sufferers of melancholia.[54] Pat Benatar's classic rendition of G. Gill and C. Wade's 'Heartbreaker', for example, is hardly a hysterical lament for lost love, with its steady, methodical motion and insistence on its tonal centre. It is instead the auditory image of powerful control in hopeless love, rendering the singer into the object of desire instead of rejection. 'Love in itself, in the form of longing and deprivation, lowers the self-regard; whereas to be loved, to have love returned, and to possess the beloved object exalts it again', says Freud.[55] Benatar's singing voice, like Strozzi's soprano narrator long before her, substitutes the exultation of music for deprivation and thus conveys musically the return to self-regard.

Opposite these bright, lively, and occasionally humorous songs of unfulfilled desire and their message that music can assuage the listener's own erotic turmoil, stands a darker, more solemn group of songs that instead invite the auditor to share in the age-old sorrow of loss and perhaps the melancholy isolation of artistic genius.[56] The darker side of rock includes destruction, despair and the dusky shadow of violence that has stalked modern popular images of love for well over a century, but reaches its narcissistic zenith beyond all of these in the desire for something unknowable and unfocused, just out of reach. The nineteenth- and twentieth-century artist has often returned to the ancient link between sexual desire and frenzied artistic inspiration by a self-conscious and inward-focused transformation of love into art.[57] 'my reflection, dirty mirror / there's no connection to myself / i'm your lover, i'm your zero / i'm the face in your dreams of glass', snarls lead singer Billy Corgan of the Smashing Pumpkins in brief, nearly static fragments over a descending *basso ostinato* in the 1995 song 'Zero'. Here is no cupid to reflect the sunshine of heavenly love onto lover and beloved through inaudible harmony, no earthly solace promised in the magic mirror. 'i'm in love with my sadness', proclaims the hard-edged, depressive voice shortly after it has pronounced its own emptiness and that of god, starkly alone and unaccompanied. This brief affirmation of love and beloved object mirror each other on either side of a short pause as antecedent and consequent halves, complementary opposites in the glass of self-reflection. Here, his love drops and then rises around a tonal centre a fifth away from the opposed rise and fall of his sadness, pulled towards each other over shared harmonic support. In contrast, in the end it is the mysterious 'she' addressed by the text who is simple, monolithic and literally monotonous as the instrumental accompaniment drops away from the voice to render her final auditory image a lonely, dropping 'only'. The singer-narrator's melancholy is the jagged, broken glass of the narcissistic mirror, in which self and lover/other are cast into the same empty world of undefinable loss that had neither beginning nor clear and shining object. It includes the identifying 'rhythm slowed down or interrupted' of the living death of melancholy, yearning at once for both sides of the mirage.[58]

More commonly, however, the melancholy strain in rock has had a softer sound, a gentle longing for a distant place of comfort to which no living body can ascend, the desire for a phantasmic object or missing part of self that no lover can fulfil. Through an indefinite sense of love and loss, such songs move beyond mere lovesickness and return to an overarching sense of melancholia. Here is revealed the paradoxical search in love for an external object to answer the inner cry of desire, the consequent introversion of self, and yearning for the object of first loss. 'The child king becomes irredeemably sad before uttering his first words', explains Kristeva:

> this is because he has been irrevocably, desperately separated from the mother, a loss that causes him to find her again, along with

> other objects of love, first in the imagination, then in words ... led to ponder over not only the amatory state but its corollary as well, melancholia. ... [I]f there is no writing other than the amorous, there is no imagination that is not, overtly or secretly, melancholy.[59]

Reynolds and Press have suggested that the most melancholy voices of rock music come from its most aggressive, dominant, strident men in contemplative moods, 'psychedelic mothers' boys singing wistfully', defined by 'an undefinable sense of lack', men of phallic potency like Jimi Hendrix or Ian Curtis seeking an indefinite feminine element through their own pensive lullabies.[60]

Led Zepplin's 1971 song 'Stairway to Heaven' includes features that would have been recognized as melancholic over three hundred years previously: its slow tempo, its frequent and sometimes unexpected pauses, and especially its fantasy-like opening section, shared between acoustic guitar and recorder consort in a strange and incongruous borrowing into acid rock from the coincident early music movement. Here is a virtually seamless blend of several varieties of the nostalgic yearning, search for authenticity, and popular mysticism associated with unrequited love and melancholy longing in the modern world.[61] As Laurence Dreyfus and Robert Morgan have pointed out, the early music movement, which reached its popular peak during the late 1960s and early 1970s, largely represents a search for lost authenticity of musical sound and a rebellion against the forbidding, modern ways of the élite musical mainstream. Paradoxically, it also enabled an aesthetic of novelty through auditory metamorphosis of the familiar into something slightly alien.[62] The same improbable blend of nostalgia and novelty becomes evident immediately in 'Stairway to Heaven'. Its clear, resonant neo-Elizabethan opening and its simple, square phrase structure are a far cry from the band's more usual metallic distortion. The recorder, the most uncomplicated instrument of the early music revival, additionally evokes the memory of childhood sounds and first enchanting musical experience. For its gentle timbre suggests the simple melodies first learned on inexpensive, mass-produced versions in many a British school, first pre-adolescent awareness of musical capacity. Even more nostalgic is Robert Plant's periodic punctuation of the text with soft, wordless repetitions of melodic fragments from the song, suggestive of the mother's first reassuring lullaby and the infant's first echo of her beloved voice.[63]

Centuries earlier, the airy sweetness of the recorder had been associated with celestial purity and revelation. Here, in an alien auditory world, it again guides the listener to a mysterious heavenly presence, the lost mother of infinite resource buying a stairway to heaven. Robert Plant's unusually restrained and even occasionally wistful voice articulates a text of an equally old-fashioned sort, a hypnotic, fairy-tale-like evocation of cosmic good, evil and free will, set mostly in the key of a minor with occasional tension against C major. He is beyond gender, beyond genre, beyond erotic desire, beyond time. Even his unexpected burst into the rapid, electrified frenzy and acoustically more brilliant head-voice more typical of the band, accompanied by Jimmy Page's switch from acoustic to electric guitar, merely provides a central temporal contrast to its idyllic auditory frame, recalling that mania is often the inspired flip side of melancholy quietude.[64] The listener, too, becomes called into 'the opening of a dimension that can never again be closed', the moment in which idea and sensation merge through musical performance.[65] But in the modern world in which sophisticated, amplified sound has become the auditory and aesthetic norm, we can never again return home safely to the pure sweetness of simple, originary acoustic music. In this hypnotic song, the listener is called by 'the piper' into a quasi-mystical world populated with auditory and verbal evocations of cherished things that have been lost, relegated to childhood stories or the half-remembered teachings of religions that have no place in the knowing, fleshly world of rock music. Such songs provide a warm, dark retreat from the genre's auditory norm. Here is a wistful reminder of unnamed loves lost and sounds forgotten long ago, a comforting, genderless refuge for and from a world dominated by boastful, super-rational masculinity. 'Many men are made melancholy by hearing music', wrote Burton over three centuries before Plant was born, 'but it is a pleasing melancholy that it causeth, and therefore to such as are discontent ... it expells cares ... and easeth in an instant'.[66]

Notes

1. Burton (1632), 294.
2. For further information on humoural theories of healing, especially in relationship to melancholy, see Gouk (2000); Jackson (1986), 7–10; and Schleiner (1991), 32–5.
3. Beier (1987), 8–19, and Henry (1991).
4. Ficino (1989), 20–23; Heffernan (1995), 5–25; Jackson (1986); Klibansky et al. (1964); Kristeva (1989), 6–8; see also Battersby (1989).
5. Couliano (1987), 47–51; Freud (1917/1959), 152, 164–7; Jackson (1986), 249–73, 373–80; Klibansky et al. (1964), 217–40; MacDonald (1981), 151–3, 157.
6. Ostow (1970), 10–11, 41.
7. Barrough (1596), 45–6.
8. Cataldi (1993), 100–107; Freud (1917/1959), 153; Jackson (1986), 373–80; and Otis (1994), 3–10.
9. Kristeva (1989), 4.

10. Ibid., 8; Lepenies (1992), 3–20.
11. See, for example, Babb (1951); MacDonald (1981), 148–52; also n. 29 below.
12. Enterline (1995), 8–9, 126–8, 140–44; and Schiesari (1992), 96–101.
13. On the symptomology of erotic melancholy in the pre-modern West, see Babb (1951), 132–7; Couliano (1987), 18–21; Jacquart and Thomasset (1988), 83–6; Lowes (1913–14), 491–546; and Wack (1990), p. xi.
14. Ravenscroft (1614), sig. A3^{v}.
15. Ferrand (1640), 2; and *The Praise of Musicke* (1586), 61.
16. See Austern (1993) and Wells (1994), 83–4, 170–75.
17. Burton (1632), 488.
18. Enterline (1995), 1, 7–8, 156–64.
19. Ficino (1989), 360–61, 388–9; Tomlinson (1993), 87–8, 112–14; see also Gouk (1999), Voss (2000) and D. P. Walker (1985).
20. Burton (1632), 540; and Ravenscroft (1614), sig. B2^{v}.
21. Sinibaldi (1657), sig. F7^{v}.
22. Dart (1961), 40–42.
23. Wright (1604), 172; Gouk (1991), 96–7, 100–103.
24. Bacon (1683), 128; Austern (1996), 134–43; Finney (1962), 139–58.
25. T. Bright (1586), 247–8.
26. Austern (1993), 348–53; Finney (1947a), 158–60; Finney (1947b), 283.
27. Burton (1632), 203–4, 296, 488–90.
28. Austern (1993), 348–53; Fontanus (1652), 71–2; and Wack (1990), 13.
29. Rooley (1983), 6–20; and Wells (1994), 185–207.
30. For thorough analyses of the musical-rhetorical structures of two of Dowland's darkest and most famous songs of melancholy despair, see Toft (1993), 128–53. For an insightful discussion of the ways in which Dowland's lute songs imitate passionate experiences, see Fischlin (1987–8), 52–86.
31. Couliano (1987), 18–19, 38–9 and 50–51; Jacquart and Thomasset (1988), 94; Kristeva (1989), 5–6, 8; and Wack (1990), 21.
32. Recordings of this song are widely available on compilations of Elizabethan and Jacobean lute songs and collections devoted to the works of Dowland. The standard score in modern notation is Dowland (1603/1970); for a facimile see Dowland (1603/1977).
33. *The Praise of Musicke* (1586), 34.
34. For the standard modern score of this madrigal, see Monteverdi (1929), 286–94. Recordings of this work are widely available in collections of Monteverdi's late madrigals and a number of general Italian madrigal collections of the era.
35. The most ground-breaking and influential analyses of recent years may be found in McClary (1991a), 86–90; Rosand (1979), 351–2; and Tomlinson (1993), 236–46.
36. MacDonald (1981), 159–60. For greater insight into the cultural meaning of pieces of music which re-create such conditions, see Cusick (1994), 37.
37. Foucault (1967), 89–91; and Wack (1990), 13. Even in our own day, tears and orgasm, or the desire for orgasm, have been linked in clinical study of female depressives or melancholiacs; see Ostow (1970), 22–3.
38. Burton (1632), 202–3.
39. Barrough (1596), 46; and Sinibaldi (1657), sig. D1^{r-v}.
40. Sinibaldi (1657), sig. D1^{r-v}.

41. See McClary (1991a), 86–7.
42. For the facsimile score of this work, see Strozzi (1986), 25–6. The cantata is recorded on 'Glenda Simpson Sings Barbara Strozzi, with the Camerata of London' (1988). London: Hyperion Records Limited.
43. For a discussion of Strozzi's compositional style, see Rosand (1986), 177–87.
44. Cataldi (1993), 123; Shepherd (1977/1980), 106; and Small (1996), 60–61, 80–83. See also Gouk (1999).
45. McClary (1991b), 53–79; Shepherd (1977/80), 107–8; Shepherd (1991), 122–3; and Small (1996), 94–5.
46. Cataldi (1993), 100–107, 129; Kern (1992), 61–3; Merleau-Ponty (1968), 149–51; and Schwartz (1997), 7, 14–15.
47. Merleau-Ponty (1968), 149–50; see also 152–3.
48. For further discussion of such forms of deliberately marginalized cultural protest and escape from mainstream structural commitment and sensory compartmentalization, particularly in the Western arts after the Renaissance, see Turner (1974), 260 and 264–5.
49. In particular, see Walser (1993), 21, 26–34, 39–41.
50. Adorno (1976), 26–7. See also Vulliamy (1977/1980), 188–90.
51. Adorno (1976), 27; and Reynolds and Press (1995), pp. xiii–xiv.
52. Vulliamy (1977/1980), 189; Shepherd (1991), 166; and J. W. White (1997), 1–5.
53. Shepherd (1991), 165–8. See also O'Brien (1995), 2–3, 105; and Reynolds and Press (1995), pp. xv, 234–5.
54. Ostow (1970), 22–3.
55. Freud (1914/1959), 57. For information on the application of Freudian psychology to modern clinical music therapy, see Priestly (1994), 155–68 and 181–5.
56. Freud (1917/1959), 159–63; Kristeva (1989), 5; Ostow (1970), 44–5.
57. See Freud (1917/1959), 162; and Kern (1992), 116–17. The narcissistic longing for reunion with a lost object that leads to a desire for death finds roots in the ancient Western link between the soul and male genitalia; see Brown (1990), 128–30.
58. Kristeva (1989), 4.
59. Ibid., 6. See also Freud (1914/1959), 31–7; Freud (1917/1959), 159–63.
60. Reynolds and Press (1995), 211–27. See also Shepherd (1991), 155–6.
61. From *Zoso*, Atlantic Recording Corporation. See Jackson (1986), 373–80; and Ostow (1970), 130–32.
62. Dreyfus (1983), 299, 305, 314–15; and Morgan (1988), 75–6.
63. Schwartz (1997), 16, 20–21.
64. Freud (1917/1959), 164–5; and Jackson (1986), 249–73.
65. Merleau-Ponty (1968), 151; and Schwartz (1997), 7.
66. Burton (1632), 297.

CHAPTER EIGHT

Soul music as exemplified in nineteenth-century German psychiatry

Cheryce Kramer

Introduction

One late summer day in 1848 a gymnastics instructor working in a psychiatric asylum near Dresden asked his class to assemble in a pinwheel formation. The group was to make the pinwheel rotate left and right in accordance with his shouted commands and a rhythm he clapped to mark each stride. The patients had executed this formation many times before and enjoyed performing it both for the asylum community and audiences at large. But its primary purpose was therapy rather than entertainment. The psychiatric opinion of the day held coordinated, cadenced activity, such as would be required to execute the above formation, to be conducive to mental well-being.

On this particular day, however, the therapeutic effect was absent. One patient on the periphery of the pinwheel formation was unable to keep in step with her fellow gymnasts. As a consequence the pattern of movement was neither coordinated nor cadenced and the pinwheel resembled a bicycle wheel after collision with a tree. To save the formation, and its medicinal potential, the instructor placed the offending gymnast in the very centre of the pinwheel where she needed only to rotate on the spot. Unable to carry out the leg movements associated with the first position, the patient was perfectly able to execute the pivoting turns required for the second. After this simple adjustment, coordination and cadence permeated the group's movement and, we are told, the pinwheel rotated unimpeded.[1]

The casual simplicity of this episode masks a complex set of cultural relations organizing the music therapy practised in a nineteenth-century German asylum which pioneered an approach to psychiatry emphasizing sensory stimulation over pharmaceutics or routines of persuasion. It would lead too far astray here to present this psychiatric approach in all its diagnostic, etiologic and therapeutic distinctiveness,[2] or equally to attempt an exhaustive description of the cultural conditions which organized that approach.[3] Yet we cannot appreciate the music therapy it spawned without recognizing that pre-Freudian German psychiatry was directed towards a peculiar soul-organ called the *Gemüth*, which, by all accounts, suffered its own forms of illness, required its own forms of treatment and was peculiarly susceptible to sensory stimulation, especially music.[4] A historical example will serve to characterize the peculiar brand of music therapy which arose within the context of the psychiatry of *Gemüth* and forms the subject of this chapter.

The example is based upon psychiatric practice at the Cure and Nursing Home Illenau from 1842 to 1889, a period of relative continuity in the perceived purpose and daily management of the asylum. The Illenau case is illustrative because every aspect of Illenau's institutional culture, from the landscape to its spatial arrangement, social structure and daily schedule, reflected and reinforced the phenomenal proclivities of *Gemüth*; Illenau physicians conceived the asylum complex to be a purpose-built receptacle of *Gemüth* and its inner life to be a manifestation of a collective *Gemüth*. Due to the emergent habits of sentience, i.e., the phenomenology associated with a soul thus configured, Illenau's music therapy comprised everything from the music at asylum concerts to the patterns of movement in gymnastics and the quotidian cadence of asylum life.

The Illenau *Gemüth*

The Illenau literature abounds with references to *Gemüth*. Yet its prominence is not unique to this literature. *Gemüth* was a national preoccupation in Biedermeier Germany from roughly 1815 to 1848.[5] Women's magazines enumerated its virtues, and priests, educators and doctors directed their appeals for health, happiness and prosperity to its munificent influence.[6] Prominent thinkers such as Kant, Schiller, Schelling, Novalis, Hegel and Schopenhauer employed it in their philosophical investigations, and Heinrich von Kleist wrote an entire short story, 'Über die Vollendung der Gedanken beim Reden' (On the completion of thought while speaking), plotting the movements of *Gemüth* in a dialogue where one party speaks before knowing what to say and the other responds before hearing what is said. By 1830 talk of *Gemüth* was so ubiquitous that Goethe complained that the concept was becoming almost devoid of meaning: 'Germans should not utter the word *Gemüth* for a period of 30 years, then perhaps bit by bit *Gemüth* would be regenerated.'[7]

At a very general level of description *Gemüth* can be defined as a collectively instantiated soul rooted in sentience. But this definition is hardly illuminating. Despite or perhaps because of its pervasive influence, the concept of *Gemüth* is highly elusive. In Grimm's etymological dictionary alone the term spans 32 pages of definitions, many of which are mutually contradictory. For a more practical definition of *Gemüth* it is helpful to turn to the Illenau School of Psychiatry. It furnishes a fairly vivid demonstration of the cultural assumptions which framed experiences of *Gemüth* because its practitioners held mental illnesses to be, literally, 'illnesses of the *Gemüth*' (*Gemüthskrankheiten*) and, consequently, geared their treatment methods towards observing, regulating and cajoling the afflicted organ.

Illenau physicians construed the *Gemüth* to be a soul-organ with two central attributes: it was the unifying element between body and soul; and it was a collectively instantiated subject. The first attribute was associated with the *Gemüth*'s capacity to mediate sensations by connecting states of body with states of mind. It enabled the *Gemüth* to serve both as the exponent and carrier of aesthetic experience. Just as bodies are physical entities which respond to medication and minds are psychological entities which respond to language, the *Gemüth* was understood to be a phenomenal entity which responded to the aesthetic configuration of its environment. Sensations were absorbed into this entity and then radiated throughout its structure, where they continually merged in a diffuse nexus of sensations constituting the state of *Gemüth*. Music was one of the ambient factors used to regulate the state of *Gemüth* amongst Illenau patients.

The second attribute, namely that the *Gemüth* was a collectively instantiated subject, describes the way in which psychological space was carved up at Illenau, where lived reality was an aggregate rather than atomic phenomenon. Asylum life posited no dichotomy between the experience of one and many because the *Gemüth* of individual patients and the *Gemüth* of the asylum population formed a single psychological continuum. The Illenau *Gemüth* was not, as we might imagine, distinct from the individuated subjectivity of each asylum inhabitant but rather was comprised of, and itself determined, the subjectivity of all inhabitants. Sensations apprehended by individual members of the Illenau community were considered to radiate throughout the entire asylum population, continually merging in the diffuse nexus of apprehensions constituting its collective *Gemüth*.

This collective, sentient subject is virtually impossible to comprehend for a modern reader, whose experience of psychic life is individuated and governed by unconscious rather than aesthetic impulses. There is no equivalent register of feeling today; a contemporary German has no more access to this nineteenth-century state of being than a foreigner. Yet without taking account of the *Gemüth*'s defining spiritual faculties, i.e., aesthetic resonance and collective attunement, we cannot understand the musical cures employed at the asylum and, hence, the significance of the gymnastics episode narrated above. The music therapy practised at Illenau reflected and reinforced the experience of *Gemüth* by employing three domains of coordinated, cadenced activity, namely the asylum concert, gymnastics exercise and daily schedule.

The asylum concert

Music was administered to patients via the staged, public concert. In the year 1875 alone asylum officials arranged for 140 concerts to be held at Illenau.[8] The asylum maintained a house choir, marching band and chamber orchestra and employed a full-time music instructor who worked in close collaboration with the physicians. Every piece of music performed at the asylum had to receive prior medical approval, and compositions deemed aesthetically too demanding for those suffering from an affliction of *Gemüth* had to be rewritten by the music instructor.[9] The asylum published the *Illenauer Liederbuch*, a book of special hymns for mental patients that became the standard text for psychiatric asylums throughout Germany. But musical selections were not modified solely according to medical criteria; the musical talent assembled at the asylum also exerted an influence on the final form of each composition. In the early years, for example, the harmonium featured prominently in Illenau's concert because that was the preferred instrument of the asylum's first music instructor.

In keeping with the standard concert practices of the period, the Illenau concert consisted of selected miniatures by nine or twelve composers and rarely included more than one small movement from a larger piece of music. A typical performance would take a form similar to the concert held in the Illenau assembly hall on 18 January 1883:

Overture to 'Iphigenie in Aulis' by Gluck for piano
'Pilgerspruch', choral piece by Mendelssohn-Bartholdy
'Vespergesang', choral piece by Bortniansky
'Die drei Liebchen', solo for baritone by Speyer
'An das Vaterland', choral piece for male choir by Kreutzer
'Waldlied', choral piece for male choir by Mangold
'Ave Maria' by Stradella for piano, harmonium and violin
'Der Spielmann und sein Kind', duet by Weidt
'Seliger Tod', choral piece for male choir by Isenmann
'Silbernes Bächlein', choral piece for male choir by Isenmann

Allegro movement from the C Major Sonata for Piano and Violin by Mozart
Cantata for mixed choir by Palmer.[10]

Contrasting pieces were combined to span a wide field of aural sensations: sacred and popular, major and minor, fast and slow, lyrical and marching, instrumental and vocal, solo and choral. These concerts frequently featured children's pieces, rarely touched upon romantic themes, and elided highly chromatic sequences of pitch as well as complicated harmonies. The Illenau concert used modulations of sound to combine a heterogeneity of sensations into a single balanced experience that would be conducive to the flourishing of *Gemüth*.

It is no accident that one of the most popular composers at Illenau and of the period was Mendelssohn, his musical style being ideally suited to the phenomenal proclivities of *Gemüth*. In the words of Charles Rosen, the concert pianist and music historian:

> Mendelssohn rounds off his phrases, his paragraphs, and eventually his sections with a certain comfortable sweetness... . The *Songs Without Words* have a Mozartean grace without Mozart's dramatic power, a Schubertean lyricism without Schubert's intensity. If we could be satisfied today with a simple beauty that raises no questions and does not attempt to puzzle us, the short pieces would resume their old place. In the concert repertoire. They charm, but they neither provoke nor astonish. It is not true that they are insipid, but they might as well be.[11]

The aesthetic experience Mendelssohn strove to create through music mapped perfectly onto the experience coded into every aspect of Illenau's institutional arrangement. For Illenau physicians the restorative potential of music resided not primarily in the rhythmic and tonal qualities of individual sounds but, more importantly, in the aesthetic effect of an entire composition with its balance of tone, harmony, rhythm and cadence.

Just as important as the aesthetic configuration of an asylum concert was, however, its ability to further the dissolution of self in the asylum community. The music therapy practised at Illenau was quite unlike music therapy today in that remedial doses of sound were administered to groups of patients rather than individual ones. The concert served as a vehicle enabling members of the asylum community to fuse and harmonize in a shared aural experience. In this respect the asylum concert formed part of Illenau's overall psychiatric strategy to immerse the patient population in an aesthetically structured environment that would both serve to equilibrate every individual instantiation of *Gemüth* while simultaneously forging a collective instantiation of *Gemüth*.

Gymnastics exercise

Gymnastics exercise extended Illenau's musical cures into patterns of movement. The asylum had its own gymnastics hall, a full-time gymnastics instructor and usually provided guitar accompaniment for gymnastics classes. Its gymnastics handbook featured a comprehensive list of disorders and corrective movements. So, for example, the prescription for dreamers was rope-jumping because the rope would knock them in the head if attention strayed; for garrulous patients it was lifting such weights that the sheer physical strain of exertion would prevent them from speaking. The presence of a physician during class insured that the pace, rhythm and complexity of each exercise was tailored to the specific affliction of each patient.[12]

At first glance it might appear that gymnastics was directed towards regulating the behaviour and experience of individual patients. The key to understanding the phenomenal texture of Illenau's exercise programme is, however, to look at the structure of a standard class. Like the asylum concert, gymnastics was directed towards the psychological coordination of groups of patients called *Riegen.*

> I. Order Exercises – groups of gymnasts execute formations and patterns involving march steps, countermarches, chains, figures, loops and walking in circles.
>
> II. Free exercises – gymnasts stretch their legs, arms and torso by holding sustained postures as well as jumping, skipping and sway walking.
>
> III. Apparatus exercises – gymnasts execute jumping exercises involving large and small ropes, double bars and vaults as well as obstacle runs and stilt-walking.
>
> IV. Games – gymnasts assemble for ball games, races and catch games such as hide-and-go-seek.[13]

Traditionally gymnastics as proposed by *Turnvater* Jahn, the founder of the gymnastics movement in Germany, had consisted in the last three categories of movement.[14] A class would begin with the confrontation of the self with itself in arm and leg movements; proceeded to the confrontation of the self with the non-self through the use of ropes, double bars and the vault; and concluded with the confrontation of the self with the other in a variety of competitive team sports and games like hide-and-go-seek. But asylum physicians introduced a new category of exercise called 'order exercises', which involved patients assembling in formations such as the human pinwheel mentioned in the introductory passages of this chapter.

Strikingly, these order exercises did not involve *confrontation* of any kind. Instead they were designed to enhance *cooperation* and actualize collective experience. The only way to maintain the rotation was for all gymnasts to focus on the collective pattern of movement instead of their own steps. The pinwheel was sustained not as a result of each gymnast performing the *same* action but rather performing an action commensurate with his or her place in the formation. It is striking evidence of the purported value of collective experience that formation exercises constituted the first order of business in the gymnastics classes held at Illenau. Prior to limbering up the patients' bodies, asylum physicians limbered up the patients' souls. And they did this by stimulating the registers of psychological coordination and literally strengthening the class's collective *Gemüth*.

The rhythmic punctuation of asylum life

Through the highly prized and much discussed 'House Schedule' (*Hausordnung*) Illenau's musical cures even extended into the quotidian cadence of asylum life. This schedule, one of the first of its kind in German-speaking territories, was ratified by the State Medical Commission of Baden, where Illenau was located, and published as a separate booklet to be issued to new members of the Illenau community upon arrival.[15] The schedule specified the daily routine of doctors, patients and employees respectively while ensuring that this routine was sufficiently varied so as not to become monotonously repetitive. Illenau physicians held that occupation could be a panacea for spiritual discomfort provided it was administered in correct doses and with sufficient diversity to produce an engrossing way of life. The daily schedule was composed around contrasting occupations which, like the asylum concert, were combined to span a wide range of mental states so as to strike a restorative balance between periods of rest and work, play and discipline, activity and passivity, structured time and free time. Illenau's daily routine enhanced the aesthetic ordering and collective attunement of experience through coordinated, cadenced activity.[16]

Asylum life comprised a pharmacology of experience in which each ward constituted a separate life-world; that is to say, it had a distinctive spatial, temporal and social configuration which was correlated with a distinct set of psychological predispositions. The physician's task was to move patients between its variegated wards, i.e., between different forms of experience, according to their shifting psychiatric needs. This skill depended most crucially on timing or, as Illenau physicians said, *Takt* (beat or cadence). Since asylum officials conceived the asylum as an organism this *Takt* was comparable to a communal pulse. An article in the *Wochenblatt* spoke of music exerting a 'favourable, pleasurable,

8.1 Patient etching. Privatarchiv Hugo Huber, Achern.

animating and uplifting' influence on 'Illenau's collective being',[17] language which related the effect of music to the vitality of a communal pulse. The *Gemüth* was an inherently rhythmic entity. Indeed illnesses of *Gemüth* were also called 'arrhythmia'.[18] To combat the arrhythmia of individual patients, Illenau doctors created an institutionally grounded, ritualized way of life with its own curative pulse. The asylum's musical cures, or in other words the coordinated, cadenced activity manifest in its concerts, gymnastics and daily schedule, served to regulate the pace and strength of that pulse.

A drawing by an Illenau patient alludes, by way of visual suggestion, to the ubiquity of this communal pulse and its association with musical performances. The picture shows a patient handing her attendant a sheet of music (see Figure 8.1). The scene likens the relationship between the individual and the community at Illenau to the relationship of single notes in a musical composition. The asylum world is marked by a few lines resembling a musical score in the background of the picture. The patient and employee are placed within this asylum score as two individual notes: one dressed in white, like a minim or half note, and the other in black, like a crotchet or quarter note. The implication is that asylum life was essentially musical in that individual members of the Illenau population contributing their personal pulse, or *Takt*, to the cadence of the asylum community were simultaneously constrained by its pulsating beat.

Conclusion

This chapter has explored the phenomenal process that characterizes music therapy in general by relating the efficacy of Illenau's musical cures not primarily to the music *per se*, although that too, but to their reception in the cultural context of nineteenth-century Germany. It has demonstrated that Illenau's musical cures encompassed different forms of coordinated, cadenced activity, specifically asylum concerts, gymnastics exercise and the daily schedule. In its interpretive framework the efficacy of these cures was associated with the aesthetic ordering and collective attunement they generated in a patient population governed by the movements of *Gemüth*.

So what does the musicality of Illenau's institutional culture have in common with the musical cures described in the other chapters in this volume? At first glance very little. Every culture produces its own forms of musical healing which are quite unlike each other. One of the confounding difficulties in the discussion preceding this volume was that the presumed attributes of a musical cure kept shifting in accordance with each speaker's area of expertise: the location for performing curative music emerged as no more constant than the position music occupies in the therapeutic ritual as a whole, the selection of instruments upon which it is played, the afflictions it is used to treat, the number of participants in a performance, its composition and duration.

But different musical events come to look quite similar if we focus not on the content of individual healing rituals but on their cultural function. The efficacy of music therapy is a result not of the music alone but of its apprehension in experience. Due to this dependency on experience, the therapeutic influence of music is necessarily governed by an extant phenomenal framework organizing the musical experience for its participants. That is to say the same cultural conditions which legitimate certain therapeutic practices also render the target audience susceptible to the influence of those practices. This general feature of healing cures is especially apparent in the case of rituals employing music because the shared assumptions, habituated expectations and conditioned emotional responses which uniquely identify a given cultural context are also coded into the music itself. Music does not merely represent a given phenomenal order, it also modifies that order immediately it is intoned by arousing in its listeners a series of discrete emotional states whose cultural significance is variable.

The analysis of this chapter presumes a certain congruence between available forms of music therapy and the extant configuration of soul in a given cultural situation. A similar assumption underlies several of the other chapters in this volume, although the authors have not necessarily made it explicit. So, for example, Henry Stobart relates the 'aural landscapes' of Bolivian shepherds to the influence of *animu* and John M. Janzen relates the 'musical enchantments' of African healers to the influence of 'spirits'. The methodological linking of different soul types, such as *animu*, 'spirits' and *Gemüth*, with specific musical cures, such as 'aural landscapes', 'musical enchantments' and 'coordinated, cadenced activity', suggests that this assumption reflects an intrinsic feature of music therapy.[19] Indeed it suggests that music therapy might be defined as the art of making 'music for the soul', that is to say music congruent with the configuration of soul deemed most restorative at a given time and place, or in short 'soul music'.[20]

Gary Ansdell, a fellow contributor to our 1997 symposium on 'Music, healing and culture' and practising music therapist, made the intriguing observation in response to questioning after his paper that musical cures work because 'they enable patients to see how they are being perceived by others'.[21] On his construal music therapy is an exercise in self-actualization whose appeal is fundamentally narcissistic. This is in direct contrast to the appeal of the human pinwheel for

Illenau patients who sought the dissolution of self in cadenced, coordinated sensation. Ansdell's observation does not identify an eternal truth about music therapy because it does not hold true everywhere and at all times. But it does provide a vivid illustration of the dominant configuration of soul in the contemporary Western world – or, not to put too fine a point on it, of us. The 'Oedipal subject', for lack of a better term, desires more than anything else to know how it is being perceived by others. And, like other types of soul in history, it has learnt to engage music as a tool for achieving the desired self-understanding.

Notes

1. Löschke (1849), 27.
2. I have done so elsewhere: see Kramer (1998).
3. Whereas several authors have pointed out that the cultural situation in Biedermeier Germany was premised upon the doctrine of *Gemüth*, a detailed portrayal of both the situation itself as well as the role of *Gemüth* in producing and maintaining that situation have yet to be undertaken. For partial discussion, see Bernhard (1983), introduction; Geismeier (1982); Sengle (1970).
4. There is no equivalent for *Gemüth* in English. A variety of translations have been proposed, such as 'soul', 'temperament', 'state of being' or 'sentient mind'. Each of these translations conjures up a certain quality of experience which differs from that associated with *Gemüth*. To emphasize the specificity of this quality of experience I will use the original German term throughout this chapter.
5. Although these dates are frequently cited in the secondary literature on *Gemüth*, the periodization is very approximate. As late as 1926 a popular magazine was still being published in Stuttgart entitled: *Der Türmer, Monatsschrift für Gemüth und Geist* (The Tower Watchman – a Monthly for *Gemüth* and *Geist*).
6. The entries in journals such as Stolle's and Drezmann's *Die Gartenlaube* and Lewald's *Europa – Chronik der gebildeten Welt* document the widespread appeal of this concept in the general population.
7. Quoted in the article on 'Gemüt' in *Deutsches Wörterbuch* (Grimm 1897), vol. 4, pp. 294–327.
8. Petition dated 5 June 1880. In: Staatsarchiv Freiburg, Employee Records for Illenau: Fidel Ehinger, B 821/1 Nr. 514.
9. Roller (1831), 202.
10. *Illenauer Wochenblatt* (Illenau Weekly) (1883), No. 4, p. 17.
11. Rosen (1995), 571, 589.
12. 'Das Turnen' (Gymnastics), in *Illenau Wochenblatt* (1878), Nos 30–33.
13. *Illenau Wochenblatt* (1870), No. 28.
14. See Jahn and Eiselen (1816).
15. Brandt (1903), 15.
16. The House Schedule is given in Roller (1832), 58–163.
17. *Illenau Wochenblatt* (1886), No. 19, p. 76.
18. Roller (1831), 163.

19. This methodology has been applied in an anthropological context by Steven M. Friedson in his *Dancing Prophets* (1996).
20. The term 'soul music' in this sense is almost entirely divorced from its associations with Motown, choral trumpets and syncopated bass licks (I say 'almost' because the kinds of cultural forces that have rendered soul music so eminently danceable for the last several generations are no doubt akin to those governing the efficacy of music therapy).
21. Ansdell (1997).

CHAPTER NINE

The dancing nurse: *kalela* drums and the history of hygiene in Africa

Lyn Schumaker

What is a drum?[1] In both Africa and the West a drum is a musical instrument and much more. In the West drums help to set and control the pace of other musical instruments and direct the movements of dancing or marching bodies. They can be symbols of high office, especially in the military. Certain of their rhythms perform ceremonial functions, such as in the expression 'to be drummed out'. In Africa drums also do these things and in addition may 'talk' – by providing the means to send messages across long distances or by summoning spirits through the playing of their characteristic rhythms. In Africa the role of drums in healing is central, so central that the term for drum, *ngoma*, refers to a widespread and ancient complex of healing activities and to individual members of this complex, whether or not actual drums appear in their performance. As in Victor Turner's famous title, *Drums of Affliction* (1968), a 'drum' is the name of the association of healers and novices who practise a particular healing ritual.

Given this, what do we make of another drum, *beni ngoma* – the drum bands or dance associations historically widespread over eastern and central Africa? I will argue in this chapter that beni ngoma reveals neglected aspects of the nature of healing in Africa. In beni ngoma, as well as in the healing ngomas, the drum is an instrument of transformation and control. And it also 'talks', enabling those who dance to its rhythms to speak of a different range of affliction from that which has been studied in relation to the healing ngomas. These are political and economic afflictions, and the drum articulates these afflictions and makes them heard across the huge distances that separate the poor from the powerful.

The history of these ngomas also illuminates a side of the history of Western medicine in Africa that has not received sufficient attention – the realm of hygiene and its interpretation and deployment by Africans. A crucial part of this history can be told through the history of drums in Africa and, particularly, through the meeting of two kinds of drum – the drums of Europe's colonizing armies and the drums of eastern Africa's dance associations.

Drawing on this history, I will analyse the African and Western technologies of healing that converge in one type of beni ngoma – the *kalela* dance of Zambia's Luapula Province and Copperbelt towns. The kalela dance and its *beni* antecedents, unlike other African 'traditional' dances, are called 'smart' dances. The important feature of a smart dance is not vigorous steps or dramatic movement but cleanliness, dignity, and the display of fine dress. In the history of these dances and the associated development of the African concept of 'smartness' one can discover the hybridization of African and Western notions of hygiene.

Historically, kalela dancers have used drumming, coordinated movement, characters, and lyrics to comment on modern life in colonial and post-colonial times and to attempt to shape its terms. These elements become tools of articulating and transforming processes that take place in the dance through the medium of healing and hygiene metaphors and technologies. The technologies of healing and hygiene employed in kalela parallel some of the practices of *muchape* – a witchcraft eradication movement whose historical and geographical range overlaps with that of beni ngoma dances like kalela. Muchape rituals seek to intervene in the changing socio-economic and political order, cleansing witchcraft and healing distressed communities. Muchape rituals blend Western and African healing and hygienic elements to accomplish a form of public, communal healing.

Because of these parallels, I will consider in what ways kalela may constitute a type of public healing. The lyrics of kalela address public afflictions of various kinds, from witchcraft to bad political leadership – while the coordinated movements and rhythmic drumming of the dance express a variety of hygienic concerns, from individual bodily cleanliness to communal witch-cleansing. Issues of identity also enter into the dance, particularly in the dancers' choice of dress – that which symbolizes the 'smart' modern urban African. Especially important to the theme of music, healing and culture is the figure of the dancing nurse, whose identity and behaviour combine elements of both Western and African healing traditions. When ministering to the kalela dancers, she employs 'charged objects' – a mirror and a cup of 'medicinal' water – that resonate with the use of similar objects in muchape witch-cleansing rituals.[2]

The kalela dance

Beni ngoma dances derive their elements from several sources, the most prominent of which are the dance associations formed by pre-colonial urban political factions in the Swahili coastal cities of eastern Africa

9.1 *Kalela* drummers, Luanshya, Zambia, 1996.

and the later military bands of German and British colonial armies in the same area. Forms of beni ngoma travelled from the coastal areas of eastern Africa into the interior by way of central African labour migrants or Africans drafted for military service, who learned the dances in those contexts and then carried them back to their homes. Kalela shows evidence of these sources in its use of costumed dancers representing some of the ranks in a European-style hierarchy – king, doctor and nurse, for example. It also employs regimental formations and, depending on the number of dancers, either has a line of individual dancers or a regimental-style group that circles around in a drill step and lines up in formation to be inspected.

Three drums, made from large tree trunks in the countryside or from discarded oil drums in the towns, provide the central focus of this circling dance (see Figure 9.1). Beaten with huge banana-shaped sticks, these drums make an enormous sound that always calls a crowd to gather. The anthropologist who first studied the dance in colonial Zambia in the 1950s could hear these drums from his home in the segregated European quarter of the Copperbelt town where he lived.[3]

At intervals in the dance, the drums stop and the dancers pause to sing songs composed by the dance leader and other members of the group. Broadly characterized, the songs deal with life and its problems in the Copperbelt towns. Some of the songs discuss ethnic or political competition, others proclaim the singer's dancing or sexual prowess. Others discuss poverty, thievery and witchcraft. When danced in the countryside, kalela's lyrics also discuss local complaints, intended to reach the ears of the chief or village head indirectly in this way.

The kalela dance as an urban form of popular entertainment in Zambia's Copperbelt towns was first described by J. Clyde Mitchell in pioneering work of the 1950s. Later Terence Ranger included it in a wider historical study that traced the beni ngoma dances to sources within the eastern African context.[4] Mitchell analysed the dance primarily in terms of what it said about African ethnic identity and prestige in the colonial urban setting. Bernard Magubane later criticized this interpretation for its focus on clothing and other aspects of the dance that seemed to show that Africans were 'aping' Europeans in their competition for prestige. This critique, however, misrepresented Mitchell's work, which in many respects foreshadowed current interpretations of dress and identity that stress Africans' appropriation and reinterpretation of European practices and commodities in their development of an African style of modernity.[5]

John Janzen's study of the regional ngoma complex of dances mentions kalela but focuses on ngomas that fit clearly into a healing tradition.[6] He draws a distinction between healing types and entertainment types, the latter having resulted from a process of folklorization partly guided by the state, while healing ngomas are 'very central and formative'.[7] Nevertheless, this chapter will show that strong similarities exist between the forms and routines of the healing ngomas and the entertainment ngomas. Kalela, for example, contains both Western and African healing regimens, objects, and characters that play ambiguous and complex roles in its performance: dancers acting as doctors and nurses, mirrors and movements reminiscent of muchape, and drums that go 'deep in one's heart'.[8] The fact that post-colonial states have been interested in folklorizing the entertainment ngomas may provide a clue to their political significance, for these dances have often addressed issues of social, political and economic power. The lyrics of kalela directly address politicians and, indeed, often criticize the most powerful leaders of the state. The folklorization of kalela that has taken place in the capitol city of Lusaka, for example, has made versions of the dance there into representations of so-called traditional life in the ethnic area from which kalela supposedly emerged, while playing down the songs that historically have focused on modern concerns.

Contrary to this folklorization, the history of kalela illustrates how Africans assimilated Western healing idioms into a form of expression that responded to problems of change in both the countryside and Copperbelt towns in the colonial period in Zambia – the dance made sense of, or reconceptualized, certain aspects of the colonial situation and expressed the responses of a particular set of Africans to the new relationships being created by colonialism. The specific colonial context that produced kalela (though not the sole referent of the dance) was that of labour migration and the problems faced by migrants both when arriving in urban areas and when returning to their rural villages. The African form of expression most pertinent to kalela (but again not the sole form involved in the construction of the dance) was the dancing of the smartly dressed migrant, which employed some of the elements of the African tradition of the praise poem.[9] The migrant's situation was not conceptualized simply as one of arrival in a new urban environment or triumphant return to a home village, however, for his fears of envy and witchcraft directed at the wealth he had obtained were also expressed in the dance.

Some of the dance's movements and the objects and characters that appear in it may have originally referred to this situation, a context shared with the muchape witch-cleansing movement. Muchape also responded to migrants' fears of witchcraft and took communal measures to heal its affliction. The dance's movements also refer to other situations meaningful to the dancers in particular places during particular historical periods. Some of these objects, characters and movements derive from the beni ngoma dances that precede and surround kalela throughout its history, elements of which act as markers of its identity despite shifts in their meaning.[10] Following is a brief history of beni ngoma and a description of the colonial and post-colonial forms taken by the kalela dance.

'Oh, Jesus, what clothes shall I wear on this earth?'

> The idea was to put on suits and look different from others, like those from Eastern Province who did *nyau*, who wore skins and kicked legs up all over the place. Whenever a man came here [to the Copperbelt] to work, he would watch the dancing and if he wanted to participate he had to buy that gear.[11]

Kalela is a 'smart' dance. If the dance has an essence then smartness is that essence – it is the marker of identity that is common to all the histories that various people have used to explain the dance.[12] In the smart dances, the term refers to orderliness and synchronicity of movement, as well as to correct and sometimes uniform dress. In kalela individual appearance and deportment receive focused attention during pauses in the dance. When asked its meaning, current informants say the term kalela itself refers to an article of clothing – the 'flashy' trousers worn by dancers in the colonial period.[13]

A recent history of soap and cosmetics in Africa describes the relationship between the acquisition of European clothing and the emergence of new standards of cleanliness, including the labour routines and the commodities required to keep the clothing clean.[14] Dances like kalela speak of this transition from earlier African standards of hygiene to new European demands. According to one of Mitchell's informants, a beni ngoma dance called *mbeni* that arrived in Malawi in the 1920s took the form of a mock military band with a European-style two-sided drum. The dancing expressed order, fineness, dignity, and cleanliness – the elements of smartness – in a number of ways:

> This was a clean dance because everyone wore good clothes. People who came dirty were not allowed to dance. Whenever they were called they brought their drums with them and they wore garments [costumes?], like the King. When they reached the courtyard, where the dance was to take place, they appeared splendid. Also the women were very clean. They danced slowly and gently, the women on one side and the men on the other; at daybreak they looked as clean as if they had not been dancing at all.

Mbeni preceded kalela in the Copperbelt towns, most likely carried by African clerks recruited from colonial Malawi by the government and the mines because of the greater availability of education for Africans there. Both dances stressed clothing and clean appearance. Indeed Mitchell, observing in the early 1950s, found kalela 'prosaic', no doubt because of the absence of vigorous, dramatic motion. Displaying clothing and keeping it clean in the course of the dancing was the main point of the dance. Today, dancers say that they make the movements of a dance 'large' when they wish to show off the dance itself, but they keep the movements small when it is the costume or clothing that is being displayed.[15]

According to Ranger, kalela developed out of the diaspora of beni ngoma dances from the Swahili coast to the east and central African hinterland, which mainly took place after the First World War, a time when Africans who had been recruited for the war in East Africa returned to their villages. In Mitchell's account, a particular man, Kalulu, developed the kalela dance in the Bangweulu region of Zambia in the 1930s. Because of his musical ability, Kalulu was allowed to take his drums with him when he left for military service in the Second World War. Mitchell speculates that after the war the dance may have been brought to the Copperbelt by labour migrants from Bangweulu familiar with the dance.[16]

Zambians telling the history of kalela mention its place in a succession of dance styles brought to rural villages by returning labour migrants. Kalela, in these accounts, displaced *kapoya*, a European-style dance involving well-dressed couples. Local missionaries did not approve of *kapoya* because of the coupled dancing, but encouraged kalela because men and women danced in separate lines.[17]

Although kalela has roots in beni ngoma and the East African Swahili context, it also has roots in other more local Zambian experiences. The photos of the Rhodes–Livingstone Institute anthropologist Max Gluckman (who worked among the Lozi of western Northern Rhodesia, far from the Copperbelt and Bangweulu), contain literally hundreds of images of traditional costumed *makishi* dancers, with one interesting exception. The exception is a photo of a dignified man dancing in a white shirt and sharply creased trousers being watched by other Lozi men dressed in shorts. The caption reads, 'A man returned from the Rand gives a solo'.[18] This suggests that returning migrants may have danced singly to show off their smart clothes even before group dances like *beni* arrived, though it is possible that *beni*-like dancing may have been familiar to former Lozi miners from contact with people who migrated from eastern Northern Rhodesia to work on the Rand, South Africa's gold-mining region, which drew migrants from many parts of central Africa. Nevertheless, the boasting aspects of kalela lyrics suggest links to an older African tradition of praise-singing that includes self-praise (appropriate to a wealthy returned migrant), as well as praise of one's chief and homeland.

Zambians who describe the history of kalela insist that the dance has always included women, which is observable in post-colonial kalela dance groups.[19] There is, however, no reason to doubt Mitchell's observation that no women participated in the dances he studied in the 1950s. Women may have been involved in separate groups or non-dancing roles in the 1950s, but one could speculate about other factors that might have caused their absence. Women from the regions sending male labour migrants – including the Luapula and Bangweulu regions where kalela was danced – were certainly less numerous than men from those areas in the Copperbelt towns in the 1950s, though their numbers increased in the course of the decade. There may not have been enough of them to form kalela organizations parallel to the men's, unlike those *beni* groups cited by Ranger in East Africa that had parallel women's organizations.[20]

On the other hand, urban women in Zambia may have *avoided* group dancing of this sort, to contrast themselves with less 'civilized' village women who joined in when the dance was performed in the countryside. Although they took part in ballroom couple dancing and even engaged in ballroom dance competitions, urban women may have seen outdoor kalela dance performances as more like sports competitions than dancing.[21] Urban and educated African women may have had an aversion to sports because of a fear of appearing undignified. This could have also been in response to domestic training given by European women who emphasized rigid gender differences, themselves subject to the stark contrast between European male and female roles common in colonial settler societies.

If women could be selective in their choice of which dances to join, men could also be selective in their choice of smart dress for the dancing. Mitchell analysed the kalela dancers' choice of European dress as a response to the meaning of such dress in an African prestige system, associated as it was with African clerks who enjoyed the highest salaries and best jobs allowed to Africans in the colonial period. Ranger also points out the importance of clerks and their style of dress in the movement of beni ngoma from the Swahili coast to the east African hinterland. Membership of beni ngoma dance organizations shifted as these clerks, marginalized with the removal of the German administration, regained status under the new British colonial system in Tanganyika and no longer needed the dance associations for their organizational purposes or prestige. Nevertheless, other marginalized groups took up the practice of forming dance organizations,[22] and one gathers that by this time the main attraction of the smart dress chosen was its association with a successful *African* group – the clerks who originally brought the dance from the Swahili coast to the hinterland.[23]

The role of hygiene in the meaning of smart dress in kalela has not been analysed, other than in references to the importance of suits being immaculate and nicely pressed. Hygiene, however, played an important role in the racial, ethnic and moral hierarchy of the Copperbelt towns where kalela was danced. When kalela dancers emulated the dress of African clerks, they largely emulated a particular ethnic group. Nyasaland peoples – Lakeside Tongas and nearby groups – dominated clerks' jobs because of their greater access to mission-sponsored education.[24] The areas of Northern Rhodesia from which miners and general labourers came suffered from extremely poor educational opportunities, and these included the areas from which kalela dancers came. Clerks, as well, frequently considered miners and labourers to be savages because of their poor wages and living conditions. Possibly they also made this evaluation because miners worked in the hot lower regions of the mines in a state of near nakedness, nakedness being denigrated by the missions and mission-educated Africans as a sign of savagery.[25]

This evaluation of moral and civilized status had a hygienic dimension: even into the post-colonial period, the tiny African middle class in

Zambia would sometimes be referred to as 'the clean ones' and their housing areas similarly designated.[26] This was because the racial and sanitary defences of the colonial project involved not only segregating Europeans from Africans, but also segregating Africans among themselves according to dress, levels of education, and other signs of Europeanization. Because employers such as the mines and government provided housing for their African employees, they could express this hierarchy in the houses given to different grades of employee.

The size of the house was one indicator of status, but just as important were the sanitation and hygiene facilities – better and more private in housing areas for clerks. Another factor was the distance from the workplace or from European employees, also hygienically motivated. Only more civilized African employees' families would be tolerated nearer to Europeans, a concern that expressed European hygiene anxieties. But African hygiene concerns found satisfaction in the shorter distance to work and the clerks' ability to purchase bicycles to ease the journey, since both of these helped smartly dressed clerks to avoid sweating and getting their clothes and shoes dusty – and the consequent association with menial labour and lack of cleanliness. When sweat and dust were unavoidable, clerks, teachers and other educated people conspicuously used white handkerchiefs to address the problem, a gesture also found in kalela.[27]

Indeed, one might speculate that the preference for slow, dignified movement and aversion to sweating in kalela and beni ngoma dances may signal an African notion of health and hygiene very different from colonial European beliefs. White settlers and government officers, for example, believed in the connection between vigorous exercise and health and carried this to extremes in their attempt to maintain vigour and avoid 'tropical inertia' by engaging in tennis in the late afternoon heat, as advised in the practical manuals of tropical hygiene at the time.

In the colonial period, clothes functioned as signs of the order dictated by tropical hygiene. Certain objects may function similarly in specific kalela dance movements. Just as pith helmets and vigorous sports distinguished Europeans who observed hygienic rules from those who degenerated and went native, objects used in kalela distinguish the dancers as hygienically different from other Africans. The cane that some dancers carry is used not only to support the dancer or indicate his status, but more importantly to brush dust from the trouser cuffs. A motion indicating this practice is incorporated into the dance, even when actual canes are absent. The handkerchief flourished by a dancer is often used to wipe the shoes, and not the brow, as we might assume.[28]

Shoes represented an important source of distinction in the Copperbelt context of the dance: the dancers who 'kick legs up all over the place', pejoratively described in the quotation at the beginning of this section, are probably not Cewa *nyau* dancers but members of the Ngoni ethnic group who performed their own distinctive dances in the same Copperbelt venues as kalela.[29] Their ngoma dance involves kicking high into the air and stamping on the ground with miners' boots, trying to reproduce the noise of a drum with their feet – and also raising clouds of dust over the dance ground.[30] On the other hand, for kalela dancers, polished dust-free clerks' shoes ranked high above dusty miners' boots in the scale of smartness, as well as in the civilized order of the colonial Copperbelt town.[31]

Such concern with white handkerchiefs, canes and dust-free shoes were not trivial. In Africa, and particularly in the towns, European settlers used hygiene to control the movement and behaviour of Africans, perceiving them as dangerous, immoral and diseased. Boundaries between town and country and within the towns followed racial lines often justified by these hygienic concerns. Burke's study shows that clothing and Western standards of cleanliness formed a key part of the 'racially coded borders of consumption' in Zimbabwe. Because of this, white settlers often perceived well-dressed Africans as challenging their racially superior position.[32] Africans did, indeed, use clothing and other commodities to challenge racial boundaries, and this is part of the meaning of fine clothing and dignified movement in kalela. Those who danced kalela in the colonial Copperbelt towns came from the poorest economic groups with the least security of urban residence.[33] Africans had no legal right to be in the towns and were only allowed to pass through or reside there on the basis of employment or relation to an employee. By acquiring good clothing and dancing to display it, those at the bottom contested the social and racial order that placed them in a marginal position, and they used the dance to transform their identity into that of modern prosperous urban people, deserving of a place in the towns.

This contested colonial order provided the context for the song of a blind African minstrel recorded by Peter Fraenkel in Zambia in the 1950s, in which the central and repeated refrain is a question about clothing and the presentation of self in a racially unjust world:

> I do not know the way to God,
> Else I would have gone to complain.
> Oh, Jesus, what clothes shall I wear on this earth?
> White men have no sympathy.[34]

Nurses and mirrors

> There was a Bemba, who married one of my aunties, who had eight suits even as a retired man, and now I understand why – they were needed for [*mbeni*] dancing.[35] In kalela you just dance a little and don't want to sweat, because the point is the nice clothes being shown off... . The dancers are always watching themselves.[36]

Clothing involved more than self-presentation and a challenge to the colonial order. Like hygiene, clothing also implies protection, sometimes of a magical kind. Maintaining its protective power, however, requires ritual activity and the intervention of powerful figures. In kalela these ritual actions and powerful figures derive from a convergence of African and European practices, meanings and identities. This convergence is best illustrated by the figure of the nurse with a mirror.

Among the objects such as canes and handkerchiefs that one finds in kalela, one object especially resonates with the theme of hygiene and magical protection – the mirror. Among the costumed characters who dance kalela are two medical figures – a doctor and a nurse – who inspect the dancers individually and when they line up in regimental formation. During the individual inspection, the nurse walks along the line of dancers holding up a mirror to each person's face.

In Africa, as in Europe, mirrors appeared in a variety of situations associated with cleansing and hygiene. From the beginning of European exploration, Africans observed Europeans using mirrors when washing the face, shaving and checking the appearance of clothing and hair, and they soon joined in these activities, using the mirrors that entered the continent as trade goods in the pre-colonial period. During the colonial period, soap and cosmetics companies gave away mirrors with their products, instructing people on how to use them to achieve European standards of personal hygiene.[37]

Mirrors appeared in the muchape witch-cleansing rituals that began in the colonial period around the 1930s and which have reappeared at intervals up to the present.[38] Indeed, in some of its incarnations, the muchape movement has been identified with the mirror, as in the *Wacilole* movement discussed by Roy Willis, the name itself meaning 'People of the Mirror'.[39] Muchape also originated in the context of labour migration, addressing the vulnerability of labour migrants to envy and witchcraft, as, for example, in the origin story for the 1960s *Kamcape* movement in Tanzania, recounted by Willis.[40] In the origin story for the 1930s movement discussed by Ranger, a returning son brings the muchape medicine that cures his father, the headman of a village, and the medicine is later used for communal cleansing.[41] Generally in muchape movements, young people demand that their villages be cleansed of witches, accusing their elders of nefarious practices.[42] Witch-finders, usually outsiders and often regionally famous, then come with their disciples to each village, sometimes asking payment for their services. They line up villagers for inspection in a central location, with separate lines for men and women, inspect each individual to detect witches, and confiscate and destroy medicines and objects used for witchcraft. Usually a liquid medicine is given to the accused, or to all members of a community, and the newly cleansed may be physically marked or branded in some way.

Witch-finders commonly employ mirrors to discover witches or 'diagnose' the amount of witchcraft infecting the people lined up for ritual inspection. In some respects this is similar to the process of using the mirror in kalela, though the witch-finder usually turns his or her back and examines the individual's *reflection* in the mirror, while the nurse in kalela holds up the mirror for the individual to examine his or her own reflection.[43] Nevertheless, it is the nurse, like the witch-finder, who takes action when a dancer's appearance does not come up to standard. According to Mitchell's account,

> A 'nursing sister', the only woman in the group, was dressed in white, and went around with a mirror and a handkerchief to allow each dancer to inspect himself to see whether he was neat and tidy. She also wiped the sweat from the faces of the dancers as they went on dancing.[44]

When observing the dance in 1992, I saw a character who was called a nurse – although she was dressed in ordinary clothing – wiping the dancers' faces and providing drinking water. During competitive dancing between different Copperbelt teams, she and a doctor – who was also the team leader – were said to perform the same kinds of services provided by sports doctors for football teams.[45] Sports doctors in Africa, however, may also be official team traditional healers who provide football players with protection from witchcraft and who, allegedly, bewitch the opposing teams.

In addition to similarities in the forms of inspection she takes part in, the nurse in kalela also resembles the witch-finder in muchape as a character, particularly if we think of her as an African nurse rather than an African woman imitating a European nurse. In other words, the character of the nurse is more than just a costumed African imitation of an official European colonial role. Young women's concerns about fertility and the possible ill effects of envious older men and women practising witchcraft, along with young men's frustration over older men's control of wealth in economically trying times, often motivated requests for the services of muchape witch-finders.[46] Young men and women also formed the chief local support for and membership of muchape movements, and young women could play the prominent role of witch-finder.[47] In rural hierarchies of age and gender, young men and women usually occupy low positions, positions they have frequently challenged in the changing economic and political context of the colonial and post-colonial eras. Young men, discontent with their position, and young women, attempting to break free of the control of elders, could use movements such as muchape to justify their challenge to elders.[48]

The figure of the nurse also parallels that of a female witch-finder in that she is a young woman out of her proper place. Witch-finders are nearly always outsiders to the communities that they cleanse of witchcraft, and a female witch-finder is more than just an outsider – she is also a woman who has left her home area and taken a public role inappropriate for young women in most central African societies. The African nurse is similarly out of place in several ways. Historically, both the colonial authorities and African elders considered any unmarried African woman in an urban area to be out of place and collaborated in repatriating women to the rural areas. Moreover, the first African nurses trained on the Copperbelt in the 1950s found themselves criticized by older African men and women for being out of their proper place. Africans' complaints to the mining company hospitals stressed the inappropriateness of putting young unmarried women in positions of authority over older male and female patients and asked that only older married women be accepted for nurses' training courses.[49]

Many central African societies consider the sexuality of young women dangerous to the health of others and restrict their movements and contacts, particularly with in-laws or certain members of their parents' generation. Concerns such as these may have figured in older Africans' evaluation of them as inappropriate for the role of nurses. Considering the growing literature on gender, mobility and the blaming of young women found in popular African epidemiologies of sexually transmitted diseases,[50] the nurse in kalela may be seen as an ambivalent and potentially dangerous and powerful figure.[51]

The cup and the water the nurse dispenses, like the mirror, resonate with witch-cleansing activities. During muchape, the witch-finder first uses the mirror diagnostically to detect witchcraft. Then he or she may ask these suspected witches, or all the people participating in the cleansing ritual, to drink a special liquid or medicine that will poison the drinkers if in the future they revert to practising witchcraft and which may also protect them from witchcraft done by others. During kalela, the nurse gives water to the participants from a cup she carries with her, sometimes in an almost medicinal manner when dancers feign illness or heat exhaustion and the nurse conspicuously runs to their aid. This is done to 'add excitement to the dance'.[52] Entertaining the audience may not be the only point of this action, however. The cooling of dancers feigning heat exhaustion resonates with the cooling and controlling of 'musical heat' discussed by Steven Friedson in his study of Tumbuka healing in Malawi.[53] The nurse, in helping dancers to control heat, acts in a way similar to that of an experienced healer helping an apprentice to learn how to control musical heat in the context of possession. When she wipes sweat from the brow of a dancer, she is also removing the visible traces of too much heat.

The build-up of too much heat in kalela contradicts the most important *African* hygienic message of the dance – that the dancers should be smart, dignified and free of sweat. In many central and eastern African societies, 'too much heat' is associated with uncontrolled and dangerous sexuality, illness, infertility and witchcraft. 'Cooling' heat through medicines and ritual activity is the realm of healers and diviners. African and European nurses in hospitals function in a similar realm, as arbiters of hygiene and in administering medicines. They control the personal hygiene of patients and can deny access to a patients' relatives by detecting dirty clothes and sweat and objecting to its odour.[54] The medicines they administer may be seen as more than simple cures, and the colours of pills may also be associated with their function in regulating 'heat'. African patients may perceive them to have a strengthening and protective function against the dangers of illness and its causes, as do the medicines administered by traditional healers and the muchape liquid given by witch-cleansers.[55]

Clean clothing and its colour or whiteness may also provide protection or enhance protective power. Nurses' uniforms carry this symbolism of protection, as do the ritual uniforms of the African Zionist churches, discussed by Jean Comaroff.[56] Moreover, hygiene is implicated in the context of concern addressed by both kalela and muchape. The word muchape itself derives from a ciNyanja term, *ku capa*, that means 'to cleanse', as in vigorously washing dirty clothes.[57] The medicinal liquid that participants drink during muchape rituals may be seen as purifying the community in a way that is similar to the washing of dirty clothes with soap. Soap itself is sometimes used as a medicine for witch-finding in Zimbabwe,[58] leading one to speculate that both soap and clothing might magically, as well as actually, protect or seal off the body from supernatural dangers.[59]

The theme of clothing and protection also appears in a kalela song from the 1990s that links clothing and witchcraft together in the context of the politically charged death of a local politician:

> Witches, witches, the witches of Zambia,
> You have killed our breadwinners,

You have killed Simakuni
Who was looking after us.

In this odd world,
There is nothing good.
No matter how smartly you can dress and look,
The price at the end, my friend Musengu,
Is death.[60]

Drums that go deep in the heart

I will put it into the kalela drum.[61]

In this concluding section I return to my opening question and expand it: what is a drum? What is a drum when one can put things into it? And what is a drum when the things one puts into it are songs?

The words from a kalela song, above, make explicit a relationship between lyrics and drumming that is crucial to the significance of the dance. Most kalela songs today are complaints. They speak of the hardships of modern life, of politics and witchcraft, of economic troubles, of death, of thievery and suspicion. The singers also boast about themselves, mock the opposing dance teams, and comment on the latest news or rumours. By singing these songs during a pause in the dance, the dancers put them into the drum. The kalela drum is a drum that talks, that makes these complaints and observations public, that articulates the problems described in the songs and transforms them into public knowledge.

Kalela deals with political and economic misfortune and other complaints through a mixture of forms drawn from the healing ngomas and from the tradition of political criticism represented by the African 'praise poem'. As discussed above, kalela lyrics interpret and organize public opinion, a process similar to what Archie Mafeje argues is the goal of the praise poems of the South African 'bard'.[62] In the healing ngomas, and especially in those that involve spirit possession, a crucial aspect of the healing process is the patient's articulation of distress. Indeed, when defining the nature of 'poetic licence' in southern African praise poems, Leroy Vail and Landeg White use a healing model – a spirit-possession ceremony: 'Whatever is sung during these ceremonies is licensed in the sense that the complaints are expressed with impunity and that the 'free speech' of the possession songs is integral to the cure ...'.[63] Here I agree with Vail and White about the importance of lyrics in the healing process and disagree with Friedson's contention that the words are not important because they do not define the relationship between the dancer and the spirit, as he claims for the drum.[64]

Today kalela lyrics contain criticism that the singers expect to be 'overheard' by the powerful and which functions as a warning that thieving neighbours, witches and political leaders must heed.[65] The very public political nature of the complaints, however, seems to militate against the idea that a process of healing may be taking place. But one must remember that in the modern West, medicine and politics have become disconnected from each other in a perhaps culturally unique way. This separation has rarely been challenged except in some areas of psychotherapy, such as the urban psychology movement of the 1970s, which prescribed political activism as the cure for depression in American inner-city residents. In Africa, however, politics and healing make a more clearly linked pair. For example, in Steven Feierman's studies of Shambaa society in Tanzania, the concepts and practices of healers generate the metaphors that constitute political discourse – a discourse of 'healing and harming the land'.[66] Whether or not political discourse is constituted primarily from healing idioms in Zambia requires more research, but this study of kalela suggests that such may be the case.

In kalela, political problems are conceptualized as affliction on a model similar to that used for witchcraft-induced afflictions. Individual participants in kalela may not be healed or cured by their singing and dancing, but they clearly use the dance to articulate political complaints and transform their social identities in powerful ways. Hygiene provides the metaphors that constitute political discourse in this setting, and the dancers adopt inspective and protective technologies drawn from hygienic contexts as idioms of political transformation.

This sense of transformation is captured in a kalela song, written shortly after the country ended its one-party state and held democratic multi-party elections in 1991. This was a time when traditionally disenfranchised poor rural farmers and urban workers discovered their power on the national political stage. The following lyrics tell the recently elected political leaders what the dancers expect of them. The words directly address the new president, fully employing the poetic licence of the praise poem:

> In October all Zambians went to the polls.
> We elected Chiluba.
> He has brought democracy and good governance in Zambia.
> Mr Chiluba, we are warning you that if you fail to rule Zambia well,
> We shall come to your house with axes,
> Because you are our saviour whom we all rely on.[67]

In this song, people who were politically marginal in Zambia's one-party state transform themselves into politically powerful agents who speak freely to the president of the new multi-party state and threaten action if he does not respond. During the same period, but in the public political sphere as opposed to the context of the dance, people expressed this transition through party slogans and criticism focused on the previous regime's 'colonial mentality'. These forms of expression did *not* include strong warnings to the new leadership. Adulation and assimilation to the new regime's political rhetoric was required in that setting, and, indeed, the new regime very quickly took on the cultural symbols of power formerly identified with the one-party state (and with the colonial administration before independence in 1964 and with chiefly power in the pre-colonial era), including the omnipresent 'dancing women' who ululate and gyrate ecstatically at official presidential arrivals and departures.

In contrast, in the setting of a very different kind of dance, kalela, the singers could express their new political identity in more forceful and independent terms. One could speculate that when the leader of this kalela troupe composed the song and had it performed during the dance, it may have represented the first public articulation of their new political identity on the part of the dancers. Kalela songs, however, may change in meaning as the political context shifts, and in 1996 – as opposed to 1992 – some informants claimed that lyrics that challenged political leaders to do right by their constituents also expressed loyalty and the desire to protect them from the witchcraft emanating from the new opposition parties.

As a political discourse, the song employs a global rhetoric of democratization that uses terms such as 'good governance', but the song assimiliates these terms into an African form, the praise poem, as indicated by the line that reminds the president that he has responsibility as their 'saviour'. But, unlike a praise poem, the song is 'put into the drum,' as are the problems brought to a healing 'drum of affliction'. Thus, a healing and empowering transformation of identity, in addition to freely licensed political expression, may be taking place.

In support of this view, the structure of song and dance in kalela appears to parallel the healing ngomas' 'song-dance' structure, but to transform and display the dancers' new *political* identity. In kalela, drums direct the regimented movement of the dancers, and the dancers' movements embody these rhythms. In healing ngomas, distinctive rhythms call up the different spirits involved in the process of affliction and healing.[68] In some respects this structure is also reminiscent of the structure of initiation rituals in Africa. The three drums of kalela derive partly from the central bass drum in a military band, by way of the beni ngoma associations of east Africa. The rhythm of these hybrid drums may be calling up an Africanized European spirit, or – as Peter Pels argues for certain colonial-era initiation dances in Tanzania – a

European work *rhythm*, reworked into an African mode of initiation. This new mode of initiation, according to Pels, restructures relationships between the young and the old as a preparation for labour migration – or, in other words, preparation for the work *rhythms* and relationships of the town.[69] Thus a European technology of power evoked in beni ngoma (and kalela) – regimental formations, military discipline, immaculate uniforms and dominating drumbeats – provides a powerful means of reworking relationships within African rural and urban communities, between young and old, 'modern' and 'traditional', and the politically marginal and politically powerful.[70]

Words play a key role when this rhythmic reworking process takes place in kalela. The lyrics of the songs articulate affliction and, in conjunction with the drums, bring about the transformation of identity expressed in the dancing. Unlike the case of the meaning of the words used in the songs described by Friedson in Chapter 4, the meaning of the words in kalela songs is essential to the articulation of complaints and transformation of identity. It is important that the audience understands and affirms the singers' complaints – and that those in power 'overhear' them. I suspect, however, that even in healing rituals where the participants do not understand the meaning of the words of ritual songs, that the words are none the less vital to the healing process.[71] The structured pause in kalela that is reserved for singing parallels the articulation phase in ngoma healing rituals, when the sufferer speaks first of his/her troubles before dancing to establish a new identity in control of the disease. In a context of communal healing, a pause for singing may also play an articulating role in some recent muchape witch-cleansing rituals, as described by Ute Luig. She observed the activities of a witch-finder who included his own playing and singing as part of the ritual. His songs, like many kalela songs, discussed social ills and their rectification.[72]

Conclusion

Kalela was still the most popular 'traditional' dance on the Copperbelt in 1992, when all such traditional dances were subsidized and encouraged by the mines and local government. With less in the way of subsidies, expensive costumes and formal competitions, and despite the deepening poverty of those Copperbelt residents who dance it, kalela persists into the late 1990s. Thus the current dance is not the 'fossilized' form that Vail and White contend it is, continuing only because of support from the state.[73] Its popularity demonstrates that it still speaks to Copperbelt people's interests and concerns through its visual references to witchcraft, healing and hygiene, as well as through its lyrics that discuss local and national political concerns and worries about urban poverty.

In kalela, technologies of hygienic inspection, such as mirrors and regimental formations drawn from European sources, have been transformed into something new, powerful and profoundly African. The dancers use these technologies to articulate issues of witchcraft, power and trust and to engage in the political and social criticism found in kalela's lyrics. In a sense, they redirect these technologies to focus critical attention onto the problems of urban people. In muchape, regimented movement, the use of mirrors and the distinctive marking of confessed witches become a technology for public healing. In kalela, regimented movement, the use of mirrors and distinctive dress – including the portrayal of nurses and doctors – provide a technology for dealing with political and economic afflictions. In this they do for the social body what healing ngomas do for individual bodies: through the power of the drum, they bring the experience of affliction into the 'mirror of social reflection'.[74]

Notes

1. This chapter is based on fieldwork conducted in Lusaka and Luanshya, Zambia, in 1992 and 1996. Some interviews with Zambian scholars were also conducted in 1991, and I participated in the University of Zambia Dance Troupe throughout most of 1991, learning a number of dances and observing their performance by the dance troupe at public and private events. In Luanshya I interviewed members of the Mpatamato Township Kalela Troupe and observed their performances. This fieldwork is part of a larger project to examine the history of African and European medicine on the Copperbelt from 1940 to the present. Thanks are due to Terence Ranger, John Janzen, David Maxwell, Rijk van Dijk, and Peter Pels for comments on earlier drafts of this chapter. I have also greatly profited from discussions with Bryan Callahan and an earlier collaborative essay in which we speculated on the similarities among elements in muchape, kalela, and colonial anti-syphilis campaigns; see Callahan and Schumaker (1997). Special thanks are due to Timothy Mgala, who assisted me with research on drums and dances in Lusaka; to Fine Shambweka, Zambia Consolidated Coppermines (ZCCM) Deputy Archivist, who helped with my research in Luanshya; and to Dr Mapopa Mtonga, University of Zambia.
2. The term 'charged object' comes from Geschiere (1983), and it is used by Pool (1994) to link African ideas of disease causation across a single continuum. This chapter borrows Pool's usage and extends it to European therapeutic technologies and epistemologies as well, exploring the ways that Africans may have deployed these foreign imports to negotiate local struggles over the power of healing and affliction.

3. J. Clyde Mitchell, interview, October 1990, Oxford.
4. Mitchell (1956), Ranger (1975).
5. Magubane (1971). For a similar interpretation see Matongo (1992).
6. Janzen (1992), 2.
7. Ibid., 32–5.
8. Interview with Timothy Mgala, 6 September 1996, Lusaka, Zambia.
9. See Vail and White (1991).
10. Both the muchape witch-cleansing movements and the beni ngoma family of popular dances vary across time and in different localities; see de Craemer, Vansina and Fox (1976).
11. Interview with leaders of the Mpatamato Kalela troupe: Smart Ngoma, Assistant Community Development Officer and coordinator of cultural groups; Mumba Muselela, chairman (troupe king); Besa Kashimoto, treasurer (troupe leader); Edward Kafubu, vice-treasurer (troupe doctor?) (Luanshya, August 1992).
12. This is a 'family resemblance' argument, not an essentialist one: Ranger (1975), 79–83.
13. Various interviews, Luanshya and Lusaka, 1992, 1996.
14. Burke (1996).
15. Timothy Mgala, interview, Lusaka, 6 September 1996.
16. Mitchell (1956), 9–10.
17. Dr Mapopa Mtonga, interview, Lusaka, Zambia, 1991.
18. No. 30589, Album 10, Gluckman Photographs, Royal Anthropological Institute, London.
19. Interviews with members of the Mpatamato troupe, August 1992.
20. See 'The role of women in dance associations in eastern Africa', Appendix in Ranger (1975), 167–70.
21. Kalela may also have been seen as more vigorous and athletic than *beni*: Ranger (1975), 116–17.
22. Ibid., 77ff.
23. The association of this kind of dress with colonial state power no doubt added to its attraction: Comaroff (1985), 243.
24. Ranger (1975), 117–19, Comaroff (1985), 219.
25. Clerks' views of miners are discussed in 'Sundry Africans', chapter 4 of Schumaker (1994).
26. Joyce Leeson, interview, May 1995, Manchester.
27. White handkerchiefs also figure in political settings. For example, Zambia's former president, Kenneth Kaunda, always carried a white handkerchief for luck and conspicuously wiped his tears at emotional moments in his speeches.
28. Interviews with members of the Mpatamato troupe, August 1992.
29. Ethnic groups are often conflated in the urban context, with all groups from Eastern Province referred to as Cewa as in this example.
30. This ngoma dance derives from the Zulu/Nguni regimental dances of southern Africa, based on the *impis*, or age-graded regiments into which Nguni societies were divided for marriage and military purposes.
31. Male members of the Zion Christian Church, when dancing, use their feet to drum the ground, wearing distinctive white boots. Jean Comaroff interprets the whiteness of the boots as a colour that activates spiritual power, but also connotes leisure and prestige: Comaroff (1985), 243–4.
32. Burke (1996), 100.

33. Mitchell (1956) showed that most kalela dancers were casual labourers of even lower status than miners.
34. Fraenkel (1959), 224.
35. Joseph Phiri, interview, Luanshya, 1992.
36. Timothy Mgala, interview, Lusaka, 6 September 1996.
37. Burke (1996), 138.
38. A number of scholars have examined muchape in its various forms, including Richards (1935/1970); Marwick (1950); Douglas (1963); Willis (1968); Parkin (1968); Iliffe (1979), van Binsbergen (1981); Auslander (1993); and Maxwell (1995). The only comprehensive study of muchape is by Ranger (1982).
39. Willis (1968), 7.
40. Ibid., 6–7.
41. Ranger (1982), 1–2.
42. Witchcraft-eradication movements usually express inter-generational tensions, but may not always help the young against the old and may even be welcomed by the elders. See Ranger (1982), 31–7, and Kriger (1992).
43. Ranger (1982), 12, Auslander (1993), 184.
44. Mitchell (1956), 3.
45. Beresford (1997).
46. Auslander (1993).
47. Willis (1968), 6, n. 4. See also Richards (1935/1970), 449, for a dangerous and powerful female image associated with muchape (cited in L. White (1993), 760), and Ranger (1982), 8, for another powerful female figure who provides the muchape medicine.
48. Ranger (1982), 26–7.
49. ZCCM Archives; Ranger (1982), 30.
50. For examples see Auslander (1993); Heald (1995); and Weiss (1993).
51. European nurses often functioned as hygienic gatekeepers in hospitals in colonial and early post-colonial Zambia, sometimes to the point of being perceived as endangering the lives of African children by separating them from their 'unhygienic' mothers. How much of this role has carried over into the perception of African nurses will be addressed as part of my future research (Schumaker 1997).
52. Timothy Mgala: interview, Lusaka, September 1996.
53. Friedson (1996), 166; see also Chapter 4 above.
54. Schumaker (1997).
55. The distinction between medicines and cures is important for understanding African perceptions of Western medicine in the colonial period; see L. White (1995) and Schumaker (1998).
56. Comaroff (1985), 220. Male members of Pentecostal churches in Zimbabwe also attach importance to wearing Western suits to express their identity as modern Christians, and articles of a religious leader's clothing can become symbols of his power (Maxwell 1997).
57. Richards (1935).
58. Burke (1996), 176.
59. Callahan and Schumaker (1997).
60. Lyrics of kalela song: Mpatamato troupe, Luanshya, August 1992.
61. Lyrics, Mpatamato Kalela Troupe, 1996.
62. Mafeje (1967) quoted in Vail and White (1991). The American urban psychology movement in the 1970s similarly posited that political

activism could cure the psychological illnesses of members of urban black communities better than individually focused psychotherapies.

63. Vail and White (1991), 76.
64. Friedson (1996), 130–31; cf. Janzen in this volume, pp. 58–60.
65. It is difficult to judge how effective this form of criticism is or the organization of public opinion it involves; for example, see Auslander (1993), 187.
66. This is not to say that medical metaphors are absent from political discourse in the West, only that they do not provide the primary model for conceptualizing or evaluating political activity.
67. Mpatamato Dance Troupe, August 1992.
68. Janzen (1992), 126; see also Friedson (1996), 129.
69. Pels (1996), drawing on Cooper (1992).
70. See Auslander (1993), 189, and Comaroff (1985), 233–4.
71. In other historical and cultural settings words that cannot be understood by the speaker or audience, or both, nevertheless must be spoken to indicate that a tranformation in identity has taken place. For example, 'speaking in tongues' in both European and African Christianity is a sign of the speaker's contact with the spiritual world; in European history, the use of Latin by scientists and clergy acted as a signifier of esoteric knowledge and power; in Africa, healers and witch-finders often employ a foreign language as a sign of contact with powerful alien forces needed for healing.
72. Luig (1998).
73. Small village-based kalela bands still operate in the countryside, performing for weddings and other occasions. (Interview with Timothy Mgala, 6 September 1996, Lusaka.)
74. Janzen (1992), 129.

CHAPTER TEN

Sister disciplines? *Music and Medicine* in historical perspective

Penelope Gouk

> Music and medicine, Apollo and Aesculapius! What a divine alliance! ... two such noble arts could have been engendered only in the bosom of the gods.[1]
>
> ... Apollo was the father of both Aesculapius and the Muses. On this ground it may be claimed that medicine and music are sister arts. But it is no mere poetic fancy that music is related to medicine.[2]

Introduction

That music and medicine are 'sister disciplines' appears to be a rhetorical commonplace. Yet it is not at all clear that medical practitioners in general have ever needed to know anything about music – or conversely, that musicians have needed to know anything about medicine. And despite assertions to the contrary, the connection between music and healing is even hard to find in writings by ancient Greek and Roman physicians.[3] Nevertheless, the role of the physician-musician recurs as a cultural ideal across the centuries, and appears especially important to the Renaissance.[4]

Given that musical skills have never been considered a necessary part of medical training, and how rarely doctors have actually written in a professional capacity about music, I have been led to consider the following historical questions: under what circumstances have particular physicians been prompted to write about music, and what topics have they considered important when they do? And apart from doctors, who else has written on music's relevance to medicine, and for what audiences has such literature been intended? Obviously most of this kind of material today is produced by members of the music-therapy profession, and is chiefly targeted at other music therapists, and the wider therapeutic community.[5] However, what particularly interests me is the situation before music therapy existed as a recognized profession: who was writing on this subject when the identity of 'music therapist' was not yet established? Unsurprisingly, most of the non-medical discourse addressing the effects of music falls into the domain of music theory and criticism. The purpose of this chapter is to show how the literary products of individual 'medical authors' and 'music theorists' (as we indiscriminately tend to label such figures) can be situated within quite specific institutional and cultural settings. Mapping the institutional geographies where such discourses have been authored is a first step towards revealing the power relations, interests and cultural values they inevitably reflect.

The search for a proper theory and an appropriate identity has obsessed the music-therapy profession from its beginnings.[6] Yet the same tensions can be seen in Western literature long before music therapy became recognized as an independent discipline, and appear to be associated with how doctors as well as musicians have defined themselves and their practice, particularly in relation to prevailing religious norms. In societies where the cure of bodies is seen as wholly independent of the cure of souls, there is bound to be ambiguity about a praxis which occupies a liminal position between these realms. Apollo is indeed the god of both music and medicine, and Orpheus, Pythagoras and King David are three other ancient philosophers celebrated for their extraordinary musico-therapeutic skills (which ranged from dramatically altering the behaviour of humans and animals to bringing the dead to life and exorcizing demons). Musicians who have appeared to possess amazing powers have often been likened to one or other of these figures: to be identified as a 'second Orpheus' or compared to Apollo is normally seen as a compliment. But for a medical community which explicitly dissociates itself from the supernatural there is something deeply problematic about identifying too closely with pagan gods and semi-mythological figures that are implicated in theurgic cults (i.e., the controlling of demons) involving incantations, prophecy and purification of the soul.[7] Caught between the archetypes of rational doctor, priest and divinely (or demonically) inspired musician, the identity of the musical healer is inevitably compromised.

Music and Medicine: a disciplinary geography

This chapter tests these speculations through an analysis of the structure and contents of *Music and Medicine* (1948; hereafter *MM*). As its editors, Dorothy Schullian and Max Schoen, claimed, this book was the first scholarly attempt to address the historical and scientific aspects of music therapy from Antiquity to the present, and was explicitly intended to promote broader interest in music therapy. Not coincidentally, it appeared at precisely the moment when music therapy in the United States was being professionalized.[8] According to Dorothy Schullian's preface, a 'symposium' on music and medicine was first conceived of in 1944 by the Officer-in-Charge of the US Army Medical Library, Thomas Keys.[9] Schullian was assistant curator of the Library's History Section when Keys invited her to act as co-editor.[10] Publication was guaranteed by the New York publisher Henry Schuman, who soon took over Keys's responsibilities for the project. By 1946, however, Schuman had ceded this editorial role to Professor Max Schoen, Head of Education and Psychology at the Carnegie Institute of Technology.

Schullian herself leaves the reader in no doubt about the motives she felt were behind the volume: 'The tragic years of World War II witnessed a dramatic growth in the interdependence of music and medicine.' This growth was most apparent in 'the heightened role played by music therapy in military hospitals and in the increasingly frequent use of industrial music in factories'. But the times of stress 'could reduce to no ordered whole the complicated forces acting upon one another in the fields of music and medicine, and the result in too many cases was confusion and bewilderment'.[11] Schullian's words imply that these exceptional wartime events had resulted in conflict between individuals whose interests overlapped on the boundaries between medical, musical and even military expertise, as well as raising issues of professional versus non-professional interests.

With the benefit of hindsight, we might also suggest that this scholarly initiative to restore equilibrium at the institutional level reflected a deeper and more general desire to restore harmony within the social body after the disruption of war. Trying to create (or provide a model for) harmonious social relations by musical means is of course nothing new.[12] In the wake of the English Civil War, for example, a number of musically inclined academics looked to consort music as a remedy against extreme passions.[13] More generally, Plato's vision of a Republic whose guardians are musically educated and also determine the kinds of music which are allowed in society has been a recurring theme in Western literature.[14]

Unlike the present volume, *Music and Medicine* was not made up of newly commissioned pieces of writing by scholars who convened to discuss these issues, but comprised a selection of texts, most of which had already appeared in a range of scholarly books and journals.[15] This collection provides us with a unique cross-section of those whom the editors recognized as qualified to speak with authority on the relationship between music and medicine in post-war America. As we shall examine in more detail below, this select group included prominent composers and musicians, doctors and medical scientists, anthropologists

Table 10.1 Contributors to Schullian and Schoen, *Music and Medicine* (1948). Biographical information is based on 'Notes on Contributors' by Schullian

NAME	SKILLS/OCCUPATIONS IDENTIFIED	INSTITUTIONS	ACADEMIC DISCIPLINES, POSTS	CHAPTER IN *MM*	PAGES
Paul Radin	medical practitioner, linguistics	MD Columbia; Yale, Harvard, Smithsonian	Medicine, Anthropology	1. Music and medicine in primitive cultures	3–24
Frances Densmore	classically trained musician, pioneer ethnomusicologist	Oberlin, Boston, Chicago	Ethnomusicology	2. The use of music in the treatment of the sick by American Indians	25–46
Bruno Meineke	classically trained musician: violin, piano, organ; composer; classical scholar	PhD Michigan	Classics, Assistant Professor, Michigan	3. Music and medicine in classical antiquity	47–95
Henry Sigerist	medical practitioner; historian	London; MD Zurich; Munich; Johns Hopkins	History of Medicine, Director of Johns Hopkins Institute	4. The story of Tarantism	96–116
Armen Carapetyan	classically trained musician	Paris; MA, PhD Harvard	Musicology, Director Inst. Renaissance and Baroque Music	5. Music and medicine in the Renaissance and the 17th and 18th centuries	117–157
Charles Hughes	classically trained musician	MA, PhD Columbia	Musicology, Assistant Professor, Hunter College	6. Rhythm and health	158–189
Fielding H. Garrison	classically trained musician, army medical practitioner	BA Johns Hopkins; MD Georgetown	History of Medicine, Army Medical Librarian	7. Medical men who have loved music	190–217
Alfred H. Whittaker	surgeon	MD Ohio State; Wayne State University, Detroit	Occupational therapy; Lecturer, Wayne State University	8. Occupational diseases of musicians	218–43

Howard Hanson	classically trained musician; composer	Luther College; Northwestern University	Director of Eastman School of Music	9. Emotional expression in music	244–65
Ira Altschuler	psychiatrist	MD Berne; Harvard, Michigan	Director of Group and Music Therapy, Wayne County Hospital	10. A psychiatrist's experience with music as a therapeutic agent	266–81
Arnold Elston	classically trained musician; composer	MA Columbia; PhD Harvard	Musicology, Assistant Professor, University of Oregon	11. The musician's approach to music therapy	282–92
Willem Van de Wall	classically trained musician; harpist in US Marine Band, music therapist	The Hague, Leipzig	Chairman, Committee for the Use of Music in Hospitals	12. Music in hospitals	293–321
George Ainlay	classically trained musician; army surgeon	BMus Nebraska, Weslyan University, MD Nebraska	Adviser, Committee for the Use of Music in Hospitals	13. The place of music in military hospitals	322–51
R. L. Cardinell	engineer, classically trained musician; piano; conductor, composer	Stevens Institute of Technology	Director of Research, Muzak Corporation	14. Music in industry	352–66
Charles Diserens	historical, genetic and motivational psychology	PhD Cincinnati	Psychology, Associate Professor, Cincinnati	15. The development of an experimental psychology in music	367–86
Max Schoen	psychology, music and the arts, aesthetics	Vienna; BA College of City of New York; PhD Iowa	Psychology and Education; Professor, Carnegie Institute of Technology	16. Art the healer	387–406
Dorothy Schullian	classics, medical history	BA Case Western Reserve; PhD Chicago	Curator of Rare Books, Army Medical Library	Selected references Notes on contributors	407–71 473–82

and historians; in other words experts from fields right across the arts and sciences (see Table 10.1). It is clear that for the majority of medical men represented in the collection, music played an important role in their professional and/or private lives. Indeed, some of them were as highly qualified in music as they were in medicine, as well as having considerable linguistic talents. I would suggest that this combination of skills reflects the values of the culture in which each of these doctors was raised and educated.

The structure of the book itself mirrors a new phase in Western academic scholarship. In the aftermath of the Second World War the university sector was expanding enormously, with new institutions being built and new disciplines being founded in both the sciences and the humanities. This expansion was facilitated by an increasing number of scholarly publications and conferences by means of which existing disciplinary boundaries were being redefined, and also new disciplines created. The ideals and aspirations expressed in *Music and Medicine* are best interpreted within this context of expanding and newly emerging disciplines, above all in the attempt to regulate and define the use of music in relation to the medical profession and its institutions.

All the contributors evidently had very clear ideas about what the relationship between the disciplines of music and medicine *ought* to consist of, not only in the present, but also in the past and the future. As we have already seen from the opening quotations to this chapter, some authors emphasized the ancient and venerable relationship between these 'sister arts'. Attempts to develop an essentially new form of practice were to be legitimated through appeals to a long-standing tradition which could trace its origins back to classical Greece and Rome. Other contributors bemoaned the lack of a proper, 'scientific' approach to the theory and practice of music therapy, which could only be achieved through professionalization. At least four authors were directly involved in achieving this goal. Willem Van de Wall was Chairman of the Committee for the Use of Music in Hospitals, an organization to which the surgeon George Ainlay also acted as external adviser. The psychiatrist and neurologist Ira Altschuler was another pioneer in the field who taught at Michigan State University, one of the first universities offering undergraduate and graduate programmes to train music therapists. The music professor Arnold Elston is also noted as having been coordinator for one of the earliest courses on music therapy, offered at New York University in 1945.[16]

Apart from having a direct investment in the training of music therapists, what else qualified these individuals to contribute to this 'symposium'? More than anything, a university background seems to have been a necessary precondition for inclusion in the volume. All

Schullian's authors were graduates, and with a single exception had one, if not two, higher research degrees. These included at least six MDs and eight PhDs (four in musicology, two in classics, and two in psychology) from a handful of universities in Europe (notably Zurich and Vienna) and America. Columbia, Yale, Harvard, Chicago and Michigan were among the leading US institutions represented, all of which had medical faculties as well as offering degree courses in music. Although none of the contributors is easily pigeonholed into a single disciplinary specialism, they can be broadly divided into medical and musical professionals who mostly occupied positions in a variety of university departments, research institutes, music schools and military institutions.

Of the musicians, Howard Hanson (1896–1981) was altogether the most successful practising composer, conductor and music educator, having been head of the Eastman School of Music, Rochester since 1925. Armen Carapetyan (1908–92) was a leading musicologist of his generation who was devoted to the study and performance of early music. He was Director of the Institute of Renaissance and Baroque Music at Cambridge, Massachusetts, and shortly thereafter founded the American Institute of Musicology in Rome. Frances Densmore (1867–1957), the only female among Schullian's contributors, was one of the pioneering generation of ethnomusicologists who made the earliest recordings and transcriptions of native American music. Unlike her male counterparts, however, Densmore was an independent scholar who did not hold any formal academic position.[17] Arnold Elston and Charles Hughes, who were assistant professors in the music departments of the University of Oregon and Hunter College, also identified themselves as composers, but their music is completely forgotten today. In summary, all these individuals might be classified as 'musicians' by virtue of their occupational identity, but closer inspection reveals that they occupied very different positions in the academic and professional hierarchy. The range of occupations represented here also reminds us that while 'music' tends to be thought of simply as a performing art, it also has a theoretical dimension, or 'science' (*Wissenschaft*), which constitutes the discipline of musicology.

The category of 'musician' itself also turns out to be far from homogeneous. Five other authors are described as musicians on account of their practical skills, yet it is clear that they did not perform or teach (i.e., 'profess') music as their main livelihood. Bruno Meineke, for example, who was an assistant professor in the Department of Classics at the University of Michigan, is described as a violinist, pianist, organist and composer who had taught music as well as classics at several mid-Western colleges. The mechanical engineer R. L. Cardinell, from the Stevens Institute of Technology and a member of the Acoustical Society of America, is similarly described as a concert pianist, conductor and composer. Although located on opposite sides of the humanities–sciences divide by virtue of their occupations, these men evidently possessed comparable skills in music, and might just as easily have pursued some form of traditional musical career.

The same observation can also be made about three of the medical professionals in the volume who were enthusiastic musicians, all of whom (perhaps coincidentally) had army connections. Van de Wall was a harpist in the US Marine Band, as well as being active in symphonic and operatic productions, while Col. Fielding H. Garrison is well known for having made music his avocation even though his main job was as a librarian to the Surgeon-General.[18] Most exceptional, however, was Ainlay, who possessed higher degrees in music as well as an MD; he too is noted as a concert pianist, violinist and composer. While these doctors of medicine were clearly able to practise music, it is notable that none of the doctors of music could have possibly practised medicine, at least not in the sense it is conventionally understood today.[19] For in notable contrast to medicine, music can be practised by anyone without formal licence, even though there have always been attempts to regulate it as a profession.[20] Indeed, to possess a reasonable level of musical skill, and to enjoy music as part of one's leisure, has long been considered desirable among professionals who do not earn their livelihood through music.

From the 'Notes on Contributors' it is not possible to infer whether any of the other medical authors could actually play instruments themselves, but the content of their papers indicates a strong personal interest in musically related subjects. The Detroit surgeon Alfred Whittaker, for example (who was Vice-President of the American Association of Industrial Physicians and Surgeons), reflected on diseases peculiar to musicians, while Charles Diserens, an associate professor of psychology at the University of Cincinnati, had made the effect of music on behaviour his life's work. Just as we have seen in the case of 'musician', the broad category of 'medical professional' here encompasses a spectrum from the most theoretical to the most applied, with individuals engaging in private practice as well as occupying posts in hospitals and universities. Two physicians in particular were recognized for their contribution to the humanities. Paul Radin, who had an MD from Columbia, was a visiting professor in anthropology at Kenyon College, while the better-known Henry Sigerist (1891–1957) was Director of the Institute of the History of Medicine at the Johns Hopkins University and Editor of its *Bulletin*.[21] The asymmetry observed between the medical and musical disciplines is also found between medicine and the humanities more generally. A medical doctor like Sigerist, for example, who had skills in classics and modern languages, was considered qualified to be a professor of history, but a doctor of philosophy like Schullian or a doctor of music like Carapetyan could never become a professor of medicine, despite interest in the subject. This disciplinary inequality between departments reflects the high social and intellectual credibility which the medical profession enjoyed compared with most musicians and university teachers.

Despite differences in status, however, it is clear that contributors from either side of the disciplinary divide shared common intellectual and cultural values. From my own perspective as an early modern historian, I believe that this can be illustrated particularly well by the articles on 'Music and medicine in the Renaissance and in the 17th and 18th centuries' and 'The story of Tarantism', respectively by Carapetyan and Sigerist. These papers, which will be considered in more detail below, were already benchmark contributions to the study of early modern music and medicine in my graduate days. Having looked at them afresh in preparation for my own symposium on music and healing, I believe that they are best appreciated in the context of the disciplinary and institutional network represented by *Music and Medicine*, rather than being treated as isolated texts by individuals from two 'sister disciplines' whose interests just happened to coincide.

Before looking in detail at the topics which Sigerist and Carapetyan themselves considered important, let us consider how their articles fitted into the book as a whole. The way the editors organized the volume gives a fairly clear indication of how they thought the new field of music therapy should be advanced, as well as how they viewed the proper relationship between relevant disciplines. The first part of the book comprises a series of anthropological, ethnomusicological and historical papers which address the 'origins' of music therapy. These papers serve to legitimate, as well as question, modern scientific practices, and to set an agenda for future developments. There is a strongly Eurocentric focus to this material, which chiefly serves to establish the differences between the West and the 'rest', between pre-modern and modern ways of thinking. Thus, for example, the papers by Radin on 'Music and medicine in primitive cultures' and Densmore on 'The use of music in the treatment of the sick by American Indians' are placed at the beginning of the volume, signalling concern with an earlier phase in the evolution of mankind. (It should be noted, however, that Densmore herself is careful to point out cultural bias and problems of applying Western categories of thought to Indian practices.) The four historical papers which follow implicitly mark out the chronological boundaries of Western civilization from Antiquity to the present. Those by Carapetyan and Sigerist effectively span the middle ground between

Meineke's account of 'Music and medicine in classical antiquity' and Garrison's reflections on 'Medical men who have loved music', which takes the reader into the early twentieth century.

The remaining chapters by medical and musical experts are chiefly concerned with contemporary (that is, twentieth-century) developments. Some of these focus on research into the psychology and physiology of music, while others concentrate more on its practical application. All of them, however, display a similar sense of history; indeed, they share with the first group of papers the conventions that Western civilization is divided into epochs (e.g. Antiquity, Renaissance, etc.), and that historical progress is best measured in terms of the achievements of outstanding individuals. As the papers by Carapetyan and Sigerist will be used to illustrate, such achievements are typically textual in nature. In the case of music these texts are works by recognized composers, while for medicine they are the philosophical and scientific writings of medical men, especially those concerned with disease. In the next section I suggest that such notions did not arise from specialist training in history, but rather stemmed from a tradition of university education in which emphasis has always been placed on teaching 'sciences' (i.e., systematic bodies of theoretical knowledge about specified subjects) and 'philosophy' (i.e., a higher level of understanding about the causes of things).[22] This common pedagogical framework also accounts for the overwhelming consensus found among contributors – regardless of their professional and disciplinary expertise – on what music is, what the 'scientific' method involves, and what the best procedures might be for advancing knowledge about music's relationship to the mind and body.

Scientific approaches to music and medicine

The methods prescribed by both the professional composers and the experimental scientists for determining the causes of music's effects are strikingly similar. Although emphasizing the great variety in people's subjective responses to music, the musicians (Hanson, Elston and Hughes) believed that music itself is inherently amenable to analysis. They assumed that the ideal procedure for finding out how to treat people with music should be as follows: first, begin by dissecting music into its fundamental components, with 'music' of course being understood primarily in terms of composed artworks. Second, determine how each of these fundamental elements (for example, pitch, rhythm and timbre) or their combinations affect people's behaviour and emotions, by means of rigorous experimental testing. Lastly, apply this knowledge to create new works which are designed to produce particular emotional effects.

Such a methodology, while demonstrably 'scientific' in nature, was likely to have been acquired in the course of their professional training as composers. Since at least the fifteenth century, this training has centred on the ability to read and write music, and also to play (particularly keyboard) instruments. As I have argued elsewhere, these interrelated technologies of notating and performing music have given rise to the peculiarly Western view that music 'naturally' comprises a series of discrete pitches which can be combined in a variety of ways. Within this cultural framework, *making* music has come to mean the creation of compositions or works which consist of notes assembled together in a unique and original way.[23] At the same time, emphasis has been placed on the ability to represent and also move the emotions by means of these works.

This conceptualization of music as artefacts created by the minds of individual composers also dominates the contributions by mental-health experts (Altschuler, Schoen, Diserens) who sought to establish a recognized place for music in psychology and psychiatry. Although none of them apparently had any practical skills themselves worth mentioning, these men sought to discover the laws governing music's psychological and physiological effects through controlled experimental investigation, a process which involved isolating different variables such as rhythm and pitch and testing individual responses to these auditory stimuli. They concluded from these experiments that there was an almost certain correlation between musical compositions and particular moods, and were also able to confirm that listening to music produces measurable changes in bodily processes, 'namely, change of heartbeat, pulse, blood pressure, deeper and faster breathing'. In short, they proved 'scientifically' that music produces precisely the kinds of effects that composers have sought to imitate and arouse since the sixteenth century and doctors began to take seriously in the eighteenth. More specifically, they were following an experimental tradition of physiological acoustics established by the famous German scientist Hermann von Helmholtz (1821–94) in his *Tonempfindungen als physiologische Grundlage für die Theorie der Musik* (1863, 4th edn 1877).[24]

Lurking beneath the surface of this supposedly value-free science, however, was the assumption that composed art music is intrinsically 'good', in both a moral as well as an aesthetic sense. Hanson was especially confident in the distinction he drew between 'good' forms of musical expression, which he claimed had their foundation in natural laws, and 'bad' music. He asserted that the tonal material as standardized in modern Western music (i.e., sixteenth to twentieth centuries) was 'a fair approximation of the musical material *naturally available* in the overtone series of nature and, therefore, has some claim to a scientific basis'.[25] This body of classical works provided the justification for his attack on the 'queer atavistic manifestation' of the 'Boogie Woogie' craze. Together with other types of 'hot jazz' that were popular at the time, Boogie Woogie was clearly for Hanson the epitome of 'bad music'. Only half-jokingly (or perhaps entirely in earnest), he suggested that the insidious effects of this 'aural drug' which flooded American homes over the airwaves might perhaps be countered by alternative, 'good' kinds of music – presumably including his own compositions.

Although buttressed by appeals to modern science, Hanson's portrayal of jazz as a sickening influence on American society, a degenerate practice that compares extremely unfavourably with classical music, follows a long-established model. Criticisms of new forms of music (often introduced by foreigners), coupled with fears about their damaging and even effeminizing effect on modern youth, have been a feature of Western literature since the fourth century BC.[26] Musicians themselves have been particularly ambiguous in their response to new practices (which often later become accepted as convention), and Hanson is no exception to this rule. On the one hand he draws attention to the inherently natural basis of Western art music, while at the same time suggesting that jazz represents a throwback to more primitive practices. The racial and social prejudice implicit in his comments strikes a jarring note today. Yet Hanson's beliefs were not untypical for the early twentieth century, a period when condemnation of mass culture in all its manifestations was widespread among the intelligentsia.[27]

One reason why the composers and psychologists treated music in exactly the same way may have been because they occupied comparable positions in their respective professional hierarchies. As academic doctors of music and medicine they had been trained to understand the laws governing musical and mental structures. At this level of abstraction the therapeutic potential of music is most easily conceived in terms of a transaction between the medical researcher and the composer, both of them being qualified professionals. It is assumed that the doctor understands how the mind and body work, and diagnoses the disease(s) of the afflicted, while the composer supplies works which will produce predictable responses in the 'patient'.[28]

This reified view of music as something created by the composer and prescribed by the physician is rather different from the more pragmatic vision offered in three chapters which address the use of music in institutions. Since two of these were by army surgeons (Van de Wall, Ainlay) and the third was by an engineer (Caldwell), a shared professional concern with medical and industrial technologies may be taken as given. We should also note, however, that these men were equally interested in technologies of musical production and reproduction.

Indeed, all of them were instrumentalists who had personal experience of public as well as private musical performance. Their emphasis on practice rather than analysis results in a very different set of priorities than those identified in the first group.

A central theme in these more applied papers is the role that (the then) new technologies like recording and broadcasting can, or should, play in musical therapeutics. There is also a recognition of the differences between the production and consumption of music, and the implications that this may have for those trying to incorporate music into the framework of public medicine. These authors appear quite sensitive to the social and technical problems involved in using music in public institutions, especially those in which lower-class and marginalized members of society predominate. Van de Wall, for example, specialized in musical activities for inmates and personnel of reformatories, schools for the mentally deficient and the blind, mental hospitals, hospitals for crippled children and general hospitals. Ainley in particular drew attention to the musical tastes of hospital inmates (who are compared to workers in a factory or office) and how these may conflict with those of the professionals responsible for their treatment. According to Ainley's experience, listening to 'classical' music sometimes had positive effects on people. Yet patients also responded well to folk music and forms of popular music, even though these genres were disliked by many music professionals. The concept that popular music might have a better therapeutic effect than high art constrasts strikingly with Hanson's forceful attack on jazz and its supposedly detrimental effects on the health of society.

In sum, these three papers show some recognition of the differences between active performance and passive listening, and the transformation that new technologies might effect in both the making and understanding of music. Significantly, they also suggest that 'patients' do not necessarily respond well to the kind of music that experts judge to be 'good' music, which may in the end not be what is required to make people feel better. Such views are widely held by music therapists today, among whom there has been a move away from predominantly passive techniques of treatment in favour of improvisatory participation.

Sigerist and Carapetyan: from Renaissance to Enlightenment

There are many structural and methodological similarities between the papers by Sigerist and Carapetyan. Furthermore, each of these authors demonstrates an exemplary familiarity with the other's professional domain: Sigerist's essay is focused on a handful of musical works with explicitly medical connections, while Carapetyan's article concentrates on medical and natural philosophical texts from the sixteenth to eighteenth centuries which deal with music. This symmetry should not be altogether surprising, since both the history of medicine and of musicology owed their existence as disciplines to the training and legitimation of practitioners, and were accordingly framed around their professional interests.

Sigerist himself says nothing about the contexts in which his musical examples were originally produced. However, they seem to fall into three types, of which only the third might be regarded as explicitly therapeutic in nature. The first type comprises two anonymous hymns associated with particular saints: a medieval setting on the Nativity of St John the Baptist, which was believed to have a healing effect on colds, and a hymn from a German publication of 1702 which was dedicated to St Sebastian, the patron saint of plague. It is important to note that the curative effects of such hymns would have been ascribed to the power of the saints to whom they were directed, rather than to any intrinsic qualities in their music. A similar observation can be made about the second group of works by two Italian composers to commemorate medical experiences of their patrons. The hymn by the Italian composer Bonaiutus de Casentino, for example, marks an occasion around 1300 when Pope Boniface VIII was bled and purged by his doctor. Likewise, Marchetto Cara's four-voice frottola of 1517 laments the syphilis of his patron and friend the Marchese Francesco Gonzaga of Mantua. Both compositions may well have made their recipients 'feel better', but neither was actually intended to cure disease.

Only Sigerist's last two examples (dated 1643 and 1753 respectively) can be regarded as having an explicitly curative function. These are transcriptions of pieces in the form of the tarantella, a special kind of music that was played to victims of tarantism, a strange malady reputedly transmitted through the bite or sting of the tarantula, for which dancing and music was the only cure. Most cases of tarantism were found in Apulia, the region located in the 'heel' of Italy's boot, but isolated outbreaks occurred in other parts of Italy and Spain.[29] As Sigerist demonstrates, this disease was widely remarked on in early modern medical literature. The most influential account was by the German Jesuit Athanasius Kircher, whose *Magnes, sive de arte magnetica* (Rome, 1641; 2nd edn Cologne, 1643) literally put tarantism 'on the map', as well as depicting the earliest known example of music that was used in its treatment.

Kircher also figures prominently in Carapetyan's essay, which begins by mentioning some famous Renaissance doctors and their contribution to humanist learning before going on to identify the different ways in which medicine and music were interconnected during the Renaissance and beyond. His themes include the therapeutic effects of music, especially its effects on the passions, particular disease phenomena related to music (including tarantism), music and physiology (e.g., singing and the science of voice production), the social links between music and disease (e.g., courtesans playing music and the transmission of syphilis), and finally the social links between musicians and doctors (e.g., at courts and academies).

The avenue Carapetyan explores in most detail himself is the theoretical basis underpinning early modern ideas about music's psychological and physiological effects. The principal source he uses for Renaissance medical ideas about music's effects on human temperament is *Le istitutioni harmoniche* (Venice, 1558) by Giosoffo Zarlino (1517–90), who is described as 'the spokesman of sixteenth-century music theory'. Authors whom he saw linking these subjects together in the seventeenth century included the French philosopher René Descartes, the English scholar and cleric Robert Burton, the French Minim friar Marin Mersenne, and especially Kircher, whose work has already been noted. Carapetyan claims that although the seventeenth century is considered to have inaugurated 'a new scientific and philosophical as well as musical age', there was little new in the matter of music and medicine during this period. It was only from the eighteenth century, when people first began to approach the problem with a 'measurable scientific and critical attitude', that an abundance of medically qualified authors began to write about music's links with medicine. To illustrate this material he focuses on the work of a single Montpellier physician of the early eighteenth century. This was Louis Roger's *Tentamen de vi soni et musices in corpus humanum* (1748), which according to a more recent author represents 'the first clear support for music therapy in the French medical profession'.[30]

Taken together, these two articles by Carapetyan and Sigerist sketch out a promising agenda for future work across musicology and the history of medicine. Since they appeared in the 1940s, there has been a huge amount of interdisciplinary collaboration between *practitioners* of medicine and of music, even as music therapy itself has become a well-established specialism. It is therefore surprising to see just how little interdisciplinary research has been undertaken into this area over the last fifty years by scholars working in the same fields as Carapetyan and Sigerist. Paradoxically, what this absence underlines is the very power of successfully institutionalized disciplines. While such bodies are concerned to define and understand the world on their own terms, and to establish their status and legitimacy, they are not so interested in seeing how other disciplinary domains relate to their own. Thus even though the 'sister disciplines' of musicology and history of medicine have common origins in the training of practitioners (i.e., of composers and doctors respectively), those working in these two specialisms scarcely identify with each other's professional concerns.[31] Indeed, we can see that this problem of identification, of how to create a new kind of practitioner whose expertise threatens to overthrow or dissolve long-established boundaries, is a theme which recurs throughout the essays in *Music and Medicine*.

Medico-musical identities

In my introduction to this chapter I hinted at the difficulty encountered by music therapists in trying to construct an appropriate professional identity, and suggested that this issue was closely bound up with how doctors and musicians have conventionally defined themselves in relation to prevailing social norms, and come to terms with changes in those norms. The types of doctors, healers and musicians that are singled out for discussion in *Music and Medicine* – both positive and negative stereotypes – not only tell us something about the values of individual authors, but also about those of the society for whom their work was produced. Fifty years ago, the superiority of Western European culture was normally taken as self-evident among intellectuals, as was the dominance of white males in public and professional life. Since these assumptions are no longer taken for granted, their influence on post-war scholarship is quite easy to see, particularly when we look back at what was then thought to differentiate modern culture from primitive and non-Western societies.

Paul Radin's treatment of 'primitive' or 'aboriginal man's' approach to music and medicine, for example, as distinct from that found in more 'civilized' cultures, though reflecting attitudes of his day, strikes modern readers as both patronizing and offensive. Yet although his article sheds little light on the practices and beliefs of 'primitive peoples', it reveals how anxious the author was to identify himself and his fellow doctors with a tradition of 'rational' medicine stemming from the ancient Greeks. An integral part of this identification was to show how different learned medicine was from the magical rituals used by the 'priest-practitioner' in primitive cultures. Radin was hardly unique in this enterprise, however: the tactic of contrasting rational medicine with the practices of magicians and charlatans has been a rhetorical strategy used by physicians since Hippocrates.[32] This rhetoric was first successfully developed by Galen, and subsequently became institutionalized in university medical education during the sixteenth century.[33] At that time the role of the 'priest-practitioner' as such was not in question, since it was considered normal for ordained ministers to practice medicine. A more pressing issue was where to draw the boundary between true medical knowledge and belief on the one hand, and false superstition and ritual on the other. In Radin's mental universe, however, religious and superstitious beliefs appear to lie on the same side of the boundary, and are assumed to be incommensurable with the scientific knowledge of the medical expert.

Despite his efforts to distinguish medical science from magic and superstition, Radin nevertheless assumes that both the aboriginal medicine-man and the modern doctor are a special kind of man who has a privileged status within his community. While saying nothing about his modern counterpart, Radin confidently claims that the primitive healer is 'always a person of special temperament ... characterized by marked emotional instability ... he sets a high value on the necessity of acquiring wisdom and on the educative effects of suffering ... by and large [he] is selected from among the few maladjusted individuals in the community ... he is definitely the thinker in every aboriginal community'. According to Radin, music plays a significant role as 'a symbol of the priest-practitioner's power, particularly as regards his control of spirits and deities ... likewise it is an emblem of his profession'.[34] As we shall see shortly, this cultural stereotype of a gifted yet unstable individual endowed with special powers has often been drawn on by Western artists and musicians, but it hardly seems compatible with the model of rational doctor.

Bruno Meineke's paper on music and medicine in Antiquity displays a far more positive attitude towards primitive religious cults than Radin's. Meineke himself was not a doctor, and approached the historical links between doctors and music from his training in classics as well as music. He traces the diffusion of the cults of Apollo and Aesculapius, in which music was used as an indispensable part of healing. Meineke claims that it was Pythagoras above all who 'deserves to be known as "The Father of Psychotherapeutics"', since 'in his philosophy psychics and physics were inseparably mingled into a regimen of life, in which he employed an extensive musico-therapy'.[35] The essay concludes with Meineke's own arrangement of what he believed was the earliest surviving example of Greek music, a fragment of the first Pythian Ode of Pindar (522–448 BC) which is found in Kircher's *Musurgia universalis* (Rome, 1650).[36] The fact that Meineke should take the theurgic practices of ancient Pythagorean sects as a positive model for modern psychotherapeutics suggests that he had a very different view of the ideal doctor from Radin. For somone who sees the 'priest-practitioner' as a manifestation of primitive superstition, the idea of a medical doctor 'really' engaging in practices designed to free the soul from the body and bring it to unity with the divine is completely unimaginable. Loss of control and frenzy are incompatible with scientific credibility.

Enthusiam for and ravishment through music, however, does appear to be permitted when the language of ecstasy (divine mania) is treated as metaphorical, and the musician and doctor are seen as possessing similarly creative powers. Indeed, it is the superior mental qualities of such men which allow them to control the unpredictable forces of nature through their art.[37] This link between musical and scientific genius is hinted at in Fielding Garrison's paper, for example, which draws attention to individual doctors and their participation in musical culture, above all in German-speaking regions during the nineteenth century. His archetypal musical doctor is Theodor Billroth, 'the greatest German surgeon of his time', who first met Brahms at Vienna in the 1860s and formed a 'sort of musical brotherhood' with the composer that lasted for nearly 30 years.[38]

Garrison's emphasis on German culture also extends to twentieth-century America, for he notes that music was cultivated in most German-American families, and lists several American physicians and biologists of German descent who were capable performers, or even composers. He suggests that many of the physicians who have been amateurs of music in modern times 'have been in the class distinguished for original work in the exact sciences upon which medicine is based'. He observes that great physiologists such as Helmholtz have been particularly famous as musical enthusiasts, and ascribes this to the 'logical relation' between pure mathematics and its musical analogues of harmony, counterpoint and the art of fugue.[39] In short, he identifies precisely the kind of relationship between musical and scientific analysis that is assumed by most contributors to *Music and Medicine*. It is surely not a coincidence that at least five of them (Altschuler, Radin, Schoen, Sigerist, Van de Wall) were first-generation immigrants who had studied in some of the foremost German and Swiss universities in Europe.

The ideal which underpins this celebration of the natural affinity between musical and scientific skills is that of 'Renaissance man'. Carapetyan is not alone in seeing the Renaissance as a unique period which inaugurated the modern age, a time when the 'artist could be and often was a man of science, and the man of science usually a man of letters and arts'.[40] In other words, high value is being placed on artistic and scientific skills combined in a single individual, the archetypal *homo universalis* being Leonardo da Vinci. The pre-eminent message of *Music and Medicine* is that medical men should be recognized as leading contributors to this humanistic culture, and we should remember that several of the most famous Renaissance doctors were accomplished in music. This belief is absolutely central to the ideal of *Bildung* that was common to the German-speaking middle classes of both the old world and the new. Within this cultural framework, to describe a scientist as a quasi 'artist' was to pay the highest compliment.

Nevertheless, there still remains an unresolvable tension between the attributes thought to distinguish a great musician and those considered more appropriate for a doctor or hospital worker, and this tension is evident in the 1940s debates about what the ideal music therapist should be. Speaking from his own 25 years' experience of working in hospitals, Van de Wall identifes the personality traits he thought to be desirable in this new breed of professional:

> In order to be an effective hospital music worker one should be physically healthy and emotionally well-balanced and self-controlled. Over-emotional and unstable persons, handicapped by compensation mechanisms, no matter how gifted they may be as professional musicians, should not seek employment as hospital music workers.[41]

In Van de Wall's mind, the ideal music therapist is strictly incompatible with the musical or artistic genius. Flawed by emotional and mental instability, the gifted musician has more in common with Radin's unstable priest-practitioner than the figure Van de Wall had in mind. For him, the ideal 'hospital music worker' (doubtless modelled on himself) was well-balanced and self-controlled – and, of course, a man. In his ideal professionalized world there seems to be no place for all the female musicians who in their desire to assist the national war effort had flocked to the hospitals to offer humanitarian care.[42] Moreover, his account of earlier twentieth-century developments in music therapy is conspicuously silent about the major role that women had played at the time. Among the early female pioneers he ignores were Eva Vescelius, who founded the National Therapeutic Society of New York in 1903; Margaret Anderton, who in 1919 organized and taught the first course in music therapy offered through a university at Columbia University; and Isa Maud Ilsen, a musician, nurse and hospital executive who founded the National Association for Music in Hospitals in 1926. Finally, we should not overlook Harriet Seymour, the founder and President of the National Foundation of Music Therapy. Seymour was presenting lectures and classes at numerous New York City hospitals and prisons at precisely the time that Van de Wall was active between 1941 and 1944.[43]

This focus on male identities prevails throughout *Music and Medicine*; only Densmore, perhaps because she was a woman herself, mentions some women healers in her contribution. And while Carapetyan acknowledges the musical and artistic accomplishments of Italian courtesans such as Lucrezia Porzia and Veronica Franco, he does so only to highlight early modern debates about music's role in spreading venereal disease – that is, through stimulating sexual passion. That these highly cultured women also contributed positively to the Renaissance courtly environment, as well as using music in a professional capacity, is not reflected on here.

The preponderance of élite males in the volume is a fairly accurate reflection of professional life in the post-war period, but the fact that many pioneers of the emerging music-therapy profession were actually women does not come across at all, the more so since none of their writings is included. Of course, this emphasis on male identities and the absence of women from the historical picture was absolutely normal for scholarship of the time. What deserves emphasis, however, is that ambivalence is also being expressed towards a particular kind of *male* professional; namely the priest or other figure holding sacred authority. We have already noted how negatively Radin views the 'priest-practitioner', and have suggested that this attitude arises from an assumption that superstition and religion amount to the same thing. Yet there is more than personal prejudice at stake here: the absence of any contribution by a theologian or any kind of religious figure to *Music and Medicine* also needs to be accounted for, even though it might be taken for granted. Again, the structure of the book mirrors prevailing cultural norms, namely those of a society whose economy and education is controlled by secular rather than sacred authorities, where more public investment is made in hospitals and laboratories than churches, and religious practice is seen as a matter of private concern. Within such a society, far greater authority is invested in the medical doctor than the doctor of theology, and this difference in status is reflected in the university curriculum, where the discipline of theology normally occupies a relatively marginal position compared with those of medicine, the natural sciences, and even music.

In the period celebrated as the Renaissance, however, universities were still primarily regarded as training grounds for the religious life, theology was considered to be 'Queen of the Disciplines', and the church was still the most important single source of musical patronage. It should not therefore be surprising that two of the most important and influential texts identified by Carapetyan and Sigerist were written by members of holy orders. Take, for example, the 'music theorist' Zarlino, whose account of the passions and humours was presented by Carapetyan as typifying Renaissance thinking on music's effects. Although he does not say so, Zarlino was in fact a Franciscan priest, employed as a singing man in the choir of St Mark's basilica in Venice. *Le istitutioni harmoniche* (1558) was not produced as part of his livelihood but was a private initiative whose intended audience comprised the Venetian aristocracy and professional classes who avidly consumed musical culture. The book was intended to demonstrate the philosophical as well as practical foundations of polyphonic practice, which Zarlino argued had their basis in the most recent physiological and mathematical theory. Zarlino never went to university, never had any formal medical training or a licence to practice medicine, and never took a degree in music. If he had been writing in the twentieth century, what he had to say on this subject would have been completely disregarded by the editors of *Music and Medicine*. The fact that he was a Franciscan priest alone would have automatically disqualified him from pronouncing authoritatively on either medical or musical thought.

And what about Kircher, perhaps the most important single source on musical therapeutics in the seventeenth century? The case is even worse, since he was not even a composer. Nor was he a qualified medical practitioner. Instead, he was a Jesuit professor of mathematics and philosophy who in the space of 48 years published nearly 40 books on an encyclopedic range of subjects that achieved literally worldwide circulation. His writings spanned a field of knowledge which in modern society has been carved up into specialist disciplines within the humanities and social sciences as well as the physical and biological sciences.[44] Clearly it was Kircher's status and training as a university philosopher, not as a practitioner of any art, which gave him the authority to write on these topics. Moreover, we should also note that his discussion of the powers of music is framed in the context of magic (book 9 is on the 'magic of consonance and dissonance'). In his frame of reference most effects of music on the mind and body of man were to be explained in terms of occult, but purely natural, causes: in other words a form of natural magic.[45]

Given the overwhelming association between magic, religion and the healing powers of music that prevailed in the Renaissance and beyond, it is particularly ironic that *Music and Medicine* is itself so resolutely secular and rational in tone. But of course it would never have occurred to Schullian or Schoen to seek a contribution by an ordained minister who might discuss the effects of music on the soul, its capacity to exorcize demons or ability to induce ecstasy, as though these were things to be taken seriously. In their academic world – as indeed our own today – both music and medicine were self-evidently to be understood as wholly secular professions, dealing with the natural rather than the supernatural world, in a rational and scientific way. As a consequence, any discussion of individuals who combined the role of physician and/or musician with that of the priest could only take place in relation to other times and other places, as part of historical or anthropological discourse rather than a reality of contemporary Western society.

Past histories, future directions

One of the main goals in writing this chapter was to locate Sigerist and Carapetyan within the broader institutional and cultural setting represented in *Music and Medicine*. It emerged that a relatively narrow range of interests dominates the volume, especially those of men with higher university qualifications. Most of the articles assume that the relationship between music and medicine is to be defined solely in terms delineated by practitioners themselves, particularly those with academic degrees. Within this self-appointed élite two distinct types of approach to the subject can be discerned, and I suggested that these may correspond to hierarchical divisions which cut across the professions in general, rather than being particular to either discipline. On the one hand, an 'analytical' approach was notably followed by composers and medical scientists who focused on the underlying laws governing musical and mental structures. On the other, a more 'applied' approach was favoured by hospital professionals, for whom recent advances in (musical) technology opened up new ways of organizing institutional and social structures. Given these significant differences of emphasis, it is not surprising to find competing views of what music therapy ought to be, and especially who ought to control its practice. These conflicting ideals are as much evident in the papers which address pre-modern and non-Western cultures as they are in those dealing with contemporary medical theory and practice.

Another important discovery was that a majority of the authors who contributed to *Music and Medicine* had some level of musical literacy, including the doctors, and this was clearly seen as desirable even among those who did not perform themselves. Such values were by no means universally shared in early twentieth-century American society. They were geographically as well as culturally specific, being particularly associated with cosmopolitan urban life. The ideal of the musically educated doctor was particularly cultivated among members of the German-speaking community who regarded music (along with literature and poetry) as an integral part of a liberal education, of *Bildung*. Just as Billroth's relationship with Brahms was considered appropriate for a medical student in 1860s Vienna, a hothouse of musical and artistic culture, so too were social and familial links between musicians and doctors considered normal in twentieth-century New York,

Chicago and Baltimore, to name but three cities where medical students had access to some of the highest concentrations of artistic and musical activity in the United States.

This kind of access opened up new opportunities for exploring the relationship between these domains. Sigerist's inaugural talk to the Johns Hopkins Medical Society in 1938, for instance, was followed by a concert in which his musical examples were performed by a string quartet. Such a juxtapositon of skills was clearly not unusual for the university's medical community. Just like the American-German families of doctors Garrison enthused about, Sigerist's family and immediate circle included many musicians. His own daughter Nora confirms that *Hausmusik* – monthly chamber-music events where good amateurs played quartets, trios and so forth, and her mother sang German *lieder* – was a regular feature of family life in Baltimore. 'Music was a great bond' between Nora and her father.[46] There is considerable anecdotal evidence to suggest that a high proportion of medical students at Johns Hopkins and other East Coast medical schools was similarly involved in music-making at this time.[47] My sketch of the professional and personal networks embodied in *Music and Medicine* indicates a direct correspondence between texts which celebrate the therapeutic powers of music and the local culture in which these texts are produced.

This exercise of mapping the institutional relationships underpinning *Music and Medicine* is not simply intended to unmask the prejudices of a bygone privileged élite. In the first place, it underscores many of the issues already raised in my Introduction to this volume, not least the consequences of war and the role that music plays in the regeneration of communities. Second, I believe it has profound implications for present-day scholars and practitioners seeking to explore the relationships between music, medicine and healing. For all our talk of 'new perspectives' and 'inter-disciplinary approaches', it is sobering to realize that every scholarly initiative on this front today owes its existence to the very institutional structures and disciplines which contributors to *Music and Medicine* were involved in developing. The research tools and methodologies which we currently deploy as Western academics have their roots in a tiny number of institutions and their teaching traditions.[48]

In this chapter I have suggested that a relatively narrow range of professional and intellectual interests has always dominated the literature on music and medicine. It has also hinted at the existence of healing practices involving music which have escaped the historical record because they lie outside the boundaries normally recognized by musical and medical professionals. Seeing such intellectual bias is of course nothing new. Over recent decades scholars working in the fields of cultural history, feminist scholarship and gender studies, for example, have been active in the recovery of suppressed identities and the reconstruction of hidden histories. As George Rousseau and Linda Austern in particular have already shown in Chapters 6 and 7 above, this literature points towards a wealth of primary material that can offer very different perspectives on music's healing powers and their application. Only by broadening our horizons beyond the walls of academia can a new kind of history about the 'sister disciplines' of music and medicine – including the activities of sisters excluded from these disciplines – begin to be written.

Notes

1. Meineke (1948), 47. I would like to thank Fenela Childs, Jonathan Harwood, Grace Jantzen, John Janzen, David Katz and Carsten Timmerman for their helpful comments on earlier drafts of this chapter.
2. Whittaker (1948), 218.
3. West (1999).
4. See below, and also Voss (2000) and Gouk (2000).
5. In addition to specialist periodicals like the *Journal of British Music Therapy*, see also for example Davis, Gfeller and Thaut (1992); Heal and Wigram (1993); Payne (1993); Bunt (1994); Aldridge (1996); Pavlicevic (1998).
6. Aldridge (1996), Ansdell (1997).
7. See above, Chapter 1.
8. Davis et al. (1992), 30–33.
9. The Medical Library was at that time based in Cleveland, Ohio, having been moved from Washington following the outbreak of war. Schullian was using the term 'symposium' here in the sense of a collection of papers rather than an actual meeting.
10. On Schullian's career, see Wilson (1984, 1989).
11. *MM*, p. vii.
12. There are many instances of musical works written to celebrate peace treaties and dynastic alliances cemented through marriage; see for example Yates (1947), 236–74.
13. Gouk (1996), 276–84.
14. Plato, *Republic*, 376c–403c in Bloom (1968). See also Yates (1947) and Budd (1985).
15. Including *American Journal of Psychiatry*; *Bulletin of the Society of Medical History of Chicago*; *Educational Music Magazine*; *Hygeia*; *Journal of Nervous and Mental Diseases*; *Musical Quarterly*.
16. The first text outlining a course of this kind was H. A. Seymour and E. E. Garrett, *An Instruction Course in the Use and Practice of Music Therapy* (New York, 1944).
17. For further biographical details, see Sadie (1980): vol. iii, 771 (Carapetyan); vol. v, 375 (Densmore); vol. viii, 153–4 (Hanson).
18. Tietsch (1937).

19. In the early modern period, the term 'medicine' normally denoted the empirical treatment of disease through the application of surgical or medicinal therapies, and did not require a licence or specialist training. It was 'physic' which required a grasp of the causes of disease, and which could only be legitimately practised by those with a university degree; see Cook (1990).
20. Woodfill (1953).
21. For details of Sigerist's career, see Stevenson (1982) and Fee and Brown (1997).
22. The 'sciences' as they are generally understood today used to be called natural philosophy. There is no modern English term equivalent to the German *Wissenschaft*, which retains this meaning of systematic disciplinary knowledge. For further discussion, see Gouk (1999), chapter 3.
23. See Chapter 3 above; also Gouk (1999).
24. Vogel (1993) and Hatfield (1993).
25. Hanson (1948), 245–6 (emphasis mine).
26. See, for example, the Plutarchian treatise *On Music* in Barker (1984), 205–57.
27. The German social philosopher and musicologist Theodor Adorno (1903–69) exemplifies this trend. His *Philosophie der neuen Musik* (Tübingen, 1949) is a devastating socialist critique of popular music and the 'culture industry' in general. See also Adorno (1976), and Sadie (1980), i, 112.
28. For a late seventeenth-century attempt to market such musical wares, see H. Playford (1699): *Wit and Mirth: or, Pills to Purge Melancholy*. For late twentieth-century uses of specific musical works to manage mood see Maranto (1993) for professional examples, and Mistiaen (1999) for self-help techniques.
29. For further reading see Horden (2000).
30. Forman (1984), 85; see also Gouk (2000).
31. For further discussion of this point, see above, Chapter 1.
32. Lloyd (1983), 139–47, 'The Science of Medicine'.
33. Nutton (1993).
34. Radin (1948), 14–15, 22–3.
35. Meineke (1948), 53.
36. Kircher claimed to have transcribed it from a manuscript in a Sicilian monastery, but this has never been found. Whether his setting was a forgery has not yet been resolved by scholars; see Godwin (1978), 66.
37. For a discussion of the highly gendered nature of this role, see Battersby (1989).
38. Garrison (1948), 208.
39. Ibid., 199.
40. Carapetyan (1948), 118. For a discussion of the 1940s and 1950s debate on Renaissance ideology and the role of the humanities in American universities see Landauer (1994).
41. Van de Wall (1948), 316.
42. Ibid., 294. Van de Wall's claim that music only began to be used in US hospitals from around the time he arrived in the country is clearly false; see Taylor (1981).
43. For further discussion see Davis et al. (1992), 26–30. The average male to female ratio on UK training courses is less than 25 per cent male, but men

currently outnumber women by three to two in terms of PhDs in music therapy.

44. Godwin (1979).
45. See Gouk (1999).
46. Beeston (1997), 108–9.
47. Bett (1938), Marmelszadt (1946).
48. For example, three of the contributors to this volume (Austern, Janzen, Kramer) earned their PhD from the University of Chicago, and two have degrees from Cambridge (Burnett, Stobart).

Bibliography

The most important texts are indicated by an asterisk.

MM = Schullian, Dorothy, and Schoen, Max (eds) (1948), *Music and Medicine*, New York: Henry Schuman.

Abelard, Peter (1969), *Theologia Christiana*, ed. E. Buytaert, Turnhout: Brepols.

Abercrombie, Thomas (1991), 'To be Indian, to be Bolivian: "Ethnic" and "National" Discourses of Identity', in Greg Urban and Joel Sherzer (eds), *Nation-States and Indians in Latin America*, 95–130, Austin: University of Texas Press.

*Adorno, Theodor W. (1976), *Introduction to the Sociology of Music*, trans. E. B. Ashton, New York: Seabury Press.

Agawu, Kofi (1995), 'The Invention of "African Rhythm"', *Journal of the American Musicological Society*, 48 (3): 380–95.

Aikin, William (1900), *The Voice: Its Physiology and Cultivation*, London: Macmillan.

Ainlay, George W. (1948), 'The Place of Music in Military Hospitals', in *MM*, 322–51.

Akpabot, Samuel (1972), 'Theories on African Music', *African Arts*, 6 (1): 59–62, 88.

Aldridge, David (1996), *Music Therapy Research and Practice in Medicine: From Out of the Silence*, London and Bristol, Pa.: Jessica Kingsley Publishers.

Anon. (1738), 'Common Sense: On Music and Opera', *Gentleman's Magazine*, 8: 533–6.

Ansdell, Gary (1995), *Music for Life: Aspects of Creative Music Therapy with Adults*, London and Philadelphia: Jessica Kingsley Publishers.

—— (1997), 'Music Therapy in the 20th Century: Praxis, Discourse and Discipline', unpublished paper given at conference on 'Music, Healing and Culture: Towards a Comparative Perspective', London.

Armstrong, Gwenneth (1988), 'Symbolic Arrangement and Communication in the Despacho', PhD, Institute of Amerindian Studies, University of St Andrews.

Arom, Simha (1985), *Polyphonies et polyrythmies instrumentales d'Afrique Centrale*, Paris: CNRS/SELAF.

Auslander, Mark (1993), '"Open the Wombs!": The Symbolic Politics of Modern Ngoni Witchfinding', in Jean Comaroff and John Comaroff (eds), *Modernity and its Malcontents: Ritual Power in Postcolonial Africa*, 167–92, Chicago: University of Chicago Press.

Austern, Linda Phyllis (1993), '"Alluring the auditorie to effeminacie": Music and the Idea of the Feminine in Early Modern England', *Music and Letters*, 74: 343–54.

*—— (1996), '"The conceit of the minde": Music, Medicine and Mental Process in Early Modern England', *Irish Musical Studies*, 4: *The Maynooth International Musicological Conference 1995, Selected Proceedings, Part One*, ed. Patrick F. Devine and Harry White, 133–51, Dublin: Four Courts Press.

*Babb, Lawrence (1951), *The Elizabethan Malady: A Study of Melancholia in English Literature from 1580 to 1642*, East Lansing, Mich.: Michigan State College Press, 1951.

Bach, Alberto Bernardo (1880), *On Musical Education*, 2nd edn, Edinburgh and London: W. Blackwood & Sons.

Bacon, Roger (1683), *The Cure of Old Age and the Preservation of Youth*, trans. Richard Browne, London: Thomas Flesher.

—— (1915), *Opera omnia hactenus inedita Rogeri Baconi*, ed. Robert Steele, vol. 5, Oxford: Clarendon Press.

Bain, Alexander (1855), *The Senses and the Intellect*, London: J. W. Parker & Son.

Baker, Herschel (1947), *The Dignity of Man: Studies in the Persistence of an Idea*, Cambridge, Mass.: Harvard University Press.

Barker, Andrew (1984), *Greek Musical Writings*, vol. 1: *The Musician and his Art*, Cambridge: Cambridge University Press.

Barrough, Philip (1596), *The Method of Phisick*, 3rd edn, corrected and augmented, London: Richard Field.

—— (1624), *The Method of Physick, Containing the Causes, Signes, and Cures of Inward Diseases in Mans Body*, London: Richard Field.

Barry, Kevin (1987), *Language, Music and the Sign: A Study in Aesthetics, Poetics and Poetic Practice from Collins to Coleridge*, Cambridge: Cambridge University Press.

Barthes, Roland (1977), *Image Music Text*, London: Flamingo.

Bateson, Gregory (1958), *Naven*, Stanford University Press: Stanford.

—— (1972), *Steps to an Ecology of Mind*, New York: Ballantine Books.

Battersby, Christine (1989), *Gender and Genius: Towards a Feminist Aesthetics*, London: The Women's Press.

Beaudet, Jean Michel, and Martinez, Rosalia (1994), 'Music and Water in Indigenous America', paper presented at the 48th International Congress of Americanists, symposium on 'Music in Native Latin America and the Caribbean: Comparative Perspectives', Stockholm/Uppsala (4–9 July 1994).

Beeston, Nora Sigerist (1997), 'My Father, H. E. S.: A Photo Essay', in Fee and Brown (1997), 93–120.

Beier, Lucinda McCray (1987), *Sufferers and Healers: The Experience of Illness in Seventeeth-Century England*, London and New York: Routledge & Kegan Paul.

Beresford, David S. (1997), 'Africans Rely on Team Spirits', *The Guardian*, Saturday, 16 August.

Berliner, Paul (1981), *The Soul of Mbira*, Berkeley, Los Angeles, London: University of California Press.

Bernhard, Marianne (ed.) (1983), *Hermes Handlexikon. Das Biedermeier. Kultur zwischen Wiener Kongre* und Märzrevolution*, Düsseldorf: Econ Taschenbuch Verlag.

Besmer, Fremont E. (1983), *Horses, Musicians, and Gods: The Hausa Cult of Possession-Trance*, Boston: Bergin & Garvey.

Bett, W. R. (1938), 'John Hopkins' Graduate Week in Medical History', *Medical Life*, 45: 151–60.

Binsbergen, Wim van (1981), *Religious Change in Zambia: Exploratory Studies*, London and Boston: Kegan Paul International.

al-Bīrūnī (1934), *The Book of Instruction in the Elements of the Art of Astrology [Tafhīm]*, trans. and ed. R. Ramsay Wright, London: Lukacz.

Bishenden, Charles James (1869), *The Voice and How to Use It*. London: H. White & Son.

Blacking, John (1973), *How Musical is Man?*, Seattle: University of Washington Press.

—— (1985), 'Movement, Dance, Music, and the Venda Girls' Initiation Cycle', in Paul Spencer (ed.), *Society and the Dance*, 64–91, Cambridge: Cambridge University Press.

Bloom, Allan (1968), *The Republic of Plato. Translated, with Notes and an Interpretive Essay*, New York and London: Basic Books.

Boas, George (1969), *Vox Populi: Essays in the History of an Idea*, Baltimore: Johns Hopkins University Press.

Boddy, Janice (1994), 'Spirit Possession Revisited: Beyond Instrumentality', *Annual Reviews of Anthropology*, 23: 407–34.

Boethius, A. M. S. (1989), *Fundamentals of Music*, trans. Calvin M. Bower, ed. Claude V. Palisca, New Haven and London: Yale University Press.

Bourguignon, Erika (1968), 'World Distribution and Patterns of Possession States', in Raymond Prince (ed.), *Trance and Possession States*, Montreal: R. M. Burke Memorial Society.

—— (1973), *Religion, Altered States of Consciousness, and Social Change*, Columbus: Ohio State University Press.

Brandt, Friedrich (1903), *Illenau in den sechs ersten Jahrzehnten seiner Wirksamkeit*, Karlsruhe: Buchdruckerei Fidelitas.

Bright, Ruth (1993), 'Cultural Aspects of Music in Therapy', in Margaret Heal and Tony Wigram (eds), *Music Therapy in Health and Education*, 193–207, London and Philadelphia: Jessica Kingsley Publishers.

*Bright, Timothy (1586), *A Treatise of Melancholy*, London: Thomas Vautrollier.

Bristowe, John Syer (1880), *The Physiological and Pathological Relations of the Voice and Speech. Being the Lumleian Lectures 1879*, London: David Bogue.

Brocklesby, Richard (1749), *Reflections on Antient and Modern Musick, with the Application to the Cure of Diseases*, London: Cooper.

Brown, Norman O. (1990), *Love's Body*, New York: Random House, 1966; repr. Berkeley and Los Angeles: University of California Press, 1990.

*Browne, Richard (1729), *Medicina Musica*, London.

Budd, Malcolm (1985), *Music and the Emotions: The Philosophical Theories*, London: Routledge & Kegan Paul.

Bunt, Leslie (1994), *Music Therapy: An Art Beyond Words*, London: Routledge.

*Bürgel, J. Christoph (1988), *The Feather of Simurgh*, New York: New York University Press.

Burke, Timothy (1996), *Lifebuoy Men, Lux Women: Commodification, Consumption, and Cleanliness in Modern Zimbabwe*, London: Leicester University Press.

*Burnett, Charles (1993), 'European Knowledge of Arabic Texts Referring to Music: Some New Material', *Early Music History*, 12: 1–17.

—— (1996), 'Talismans: Magic as Science? Necromancy among the Seven Liberal Arts', in *idem*, *Magic and Divination in the Middle Ages*, Aldershot: Variorum.

—— Fend, Michael, and Gouk, Penelope (eds) (1991), *The Second Sense: Studies in Hearing and Musical Judgement from Antiquity to the Seventeenth Century*, London: The Warburg Institute.

*Burton, Robert (1632), *The Anatomy of Melancholy*, 4th edn, corrected and augmented. Oxford: Henry Cripps.

Button, Graham (ed.) (1991), *Ethnomethodology and the Human Sciences*, Cambridge: Cambridge University Press.

Bynum, W. F., and Porter, Roy (eds) (1993), *Medicine and the Five Senses*, Cambridge: Cambridge University Press.

Callahan, Bryan, and Schumaker, Lynette (1997), 'Magic, Healing and Killing: Western and African Healing Idioms in the *Muchape* Movement, Colonial VD Campaigns, and the *Kalela* Dance', paper delivered at Conference on Magic and Modernity, Research Centre Religion and Society, University of Amsterdam, 23–25 June 1997.

Campbell, Carol (1983), '"Nyimbo za Kiswahili": A Socioethnomusicological Study of a Swahili Poetic Form', PhD, University of Washington, University Microfilms.

Capra, Fritjof (1996), *The Web of Life: A New Synthesis of Mind and Matter*, London: Harper Collins.

Carapetyan, Armen (1948), 'Music and Medicine in the Renaissance and in the 17th and 18th Centuries', in *MM*, 117–57.

Casey, Edward S. (1993), *Getting Back into Place: Toward a Renewed Understanding of the Place-World*, Bloomington: Indiana University Press.

Castro-Klarén, Sara (1993), 'Dancing and the Sacred in the Andes: From the Taqui-Oncoy to Rasu-Ñiti', in Stephen Greenblatt (ed.), *New World Encounters*, 159–76. Berkeley, Los Angeles, Oxford: University of California Press.

Cataldi, Sue L. (1993), *Emotion, Depth and Flesh: A Study of Sensitive Space*, Albany: State University of New York Press.

Chernoff, John Miller (1979), *African Rhythm and African Sensibility*, Chicago: University of Chicago Press.

Chodorow, Joan (1991), *Dance Therapy and Depth Psychology: The Moving Imagination*, London and New York: Routledge.

Classen, Constance (1993a), *Inca Cosmology and the Human Body*, Salt Lake City: University of Utah Press.

—— (1993b), *Worlds of Sense: Exploring the Senses in History and across Cultures*, London: Routledge.

Cocteau, Jean (1930), *La Voix humaine*, Paris: Stock.

Comaroff, Jean (1985), *Body of Power, Spirit of Resistance: The Culture and History of a South African People*, Chicago and London: University of Chicago Press.

Cook, Harold (1990), 'The New Philosophy and Medicine', in David C. Lindberg and Robert S. Westman (eds), *Reappraisals of the Scientific Revolution*, 398–43, Cambridge: Cambridge University Press.

Cooper, Frederick (1992), 'Colonizing Time: Work Rhythms and Labor Conflict in Colonial Mombasa', in Nicholas Dirks (ed.), *Colonialism and Culture*, 209–46, Ann Arbor: University of Michigan Press.

*Couliano, Ioan P. (1987), *Eros and Magic in the Renaissance*, trans. Margaret Cook, Chicago and London: University of Chicago Press.

Crapanzano, Vincent, and Garrison, V. (eds) (1977), *Case Studies in Spirit Possession*, New York: Wiley.

Critchley, Macdonald, and Henson, R. A. (eds) (1997), *Music and the Brain: Studies in the Neurology of Music*, London: William Heinemann Medical Books Ltd.

Cusick, Suzanne G. (1994), '"There was not One Lady who Failed to Shed a Tear": Arianna's Lament and the Construction of Modern Womanhood', *Early Music*, 22: 21–46.

Dart, Thurston (1961), Historical Introduction to Robert Hole, *Parthenia In-Violata*, facs. edn, with foreword by Sidney Beck, New York: New York Public Library.

Davis, W. B., Gfeller, K. E., and Thaut, M. H. (1992), *An Introduction to Music Therapy*, Dubuque, Iowa: Wm. C. Brown.

de Craemer, Willy, Vansina, Jan, and Fox, Renee C. (1976), 'Religious Movements in Central Africa: A Theoretical Study', *Comparative Studies in Society and History*, 18: 458–75.

Devisch, Rene (1993), *Weaving the Threads of Life: The Khita Gyn-Eco-Logical Healing Cult Among the Yaka*, Chicago and London: University of Chicago Press.

Dilthey, Wilhelm (1985), *Poetry and Experience*, ed. Rudolf A. Makkreel and Frithjof Rodi, in *Selected Works*, vol. 5, Princeton: Princeton University Press.

Dissertation Abstracts (1999), Ann Arbor, Mich.: University Microfilms.

Dols, Michael (1992), *Majnūn: The Madman in Medieval Islamic Society*, Oxford: Clarendon Press, 1992.

Douglas, Mary (1963), 'Techniques of Sorcery Control in Central Africa', in John Middleton and E. H. Winter (eds), *Witchcraft and Sorcery in East Africa*, 123–42. London: Routledge & Kegan Paul.

—— (1966/1994), *Purity and Danger: An Analysis of the Concepts of Pollution and Taboo*, London: Routledge.

—— (1970), *Natural Symbols: Explorations in Cosmology*, New York: Pantheon.

Dowland, John (1603/1977), *The Third and Last Booke of Songs or Aires (1603)*, Facs., ed. Diana Poulton, Menston: Scolar Press.

—— (1603/1970), *Third Booke of Songes (1603)*, ed. Edmund H. Fellowes, rev. Thurston Dart, London: Stainer & Bell.

Dreyfus, Lawrence (1983), 'Early Music Defended against its Devotees: A Theory of Historical Performance in the Twentieth Century', *The Musical Quarterly*, 69 (3): 297–322.

Edwards, David (1993), 'Why Don't Arts Therapists Do Research?', in Helen Payne (ed.), *Handbook of Enquiry in the Arts Therapies: One River, Many Currents*, 5–15, London and Philadelphia: Jessica Kingsley Publishers.

Eliade, Mircea (1964), *Shamanism: Archaic Techniques of Ecstasy*, trans. Willard R. Trask, Princeton: Princeton University Press.

Ellingson, Ter (1987), 'Music and Religion', in *The Encyclopedia of Religion*, ed. Mircea Eliade, vol. 10, pp. 163–72, New York: Macmillan Publishing Co.

Ent, George (1809), 'To Make a Probable Conjecture of Tempers and Dispositions by the Modulations of the Voice in Ordinary Discourse',

Philosophical Transactions Abridged, vol. 2 (1672–83), London: Baldwin, 441–2; originally in vol. 12 (1678), no. 140, p. 1010.

Enterline, Lynn (1995), *The Tears of Narcissus: Melancholia and Masculinity in Early Modern Writing*, Stanford: Stanford University Press.

Evans-Pritchard, E. E. (1937), *Witchcraft, Oracles and Magic Among the Azande*, Oxford: Clarendon Press.

Exiner, Johanna, and Kelynack, Denis (1994), *Dance Therapy Redefined: A Body Approach to Therapeutic Dance*, Springfield, Ill.: Charles C. Thomas.

Farmer, Henry George (1926), *The Influence of Music: From Arabic Sources. A Lecture Delivered before the Musical Association, London, 27th April, 1926*. London.

Fee, Elizabeth, and Brown, Theodore M. (eds) (1997), *Making Medical History: The Life and Times of Henry E. Sigerist*, Baltimore and London: Johns Hopkins University Press.

Feierman, Steven (1990), *Peasant Intellectuals: Anthropology and History in Tanzania*, Madison, Wis. and London: University of Wisconsin Press.

*Ferrand, Jacques [James] (1640), *Erotomania or a Treatise Discoursing of the Essence, Causes, Symptomes, Prognosticks, and Cure of Love, or Erotique Melancholy*, Oxford: L. Lichfield for Edward Forrest.

*Ficino, Marsilio (1989), *Three Books on Life*, ed. and trans. Carol V. Kaske and John R. Clark, Binghamton: Medieval and Renaissance Texts and Studies.

Finney, Gretchen L. (1947a), 'Ecstasy and Music in Seventeenth-Century England', *Journal of the History of Ideas*, 8: 153–86.

—— (1947b), '"Organical Music" and Ecstasy', *Journal of the History of Ideas*, 8: 273–92.

—— (1962), *Musical Backgrounds for English Literature, 1580–1650*, New Brunswick: Rutgers University Press.

Fischlin, Daniel T. (1987–8), '"The highest key of passion": Inexpressibility and the Self in John Dowland's *First Booke of Songes or Ayres*', *Journal of the Lute Society of America*, 20–21 (1): 46–86.

Fontanus, Nicholas (1652), *The Womans Doctour*, London: John Blague and Samuel Howes.

Forman, Edward (1984), '"Musick hath charms" ... Music and Healing in Seventeenth-Century France', *17th Century French Studies*, 6: 81–91.

*Foucault, Michel (1967), *Madness and Civilization: A History of Insanity in the Age of Reason*, trans. Richard Howard, London, Sydney and Wellington: Tavistock Publications.

Fraenkel, Peter (1959), *Wayaleshi*, London: Weidenfeld and Nicolson.

Freud, Sigmund (1914/1959), 'On Narcissism: An Introduction', in *Papers on Metapsychology*, in *Collected Papers*, vol. 4, authorized translation under the supervision of Joan Riviere, 30–59, New York: Basic Books.

*—— (1917/1959), 'Mourning and Melancholia', in *Papers on Metapsychology*, in *Collected Papers*, vol. 4, authorized translation under the supervision of Joan Riviere, 152–72. New York: Basic Books.

*Friedson, Steven M. (1996), *Dancing Prophets: Musical Experience in Tumbuka Healing*, Chicago and London: University of Chicago Press.

Garrison, Fielding H., 'Medical Men who have Loved Music', in *MM*, 190–217.

Geismeier, Willi (1982), *Biedermeier*, Wiesbaden: Ebeling.

Gersh, Stephen (1996), *Concord in Discourse: Harmonics and Semiotics in Late Classical and Early Medieval Platonism*, Berlin and New York: Mouton de Gruyter.

Geschiere, Peter (1983), *Village Communities and the State*, London: Kegan Paul International.

Giese, Claudius Cristóbal (1996), 'El canto como canal o vía comunicativa entre los mundos: los cantos mágicos de los curanderos del norte del Perú (costa)', in Max Peter Baumann (ed.), *Cosmología y música en los Andes*, 437–49, Frankfurt and Madrid: Vervuert/ Iberoamericana.

Godwin, Joscelyn (1979), *Athanasius Kircher: A Renaissance Man and the Quest for Lost Knowledge*, London: Thames & Hudson.

Gose, Peter (1986), 'Sacrifice and the Commodity Form in the Andes', *Man*, 21, 296–310.

Gouk, Penelope (1991), 'Some English Theories of Hearing in the Seventeenth Century: Before and after Descartes', in Burnett, Fend and Gouk (1991), 95–113.

—— (1996), 'Performance Practice: Music, Medicine and Natural Philosophy in Interregnum Oxford', *British Journal for the History of Science*, 29: 257–88.

—— (1999), *Music, Science and Natural Magic in Seventeenth-Century England*, New Haven and London: Yale University Press.

—— (2000), 'Music, Melancholy and Medical Spirits in Early Modern Thought', in Horden (2000).

Grafton, Anthony (1988), 'Civic Humanism and Scientific Scholarship at Leiden' in Thomas Bender (ed.), *The University and the City: From Medieval Origins to the Present*, 59–78, New York and Oxford: Oxford University Press.

Gray, John (1991), *African Music: A Bibliographical Guide to the Traditional, Popular, Art, and Liturgical Musics of Sub-Saharan*

Africa, African Special Bibliography Series, No. 14, New York, Westport and London: Greenwood Press.

Green, Monica (1994), 'The Re-creation of *Pantegni*, *Practica*, Book VIII', in C. Burnett and D. Jacquart (eds), *Constantine the African and ʿAlī ibn al-ʿAbbās al-Mağūsī*, 121–60, Leiden: E. J. Brill.

Grimm, Jacob and Wilhelm (eds) (1897), *Deutsches Wörterbuch*, Leipzig: Hirzel.

Grosse, Angela (1997), 'Medizin in höchsten Tönen', *Hamburger Abendblatt*, Wed. 21 May.

Guthrie, Malcolm (1967–71), *Comparative Bantu*, 4 vols, Farnborough: Gregg.

Hammond-Tooke, W. D. (ed.) (1974), *The Bantu-Speaking Peoples of Southern Africa*, 2nd edn, London: Routledge and Kegan Paul.

Hankins, Thomas L., and Silverman, Robert J. (1995), *Instruments and the Imagination*, Princeton: Princeton University Press.

Hanson, Howard (1948), 'Emotional Expression in Music', in *MM*, 244–65.

Harrington, Anne (ed.) (1992), *So Human a Brain: Knowledge and Value in the Neurosciences*, Basel and Boston: Birkhaüser.

Harris, Olivia (1984), 'The Dead and Devils among the Bolivian Laymi', in M. Bloch and J. Parry (eds), *Death and the Regeneration of Life*, 45–73, Cambridge: Cambridge University Press.

—— (1986), 'From Asymmetry to Triangle: Symbolic Transformations in Northern Potosí', in J. Murra, N. Wachtel, J. Revel (eds), *Anthropological History of Andean Polities*, 260–79, Cambridge: Cambridge University Press.

Harrison, Regina (1989), *Signs, Songs and Memory in the Andes: Translating Quechua Language and Culture*, Austin: University of Texas Press.

Hatfield, Gary (1993), 'Helmholtz and Classicism: The Science of Aesthetics and the Aesthetics of Science', in David Cahan (ed.), *Hermann von Helmholtz and the Foundations of Nineteenth-Century Science*, 522–58, Berkeley: University of California Press.

Hayman, Ronald (1990), *Proust: A Biography*, London: Heinemann.

Heal, Margaret, and Wigram, Tony (eds) (1993), *Music Therapy in Health and Education*, London and Philadelphia: Jessica Kingsley Publishers.

Heald, Suzette (1995), 'The Power of Sex: Some Reflections on the Caldwells' "African Sexuality" Thesis', *Africa*, 65 (4): 489–505.

Heffernan, Carol Falvo (1995), *The Melancholy Muse: Chaucer, Shakespeare and Early Medicine*, Pittsburgh: Duquesne University Press.

Heidegger, Martin (1962), *Being and Time*, trans. John Macquarrie and Edward Robinson, New York: Harper & Row.

—— (1995), *The Fundamental Concepts of Metaphysics: World, Finitude, Solitude*, trans. William McNeill and Nicholas Walker, Bloomington: Indiana University Press.

Henry, John (1991), 'Doctors and Healers: Popular Culture and the Medical Profession' in Stephen Pumfrey, Paolo Rossi and Maurice Slawinski (eds), *Science, Culture and Popular Belief in Renaissance Europe*, 191–221, Manchester: Manchester University Press.

—— (1997), *The Scientific Revolution and the Origins of Modern Science*, Houndsmills and London: Macmillan Press Ltd.

Hermann of Carinthia (1982), *De essentiis*, ed. Charles Burnett, Leiden: E. J. Brill, 1982.

Hillman, David, and Mazzio, Carla (eds) (1997), *The Body in Parts*, London: Routledge.

Holmes, Gordon (1879), *A Treatise on Vocal Physiology and Hygiene, with Especial Reference to the Cultivation and Preservation of the Voice*, 2nd edn, London: J. & A. Churchill.

Horden, Peregrine (1993), 'Responses to Possession and Insanity in the Earlier Byzantine World', *Social History of Medicine*, 6: 177–94.

—— (ed.) (2000), *Music as Medicine: The History of Music Therapy since Antiquity*, Guildford: Ashgate.

Howell, Standley (1990), 'Medical Astrologers and the Invention of Stringed Keyboard Instruments', *The Journal of Musicological Research*, 10: 1–17.

Huanca, Tomás (1989), *El Yatiri en la communidad aymara*, La Paz: Ediciones CADA (Centro Andino de Desarollo Agropecuario).

Hulme, F. Edward (1909), *The History, Principles and Practice of Symbolism in Christian Art*, London: Swan Sonnenchien.

Ibn al-Jazzār, *Viaticum*; see Wack (1990).

Ijzermans, Jan J. (1995), 'Music and Theory of the Possession Cult Leaders in Chibale, Serenje district, Zambia', *Ethnomusicology*, 39 (2): 245–75.

Iliffe, John (1979), *A Modern History of Tanganyika*, Cambridge: Cambridge University Press.

Isḥāq ibn ʿImrān (1977), *Maqālah fī l-malīhūlīya (Abhandlung über die Melancholie) und Constantini Africani Libri duo de Melancholia*, ed. Karl Garbers, Hamburg: H. Buske.

*Jackson, Stanley W. (1986), *Melancholia and Depression from Hippocratic Times to Modern Times*, New Haven and London: Yale University Press.

Jacquart, Danielle, and Thomasset, Claude (1988), *Sexuality and Medicine in the Middle Ages*, trans. Matthew Adamson, Princeton: Princeton University Press.

Jahn, Friedrich Ludwig, and Eiselen, Ernst (eds) (1816), *Die Deutsche Turnkunst*, Berlin: Wilhelm Limpert Verlag.

James, William (1936/1994), *The Varieties of Religious Experience*, New York: The Modern Library.

Janzen, John M. (1982), *Lemba, 1650–1930: A Drum of Affliction in Africa and the New World*, New York and London: Garland Publishing, Inc.

*—— (1992), *Ngoma: Discourses of Healing in Central and Southern Africa*, Berkeley, Los Angeles, Oxford: University of California Press.

—— (1995), 'Self-presentation and Common Cultural Structures in Ngoma Rituals of Southern Africa', *Journal of Religion in Africa*, 25 (2): 141–62.

Joralemon, Donald, and Sharon, Douglas (1993), *Sorcery and Shamanism: Curanderos and Clients in Northern Peru*, Salt Lake City: University of Utah Press.

Kahane, Claire (1995), *Passions of the Voice: Hysteria, Narrative, and the Figure of the Speaking Woman, 1850–1915*, Baltimore: Johns Hopkins University Press.

Kassler, Jamie Croy (1984), 'Man – a Musical Instrument: Models of the Brain and Mental Functioning before the Computer', *History of Science*, 22: 59–92.

—— (1995), *Inner Music: Hobbes, Hooke and North on Internal Character*, London: Athlone Press.

Katz, Richard (1982), *Boiling Energy: Community Healing Among the Kalahari Kung*, Cambridge: Harvard University Press.

Keeling, Richard (1992), *Cry for Luck: Sacred Song and Speech among the Yurok, Hupa, and Karok Indians of Northwestern California*, Berkeley, Los Angeles, Oxford: University of California Press.

Keil, Charles (1979), *Tiv Song: The Sociology of Art in a Classless Society*, Chicago: University of Chicago Press.

Kern, Stephen (1992), *The Culture of Love, Victorians to Moderns*, Cambridge, Mass. and London: Harvard University Press.

Kessler, Eckhard (1995), 'On Achievement: A Philosophical Approach', in Penelope Gouk (ed.), *Wellsprings of Achievement: Cultural and Economic Dynamics in Early Modern England and Japan*, 77–93, London: Variorum.

*Kleinman, Arthur (1980), *Patients and Healers in the Context of Culture: An Exploration of the Borderland between Anthropology, Medicine, and Psychiatry*, Berkeley: University of California Press.

Klibansky, Raymond, Panofsky, Erwin, and Saxl, Fritz (1964), *Saturn and Melancholy: Studies in the History of Natural Philosophy, Religion and Art*, London: Thomas Nelson and Sons, Ltd.

Kramer, Cheryce (1998), 'A Fool's Paradise: The Psychiatry of *Gemüth* in a Biedermeier Asylum', PhD, University of Chicago.

—— (2000), 'Walls of Sound and Walls of Stone in a Nineteenth-Century Asylum', in Horden (2000).

Kriger, Norma (1992), *Zimbabwe's Guerrilla War: Peasant Voices*, Cambridge: Cambridge University Press.

*Kristeva, Julia (1989), *Black Sun: Depression and Melancholia*, trans. Leon S. Roudiez, New York: Columbia University Press.

*Kümmel, Werner Friedrich (1977), *Musik und Medizin: Ihre Wechselbeziehungen in Theorie und Praxis von 800 bis 1800*, Freiburg and Munich: Karl Alber.

Lan, David (1985), *Guns and Rain: Guerrillas and Spirit Mediums in Zimbabwe*, Berkeley and Los Angeles: University of California Press.

Landauer, Carl (1994), 'Erwin Panofsky and the Renascence of the Renaissance', *Renaissance Quarterly*, 47: 255–81.

Langer, Susanne (1982), *Mind: An Essay on Human Feeling*, Baltimore: Johns Hopkins Press.

Leach, Edmund (1966), 'Ritualization in Man in Relation to Conceptual and Social Development', *Philosophical Transactions of the Royal Society of London*, 241, Ser. B, 772: 403–8.

—— (1976), *Culture and Communication: The Logic by which Symbols are Connected*, Cambridge: Cambridge University Press.

*Lepenies, Wolf (1992), *Melancholy and Society*, trans. Jeremy Gaines and Doris Jones, Cambridge, Mass. and London: Harvard University Press.

Lewis, I. M. (1971), *Ecstatic Religion: An Anthropological Study of Spirit Possession and Shamanism*, Baltimore: Penguin Books.

Lex, Barbara W. (1979), 'The Neurobiology of Ritual Trance', in E. d'Aquili et al. (eds), *The Spectrum of Ritual: A Biogenetic Structural Analysis*, 117–51, New York: Columbia University Press.

Lloyd, Geoffrey E. R. (ed.) (1983), *Hippocratic Writings*, Harmondsworth: Penguin Classics.

Löschke, J. (1849), *Über das Turnen Geisteskranker im Allgemeinen*, Pirna: Keller und Sohn.

*Lowes, John Livingston (1913–14), 'The loveres maladye of heroes', *Modern Philology*, 11: 491–546.

Luig, Ute (1998), 'The Bacape Movement: Negotiating Local Identity and Transregional Practices', unpublished MS.

*McClary, Susan (1991a), 'Excess and Frame: The Musical Representations of Madwomen', in *eadem*, *Feminine Endings: Music, Gender, and Sexuality*, 80–111, Minneapolis: University of Minnesota Press.

*—— (1991b), 'Sexual Politics in Classical Music', in *eadem*, *Feminine*

Endings: Music, Gender, and Sexuality, 53–79, Minneapolis: University of Minnesota Press.

*MacDonald, Michael (1981), *Mystical Bedlam: Madness, Anxiety, and Healing in Seventeenth-Century England*, Cambridge and New York: Cambridge University Press.

Mafeje, Archie (1967), 'The Role of the Bard in a Contemporary African Community', *Journal of African Languages*, 6 (3): 193–223.

Magubane, Bernard (1971), 'A Critical Look at Indices Used in the Study of Social Change in Colonial Africa', *Current Anthropology*, 12: 4–5.

Maranto, Chery Dileo (1993), 'Applications of Music in Medicine', in Margaret Heal and Tony Wigram (eds), *Music Therapy in Health and Education*, 153–74, London and Philadelphia: Jessica Kingsley Publishers.

Marmelszadt, Willard (1946), *Musical Sons of Aesculapius*, New York: Froben Press.

Marwick, Max G. (1950), 'Another Modern Anti-Witchcraft Movement in East-Central Africa', *Africa*, 20 (1): 100–12.

Matongo, Albert B. K. (1992), 'Popular Culture in a Colonial Society: Another Look at Mbeni and Kalela Dances on the Copperbelt, 1930–1964', in Samuel N. Chipungu (ed.), *Guardians in their Time*, 180–217, London: Macmillan.

Maxwell, David (1995), 'Witches, Prophets and Avenging Spirits: The Second Christian Movement in North-east Zimbabwe', *Journal of Religion in Africa*, 25 (3): 309–39.

—— (1997), 'Sacred Lives: Secret Lives – the Biography of Emmanuel Guti, Founder of the Zimbabwe Assemblies of God', paper for the Britain Zimbabwe Research Day, 7–8 June 1997, St Antony's College, Oxford.

Meineke, Bruno (1948), 'Music and Medicine in Classical Antiquity', in *MM*, 47–87.

Merleau-Ponty, Maurice (1968), *The Visible and the Invisible*, trans. Alphonso Lingis, ed. Claude Lefort, Evanston: Northwestern University Press.

Mistiaen, Veronique (1999), 'Bizet Does It', *The Guardian*, Tuesday, 2 March.

*Mitchell, J. Clyde (1956), *The Kalela Dance*, Rhodes–Livingstone Papers, 27, Manchester: Manchester University Press.

Mollet, L'Abbé (1752), *Lectures in Experimental Philosophy*, London: Printed for J. Wren.

Monteverdi, Claudio (1929), *Tutti le opere*, vol. 8, ed. G. Francesco Malipiero, Asolo.

Moore, Stan (1998), 'Urban Uganga in Dar es Salaam', PhD, University of Kansas; Ann Arbor: University Microfilms.

Morgan, Robert P. (1988), 'Tradition, Anxiety, and the Current Musical Scene', in Nicholas Kenyon (ed.), *Authenticity in Early Music: A Symposium*, Oxford and New York: Oxford University Press.

Needham, Rodney (1967), 'Percussion and Transition', *Man*, 2: 606–14.

Neher, A. (1962), 'A Physiological Explanation of Unusual Behavior in Ceremonies Involving Drums', *Human Biology*, 34 (2): 151–60.

*Neubauer, Eckhard (1990), 'Arabische Anleitungen zur Musiktherapie', *Zeitschrift für Geschichte der arabisch-islamischen Wissenschaften*, 6, 227–72.

Nietzsche, Friedrich (1965 [1870–71]), 'The Birth of Tragedy', in Robert W. Corrigan (ed.), *Tragedy, Vision and Form*, 443–50, Chandler Publishing, Chicago.

Nutton, Vivian (1993), 'Greek Science in the Sixteenth-Century Renaissance', in J. V. Field and Frank A. L. James (eds), *Renaissance and Reformation: Humanists, Scholars, Craftsmen and Natural Philosophers in Early Modern Europe*, 15–28, Cambridge: Cambridge University Press.

*O'Brien, Lucy (1995), *She Bop: The Definitive History of Women in Rock, Pop and Soul*, London: Penguin Books.

Oesterreich, T. K. (1966), *Possession: Demonical and Other among Primitive Races, in Antiquity, the Middle Ages, and Modern Times*, trans. D. Ibberson, New York: R. R. Smith.

Ondaatje, Michael (1993), *The English Patient*, New York: Vintage.

Ong, Walter J. (1982), *Orality and Literacy*, London: Methuen.

Ostow, Mortimer (1970), *The Psychology of Melancholy*, New York: Harper & Row.

Otis, Laura (1994), *Organic Memory: History and the Body in the Late Nineteenth and Early Twentieth Centuries*, Lincoln, Nebr. and London: University of Nebraska Press.

Parkin, D. J. (1968), 'Medicines and Men of Influence', *Man*, 3 (3): 424–39.

Pavlicevic, Mercedes (1998), *Music Therapy in Context: Music, Meaning and Relationship*, London and Chicago: Jessica Kingsley Publishers.

Payne, Helen (1993), *Handbook of Enquiry in the Arts Therapies: One River, Many Currents*, London and Philadelphia: Jessica Kingsley Publishers.

Pels, Peter (1996), '*Kizungu* Rhythms: Luguru Chrisitanity as *Ngoma*', *Journal of Religion in Africa*, 26: 163–201.

Peters, Larry G., and Price-Williams, Douglass (1983), 'Overview: A

Phenomenological Overview of Trance', *Transcultural Psychiatric Research Review*, 20: 5–39.
*[Playford, Henry] (1699), *Wit and Mirth: or, Pills to Purge Melancholy*, London: Will[iam] Pearson for Henry Playford.
Pool, Robert, (1994), 'On the Creation and Dissolution of Ethnomedical Systems in the Medical Ethnography of Africa', *Africa*, 64 (1): 1–17.
Porter, Roy (1997), *The Greatest Benefit to Mankind: A Medical History of Humanity*, London: HarperCollins.
**The Praise of Musick* (1586), Oxford: Joseph Barnes.
Priestley, Mary, *Essays on Analytical Music Therapy*, Phoenixville, Pa.: Barcelona Publishers, 1994.
Radin, Paul (1948), 'Music and Medicine in Primitive Cultures', in *MM*, 3–24.
*Ranger, Terence (1975), *Dance and Society in Eastern Africa, 1890–1970: The Beni Ngoma*, London: Heinemann.
—— (1982), '*Mchape*: A Study in Diffusion and Interpretation', unpublished MS.
*Ravenscroft, Thomas (1614), *A Briefe Discourse of the true (but neglected) use of Charact'ring the Degrees*, London: Edw[ard] Allde for Tho[mas] Adams.
*al-Rāzī (1950), *The Spiritual Physick of Rhazes*, trans. A. J. Arberry, London: Murray.
Reynolds, Simon, and Press, Joy (1995), *The Sex Revolts: Gender, Rebellion, and Rock'n'Roll*, Cambridge, Mass. and London: Harvard University Press.
Richards, Audrey (1935/1970), 'A Modern Movement of Witch-Finders', *Africa*, 40 (3), 448–61, rep. in Max G. Marwick (ed.), *Witchcraft and Sorcery*, 164–77, London: Penguin, 1970.
Roller, Christian Friedrich (1831), *Die Irrenanstalt nach allen ihren Beziehungen*, Karlsruhe: Christian Friedrich Müller Hofbuchhandlung.
—— (1832), *Illenau die Großherzogliche Badische Heil- und Pflegeanstalt*, Karlsruhe: Christian Friedrich Müller Hofbuchhandlung.
Rooley, Anthony (1983), 'New Light on John Dowland's Songs of Darkness', *Early Music*, 11: 6–21.
Rosand, Ellen (1979), 'The Descending Tetrachord: An Emblem of Lament', *The Musical Quarterly*, 65: 346–59.
—— (1986), 'The Voice of Barbara Strozzi', in Jane Bowers and Judith Tick (eds), *Women Making Music: The Western Art Tradition 1150–1950*, 346–59, Urbana and Chicago: University of Illinois Press.
*Roseman, Marina (1991), *Healing Sounds from the Malaysian Rainforest: Temiar Music and Medicine*, Berkeley, Los Angeles, Oxford: University of California Press.

Rosen, Charles (1995), *The Romantic Generation*, London: HarperCollins.

*Rouget, Gilbert (1985), *Music and Trance: A Theory of the Relations between Music and Possession*, trans. Brunhilde Biebuyck, Chicago: University of Chicago Press.

Ruskin, John (1885–1900), *Praeterita: Outline of Scenes and Thoughts perhaps Worthy of Memory in my Past Life*, 3 vols, Orpington: G. Allen.

Sadie, Stanley (ed.) (1980), *The New Grove Dictionary of Music and Musicians*, 20 vols, London: Macmillan.

*Schiesari, Juliana (1992), *The Gendering of Melancholia: Feminism, Psychoanalysis and the Symbolics of Loss in Renaissance Literature*, Ithaca and London: Cornell University Press.

Schleiner, Winfried (1991), *Melancholy, Genius and Utopia in the Renaissance*, Wiesbaden: Otto Harassowitz.

Schopenhauer, Arthur (1974), *Parerga and Paralipomena: Short Philosophical Essays*, trans. E. F. J. Payne, 2 vols, Oxford: Clarendon Press.

Schumaker, Lynette (1994), 'The Lion in the Path', PhD, University of Pennsylvania.

—— (1997), 'A Plague of Cats', unpublished paper delivered at Keele University, 3 June.

—— (1998), 'The Clean and the Smart: Explorations towards a History of Hygiene in Africa', unpublished paper for the 14th Satterthwaite Colloquium on African Religion and Ritual, 19–22 April.

Schutz, Alfred (1951), 'Making Music Together: A Study in Social Relationship', *Social Research*, 18 (1): 76–97.

Schwartz, David (1997), *Listening Subjects: Music, Psychoanalysis, Culture*, Durham, NC and London: Duke University Press.

Sengle, Friedrich (1970), *Biedermeierzeit: Deutsche Literatur im Spanungsfeld zwischen Restauration und Revolution 1815–1848*, 2 vols, Stuttgart: J. B. Metzler.

*Shepherd, John (1977/1980), 'The Musical Coding of Ideologies', in John Shepherd et al. (eds), *Whose Music? A Sociology of Musical Languages*, 179–200, London: Latimer; repr. New Brunswick and London: Transaction Books.

*—— (1991), *Music as Social Text*, Cambridge: Polity Press.

Shiloah, Amnon (1964, 1966), 'L'Epitre sur la musique d'Ikhwān al-Ṣafā', *Revue des études islamiques*, 32: 125–62 and 34: 159–93.

—— (1972), 'Ibn Hindū, le médicin et la musique', *Israel Oriental Studies*, 2: 447–62.

Sibum, Otto (1994), 'Working Experiment: Bodies, Machines and Heat

Values', in Richard Staley (ed.), *The Physics of Empire*, 29–56. Cambridge: Whipple Museum.
Sigerist, Henry (1943), *Civilization and Disease*, Ithaca: Cornell University Press.
—— (1948), 'The Story of Tarantism', in *MM*, 96–116.
Silverblatt, Irene (1988), 'Political Memories and Colonizing Symbols: Santiago and the Mountain Gods of Colonial Peru', in Jonathan Hill (ed.), *Rethinking History and Myth*, 174–94, Urbana and Chicago: University of Illinois Press.
Silverman, Kaja (1988), *The Acoustic Mirror: The Female Voice in Psychoanalysis and Cinema*, Bloomington: Indiana University Press.
Sinibaldi, Giovanni Battista (1657), *Rare Verities. The Cabinet of Venus Unlocked, And Her Secrets laid open*, London: P. Briggs.
Siraisi, Nancy (1973), *Arts and Sciences at Padua*, Toronto: Pontifical Institute of Mediaeval Studies.
—— (1975), 'The Music of the Pulse in the Writings of Italian Academic Physicians', *Speculum*, 50: 689–710.
Sloboda, John A. (1985), *The Musical Mind: The Cognitive Psychology of Music*, Oxford: Oxford University Press.
*Small, Christopher (1996), *Music, Society, Education*, foreword by Robert Walser, Hanover and London: Wesleyan University Press.
Stevenson, L. G. (1982), 'Twenty-five Years Ago: Henry E. Sigerist (1891–1957)', *Bulletin of the Institute of the History of Medicine*, 56: 569–70.
Stewart, Garrett (1990), *Reading Voices: Literature and the Phonotext*, Los Angeles: University of California Press.
Stobart, Henry (1996a), 'Tara and Q'iwa: Worlds of Sound and Meaning', in Max Peter Baumann (ed.), *Cosmología y música en los Andes*, 67–81, Frankfurt and Madrid: Vervuert/Iberoamericana.
—— (1996b), 'The Llama's Flute: Musical Misunderstandings in the Andes', *Early Music*, 24 (3): 471–82.
Stoller, Paul (1989), *Fusion of the Worlds: An Ethnography of Possession Among the Songhay of Niger*, Chicago: University of Chicago Press.
Storr, Anthony (1992), *Music and the Mind*, New York, Toronto, Oxford: The Free Press, Macmillan Inc.
Strozzi, Barbara (1986), *Cantatas*, selected and ed. Ellen Rosand, New York: Garland.
—— (1988), 'Glenda Simpson Sings Barbara Strozzi, with the Camerata of London' (1988), London: Hyperion Records Limited.
Sullivan, Blair (1977), 'The Polyphony of the Spheres', *Viator*, 28: 33–43.
Sullivan, Lawrence (1988), *Icanchu's Drum: An Orientation to Mean-*

ings in South American Religions, New York: Macmillan Publishing Company.

Taussig, Michael (1980), *The Devil and Commodity Fetishism in South America*, Chapel Hill: University of North Carolina Press.

—— (1987), *Shamanism, Colonialism and the Wild Man: A Study in Terror and Healing*, Chicago: University of Chicago Press.

Taylor, D. B. (1981), 'Music in General Hospital Treatment from 1900 to 1950', *Journal of Music Therapy*, 18: 62–73.

Taylor, Gerald (1976), 'Camay, Camac et Camasqa dans le manuscrit Quechua de Huarochiri', *Journal de la Société des Américanistes*, 63: 231–44.

Taylor, Jeremy (1654), *The Real Presence and Spirituall of Christ in the Blessed Sacrament proved, against the doctrine of Transubstantiation*, London: Richard Royston.

Thomas, Keith (1971/1980), *Religion and the Decline of Magic*, Harmondsworth: Penguin Books.

Tietsch, F. T. (1937), 'The Colonel Played the Piano', *Bulletin of the Institute of the History of Medicine*, 5 (the Fielding H. Garrison Memorial issue), 382–403.

Toft, Robert (1993), *Tune thy Musicke to thy Hart: The Art of Eloquent Singing in England 1597–1622*, Toronto and London: University of Toronto Press.

*Tomlinson, Gary (1993), *Music in Renaissance Magic: Toward a Historiography of Others*, Chicago and London: University of Chicago Press, 1993.

Turkle, Sherry (1995), *Life on the Screen: Identity in the Age of the Internet*, New York: Simon & Schuster.

Turner, Victor W. (1967), *The Forest of Symbols: Aspects of Ndembu Ritual*, Ithaca: Cornell University Press.

*—— (1968), *Drums of Affliction: A Study of Religious Processes among the Ndembu of Zambia*, Oxford: Clarendon Press.

—— (1974), *Dramas, Fields, and Metaphors: Symbolic Action in Human Society*, Ithaca and London: Cornell University Press.

Updike, John (1997), 'Car Talk', *New Yorker*, 31 March, 108.

Vail, Leroy, and White, Landeg (1991), *Power and the Praise Poem: Southern African Voices in History*, Charlottesville: University Press of Virginia; London: James Currey.

Van de Wall, Willem, 'Music in Hospitals', in *MM*, 293–321.

Van Dijk, Rijk, Reis, Ria, and Spierenburg, Marja (eds) (forthcoming), *The Quest for Fruition: Studies of the Political and Therapeutical in Ngoma*, Oxford: James Currey.

Vansina, Jan (1966), *Kingdoms of the Savanna*, Madison: University of Wisconsin Press.

Villon Films (1996), 'Sangoma: Traditional Healers in Modern Society' [South Africa], Vancouver: Villon Films.
Vogel, Stephan (1993), 'Sensation of Tone, Perception of Sound, and Empiricism: Helmholtz's Physiological Acoustics', in David Cahan (ed.), *Hermann von Helmholtz and the Foundations of Nineteenth-Century Science*, 259–87, Berkeley and Los Angeles: University of California Press.
Voss, Angela (1992), 'Magic, Astrology and Music: The Background to Marsilio Ficino's Astrological Music Therapy and his Role as a Renaissance Magus', PhD, London: City University.
—— (2000), 'Marsilio Ficino: The Second Orpheus', in Horden (2000).
Vulliamy, Graham (1977/1980), 'Music and the Mass Culture Debate', in John Shepherd et al. (eds.), *Whose Music? A Sociology of Musical Languages*, 179–200, London: Latimer; repr. New Brunswick and London: Transaction Books.
*Wack, Mary Frances (1990), *Lovesickness in the Middle Ages: The Viaticum and its Commentaries*, Philadelphia: University of Pennsylvania Press.
Walker, D. P. (1958), *Spiritual and Demonic Magic from Ficino to Campanella*, London: Warburg Institute.
—— (1985), *Music, Spirit and Language in the Renaissance*, ed. Penelope Gouk, Aldershot, Hampshire: Ashgate.
Walker, Sheila S. (1972), *Ceremonial Spirit Possession in Africa and Afro-America*, Leiden: E. J. Brill.
*Walser, Robert (1993), *Running With the Devil: Power, Gender, and Madness in Heavy Metal Music*, Hanover and London: Wesleyan University Press.
Weiss, Brad (1993), 'Buying her Grave: Money, Movement and AIDS in North-West Tanzania', *Africa*, 63 (1): 19–35.
*Wells, Robin Headlam (1994), *Elizabethan Mythologies: Studies in Poetry, Drama and Music*, Cambridge and New York: Cambridge University Press.
Werbner, Richard (1991), *Tears of the Dead: The Social Biography of an African Family*, Washington, DC: Smithsonian Institution Press.
*Werner, Eric, and Sonne, Isaiah (1941–2), 'The Philosophy and Theory of Music in Judaeo-Arabic Literature', *Hebrew Union College Annual*, 16: 251–319 and 17: 513–73.
West, Marti (2000), 'Music Therapy in Antiquity', in Horden (2000).
White, John Wallace (1997), 'Radio Formats and the Transformation of Musical Styles: Codes and Cultural Values in the Remaking of Tunes', *College Music Symposium*, 37: 1–12.
White, Luise (1993), 'Vampire Priests of Central Africa: African De-

bates about Labor and Religion in Colonial Northern Zambia', *Comparative Studies in Society and History*, 35: 746–72.

—— (1995), '"They could make their victims dull": Genders and Genres, Fantasies and Cures in Colonial Southern Uganda', *American Historical Review*, 100 (5): 1379–1402.

Whittaker, Alfred H. (1948), 'Occupational Diseases of Musicians', in *MM*, 218–43.

Wiesner, Hillary (1993), 'The Cosmology of al-Kindi', PhD, Harvard University.

Wigram, Tony, Saperston, Bruce, and West, Robert (eds) (1995), *The Art and Science of Music Therapy: A Handbook*, Chur: Harwood Publishers.

Wilcox, Judith, and Riddle, J. M. (1995), 'Qustā ibn Lūqā's *Physical Ligatures* and the Recognition of the Placebo Effect', *Medieval Encounters*, 1: 1–50. [Qusṭā b. Lūqā]

Willis, Roy G. (1968), 'Kamcape: An Anti-Sorcery Movement in South-West Tanzania', *Africa*, 38 (1): 1–15.

Wills, A. J. (1985), *An Introduction to the History of Central Africa: Zambia, Malawi, and Zimbabwe*, 4th edn, Oxford: Oxford University Press.

Wilson, L. G. (1984), 'Dorothy Schullian Retires from the *Journal*', *Journal of the History of Medicine*, 39: 457–61.

—— (1989), 'Dorothy M. Schullian, 1906–1989: A Humanist Historian of Renaissance Medicine', *Journal of the History of Medicine*, 44: 421–9.

Winn, James (1998), *The Humanities as Performance: The James Murray Brown Lectures*, New Haven: Yale University Press.

Winternitz, Emmanuel (1979), *Musical Instruments and their Symbolism in Western Art: Studies in Musical Iconology*, 2nd edn, New Haven and London: Yale University Press.

Woodfill, Walter L. (1953), *Musicians in English Society from Elizabeth to Charles I*, Princeton: Princeton University Press.

*Wr[ight], Tho[mas] (1604), *The Passions of the Minde in Generall*, corrected, enlarged, and augmented edn, London: Valentine Simms for Walter Burre.

Yates, Frances A. (1947), *The French Academies of the Sixteenth Century*, London: Warburg Institute.

Index

References in *italics* refer to pages with figures and tables. An entire chapter devoted to a topic is indicated in bold type, e.g. **46ff.**